W9-BTG-127

WITHDRAWN

PR 6021 I35 Z53 1996

97-280

Abbate Badin, Donatella.

Thomas Kinsella

JUL 2000

JUN 2004

JUL 09

JUL X X 2015

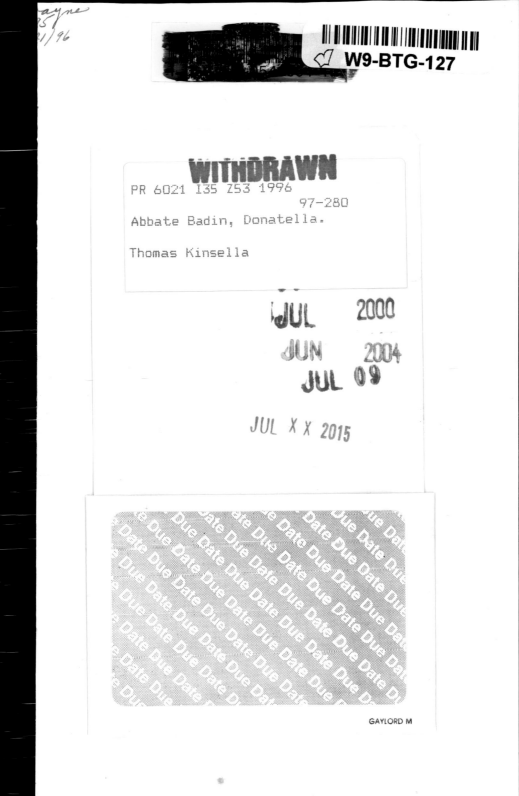

GAYLORD M

Thomas Kinsella

Twayne's English Authors Series

Kinley Roby, Editor
Northeastern University

TEAS 527

THOMAS KINSELLA
Courtesy of Tara MacGowran

CUMBERLAND COUNTY COLLEGE LIBRARY
P.O. BOX 517
VINELAND, N.J. 08360

Thomas Kinsella

Donatella Abbate Badin

University of Sassari, Italy

Twayne Publishers
An Imprint of Simon & Schuster Macmillan
New York

Prentice Hall International
London Mexico City New Delhi Singapore Sydney Toronto

CUMBERLAND COUNTY COLLEGE LIBRARY
PO BOX 517
VINELAND, N.J. 08360

97-280

Twayne's English Authors Series No. 527

Thomas Kinsella
Donatella Abbate Badin

Copyright © 1996 by Twayne Publishers
All rights reserved. No part of this book may be reproduced or transmitted in any form or by any means, electronic or mechanical, including photocopying, recording, or by any information storage and retrieval system, without permission in writing from the Publisher.

Twayne Publishers
An Imprint of Simon & Schuster Macmillan
1633 Broadway
New York, NY 10019–6785

Library of Congress Cataloging-in-Publication Data
Abbate Badin, Donatella.
   Thomas Kinsella / Donatella Abbate Badin.
      p.   cm. — (Twayne's English authors series ; TEAS 527)
   Includes bibliographical references and index.
   ISBN 0-8057-7047-X (alk. paper)
   1. Kinsella, Thomas—Criticism and interpretation.   2. Ireland—In literature.   I. Title.   II. Series.
   PR6021.I35Z53 1996
   821'.914—dc20
                                                            96-23432
                                                            CIP

The paper used in this publication meets the minimum requirements of American National Standard for Information Sciences—Permanence of Paper for Printed Library Materials. ANSI Z3948-1984. ∞ ™

10 9 8 7 6 5 4 3 2 1

Printed in the United States of America

To my mother

Contents

Preface

Thomas Kinsella is one of the most distinguished living Irish authors, and the literary establishment is lavish in its praise for his oeuvre. On the other hand, there are no book-length studies of his poetry, except one valuable but outdated volume, and in national and international conferences, very few papers deal with his work.

There are several reasons for this silence: Kinsella himself is a reticent person who does not try to attract attention through frequent public appearances, poetry readings, or press declarations; he does not belong to any literary coteries; and his poetic production is scanty and has appeared on the market through unobtrusive channels, such as the refined limited-edition pamphlets from his private press, Peppercanister, which are only later collected and more widely distributed by Oxford University Press.

Moreover, his poetry has become increasingly difficult. The early success of *Another September,* the winner of several national prizes, was followed by a series of volumes that left readers and critics baffled. There seemed to be no connection between the traditional and accessible, yet challenging, poet whose name turned up repeatedly on examination papers, and the somber, hermetic poet who since the 1970s had been publishing increasingly incomprehensible compositions. His poems have been judged ponderous and obscure, abstract and solipsistic. To follow them seems to require specialized knowledge in Jungian psychology or Irish myth. They do not correspond to what one might expect from an Irish poet: they are not topical, not musical, and are hard to place.

For all these reasons, I felt that a volume which offered some help in understanding even the more recent poetry was overdue. The insight I acquired through my translations of his poems into Italian, gave me the presumption that I could attempt to show that his early and late poetry constituted an organic whole, and that once an immersion in his themes and images was achieved, light would shine on his oeuvre and reveal great depth and superior linguistic excellence. The primary purpose of this study is to underline the continuity of Kinsella's career. By dwelling on the individual volumes, I try to point out their interdependence and show how each volume, although different in thematic interests and stylistic peculiarities, gains significance through its links with the others and the sequential organization of the poems as a whole. Kinsella's career should be viewed cumulatively; only within this perspective does his poetry reveal its treasures. I was fortunate to meet Kinsella several times and discuss with him some of the topics of my study. His words confirmed my contention: "I feel that the poems relate and accumulate among themselves. The particulars accumulate and in the development of the sequence, or of a whole career, the thing will assemble."[1]

It is therefore a challenging and rewarding experience to immerse oneself in this complex but not monolithic oeuvre, and to discover its various facets within an essential unity. Kinsella's poems range from the personal and the psychological to the satirical and the political. I attempt to show, as well, how the poems are rooted in the mythical Irish experience while always being tied to the present day and the poet's own life. "I see poetry as a form of responsible reaction to the predicament one finds oneself in . . . . It is essential to get the matter recorded before one disappears . . . . The experience of an individual *can* be significant and, if the impulse is there, it is a responsible thing to record the particularities of that experience" (see appendix, p. 199).

Kinsella has faithfully fulfilled his responsibilities in both his poetry and his prose, his translations and his anthologies, which I have also considered in this study. The resulting impression is that of a coherent, utterly serious, and engaged personality, and of a poet who has displayed great originality and the enabling strength of his tradition.

Acknowledgments

I wish to thank, first of all, Tom Kinsella and his wife Eleanor, who contributed to the making of this book by answering innumerable questions, making sure the biographical material was correct, talking, listening, writing letters, hosting me in their beautiful home, taking me for rides, cooking delicious meals, and brewing pots of tea; in other words, supporting me all along. I also thank the poet for granting me permission to quote from copyrighted material and to publish the text of the conversation we had in County Wicklow on 14–15 August 1993.

Professor Marjorie Perloff, who knows nothing about the publication of this book, was instrumental in its genesis since she first introduced me to Tom Kinsella himself in Philadelphia many years ago, and suggested I write my doctoral dissertation on his poetry and translate his poems into Italian.

My greatest debt goes to my dear Irish friends Dr. Tony Coughlan and Muriel Saidlear, who put me up whenever I had to conduct research in Dublin, gave me access to libraries, introduced me to relevant people, sent me books and reviews, assisted with bibliographical information, and, especially, helped me understand Ireland and its traditions.

Professor Tjebbe Westendorp of the University of Lejden read parts of the manuscript and gave precious advice, as did my colleague at the University of Sassari, Professor Pino Serpillo. I am grateful for the overall support and assistance of colleagues and staff at the Institute of Foreign Languages of the University of Sassari.

My husband Francesco, an economist, lovingly applied his editing skills to material that must have appeared quite foreign to him. For this, and much more, I thank him. A big hug to my nephew Matteo and my son Nicolò, who made the computer behave and solved many technical problems, including the cooking and cleaning when I was too busy to do them. The same applies to my mother (computer excepted). To all my family, thanks for the patience.

Chronology

1960   Son John born; *Moralities.*

1961   Irish Arts Council Triennial Book Award; *Poems and Translations* published in the United States.

1962   Daughter Mary born. *Downstream.*

1963   Exchange scholarship to visit U.S. poetry centers and study Irish manuscripts.

1964   The Dolmen Press incorporated; Kinsella becomes a founding director along with Liam Miller and Liam Browne.

1965   Left position as assistant principal officer in the Department of Finance to move to the U.S.

        Member Irish Academy of Letters.

1965–1970 Writer-in-residence and professor of English Literature, Southern Illinois University, Carbondale.

1966   Modern Language Association address: "The Irish Writer"; *Wormwood.*

1967   Received Denis Devlin Memorial Award.

1968   *Nightwalker and Other Poems;* connection established between Dolmen and Oxford University Press; *Poems by Thomas Kinsella, David Livingstone and Anne Sexton* published by Oxford University Press.

1968   Received Guggenheim Fellowship to spend year in Ireland to work on poetry and translation of *The Táin.*

1969   *The Táin* published by Dolmen Press (Oxford University Press, 1970).

1970   Moved to Temple University, Philadelphia, as professor of English.

1970   Received Denis Devlin Memorial Award. Second Guggenheim Fellowship.

1971   Acquired house in Percy Place; family moved back to Dublin.

1972   Derry Black Sunday; *Butcher's Dozen;* Peppercanister Press begins operation.

1973   *Notes from the Land of the Dead and Other Poems* published in the U.S.; *New Poems* in Ireland.

1973   *Selected Poems 1956–1968.*

1975   Established Temple University's program of Irish Studies in Dublin.

1978   Spent year in Ireland thanks to third Guggenheim Fellowship.

1979   *Peppercanister Poems, 1972–1978; Fifteen Dead* (Peppercanister pamphlets #1– 4); *One and Other Poems* (Peppercanister pamphlets #5–7).

1988   *Blood and Family* (Peppercanister pamphlets #8–12).

1988   Left Dublin and moved to country house in County Wicklow.

1990   Left Temple University and the Irish studies program to return permanently to Ireland.

1994   *From Centre City* (Peppercanister pamphlets #13–17).

1995   *The Dual Tradition.*

CHRONOLOGY

Chapter One

Thomas Kinsella: A Biographical Introduction—Recurring Features in Life and Poetic Career

Toward the end of the 1960s, after the Irish poet Thomas Kinsella had established himself as one of the leading voices in the Irish Parnassus, his life and career underwent a radical change. The poet abandoned his civil service career in 1965 to move to the United States and start an academic life as a writer-in-residence and professor of Irish literature. The appearance of *New Poems 1973* (titled *Notes from the Land of the Dead and Other Poems* in the U.S.), which collected several previously published poems or short sequences, announced the choice of a difficult new style quite in contrast with that which had made him famous. Moreover, several important translations from the Irish, such as *The Táin* (1969) and the texts in the anthology *An Duanaire: Poetry of the Dispossessed 1600–1900,* put Kinsella in the forefront of a movement to make Irish literature available to a wider public in an unadulterated form.

At first sight this change of direction might indicate a lack of coherence, but on closer analysis both life and poetic career reveal a surprising consistency. Kinsella's poetic career, which started in rather conservative tones and moved toward an avant-garde hermetical style, reveals the presence of many recurring features. Similarly, there is an essential unity of attitudes and concerns throughout his life, although it might appear to be disjointed. He was, in fact, a civil servant who dabbled in poetry and then turned into a professional writer profoundly committed to his art and to the cultural cause which many of his works underpin.

Although Kinsella confessed that his first poem was written as a kind of wager with himself, to prove that he could do it, poetry soon became for him a way of "eliciting order from significant experience"[1]; an extraction of form and passionate order from what appeared to be a moral and metaphysical void. At first, order meant opposing a rather traditional and strict poetic form to the shapelessness of experience. Then, as the strictures of form loosened, it came to be a quest for values and "the

1

detection of the significant substance of the individual and common past" (*Contemporary Authors*). From a difficult discipline imposed upon himself, poetry became an instrument of knowledge and understanding. As his private awareness of the importance of poetry grew, so also did his public awareness of the loss Ireland had suffered in being cut off from its Gaelic tradition. Hence the commitment, which went alongside his private pursuit of poetry, to restore this tradition through translations, editions of Irish classics, anthologies, cultural criticism, public addresses, and teaching.

One can detect a similar dedication to public commitments alongside private concerns in Kinsella's personal life and family heritage. Devotion to social engagement, on one hand, and to privacy in life and art, on the other, run through his blood. Kinsella likes to emphasize this pattern in his own life and in his narratives about his forebears.

Family

Kinsella describes with great pride his working-class family and the Dublin neighborhood in which he was born in 1928, and where he grew up in underprivileged circumstances. In some of the more openly autobiographical poems, such as "His Father's Hands," Kinsella evokes family traditions, as his father tells him with pride and hyperbolic emphasis (which in the poem is jokingly termed "Emphas- / emphasemphasis"):

> Your family, Thomas, met with and helped
> many of the Croppies in hiding from the Yeos
> or on their way home after the defeat
> . . . .
> From hearsay, as far as I can tell
> the Men Folk were either Stone Cutters
> or masons or probably both.[2]

The poet's father, John Kinsella, worked for Guinness until the early 1970s. His jobs ranged from working in the cooperage to occasionally delivering kegs to pubs. He was also a shop steward and union activist, and actually lost his job after helping initiate two demonstrations at the brewery. Besides being involved in Labor Party politics, he cultivated an interest in Irish legend and myth, and participated in literary debating societies. Kinsella talks of him as "a great reader, a very concerned person. He was a member of the Left Book Club, and had all the lively books of the thirties."[3] In "The Messenger" (*Blood and Family*), Kinsella again stresses his father's dedication to private interests and political commitment:

> He reaches for a hammer,
> his jaw jutting as best it can
> with Marx, Engels, Larkin
>
> howling with upstretched arms into the teeth
> of Martin Murphy and the Church
> and a flourish of police batons.[4]

Kinsella's grandfather also worked for Guinness, running one of the barges from the brewery jetty to the seagoing vessels in the harbor, and in his retirement was a cobbler and a fiddler. Both his grandmothers kept little shops in the Liberties, a working-class Dublin neighborhood. The ancient mother who plays such an important role in *Notes from the Land of the Dead and Other Poems* and *One and Other Poems,* is the result of an imaginative fusion of the maternal and the paternal grandmothers.

Life in Dublin

Kinsella was raised in an almost rural area in the middle of Dublin near the Guinness Brewery, along the river Liffey and the railway. Except for a couple of years that the family spent in Manchester, Dublin was their permanent home. The various streets on which his immediate family and his grandparents lived became the theater of the poet's youthful explorations and were later recalled in his poetry of memory: Inchicore, Basin Lane, Bow Lane, Irwin Street, and other such names have become as familiar to the readers of his poems as Eccles Street is to Joyceans.

Thomas Kinsella attended the local national school, the Inchicore Model School, for his primary education. He then continued on to the O'Connell School, a secondary school on North Richmond Street run by the Christian Brothers, where most of the subjects were taught in Irish. Although the teenage Kinsella was reluctant and resentful about having to learn a national language foreign to Dubliners, he ended up with a solid knowledge of Irish, which proved to be a great help in public examinations and became a lifelong source of inspiration. Excellent results in his Leaving Certificate earned him a scholarship to University College Dublin (UCD), where he enrolled in September 1946, intending to study science. He completed a couple of terms of physics and chemistry before being notified that the public examinations he had taken had opened up a civil service job for him. He accepted the position, forsaking the uncertainties of a life as a student in a field which had failed to enthuse him, and preferring the modest but secure salary of a junior executive officer of the Land Commission, Congested Districts Board.

Kinsella then began attending evening classes for the diploma in public administration, which he obtained in 1949. His life, however, even after graduation, continued to orbit around Newman House, then the hub of UCD, where he would have his meals and meet literary friends or people interested in the revival of the Irish language and tradition. About this time he also began writing poems, becoming "committed" very fast to what had seemed at first just a challenging pastime.

At the same time, although not a regular student, Kinsella played an important role in the publication of the UCD literary quarterly, *National Student*. Almost every issue from the years 1951–53 contained a poem, story, or book review by him. He was soon writing reviews for other journals as well, drawing cartoons for *Comhar* (a leading Irish language publication), and even occasionally trying his hand at writing in Irish.

By the time Kinsella moved to the Department of Finance in 1951 as an administrative officer, it was becoming evident that his chief interest lay not in administration but in literature. In those early university and civil servant days, Kinsella had become part of the generation of Irish intellectuals that had sought to free Ireland of its provincialism while at the same time establishing a truly Irish cultural milieu. Among his friends were Liam Miller, the founder of the prestigious Dolmen Press, and Sean O Riada, described by Kinsella in *Fifteen Dead* as "Ireland's foremost composer and musician."[5]

With O Riada, Kinsella shared a concern for bringing lost traditions back to life. While O Riada worked hard at popularizing and preserving native musical tradition, Kinsella started in those years to play an important role in doing the same for the Gaelic literary heritage. Long evenings spent together drinking and talking, collaboration on radio shows, and a trip to the west of Ireland strengthened their friendship, and fired the young civil servant and aspiring man of letters with a desire to devote himself to literature and the exploration of Ireland's tradition in the two languages (English and Gaelic) he came to call the "dual tradition."

The key figure of Kinsella's early years, however, was Liam Miller, as the poet was to declare in several interviews. Kinsella met Miller "more or less as [Dolmen] Press was beginning" in the early 1950s, when Miller, an architect, operated a handpress from his basement, producing elegant pamphlets. With Kinsella's help, Dolmen became the most important platform for young as well as established poets (notably the later poetry of Austin Clarke), and played a major role in Irish culture. Its luxury editions were illustrated by the outstanding artists of the moment, such as Louis Le Brocquy and Anne Yeats, among others.[6]

From the beginning, Kinsella was involved in all decisions about publication and production. He edited an anthology of young Irish poets, *The Dolmen Miscellany of Irish Writing,* and became one of the three founding directors when Dolmen was incorporated. In 1968, in connection with the publication of his translation of *The Táin,* he established a link between Dolmen and Oxford University Press.

Kinsella was also involved in the actual printing process: "I would play my part, holding the print and inserting the pieces upside down," he told Dennis O'Driscoll.[7] This was the beginning of a passion for and expertise in fine editions, which in 1972 would lead Kinsella to open his own publishing venture, the Peppercanister Press. The first results at Dolmen were the setting in type of his own early poems and translations, *The Starlit Eye* and *Three Legendary Sonnets* (both 1952). Subsequently, all his books and pamphlets received their first publication by Dolmen, often in splendidly illustrated and beautifully hand-crafted editions which have become pricey collector's items.

His work with Dolmen put Kinsella at the center of the intellectual life of the 1950s, and also fostered his interest in ancient Irish literature. Miller had asked Kinsella to find manuscripts of Irish myths, legends, or stories deserving publication in English. This resulted in the translations of *Faeth Fiadha: The Breastplate of St. Patrick* (1954) and *Longes Mac Usnig: Being the Exile and Death of the Sons of Usnech* (1954). The challenge of translating *Sons of Usnech,* a preliminary story to the great Irish saga, *The Táin,* led to his involvement in the translation of the epic poem. Besides the actual translating, this activity implied an immense editorial task in the selection of texts from among the many recensions of the saga, and would occupy him for many years.

Marriage

In 1955 Kinsella married Eleanor Walsh, whom he had first met in 1951 at UCD, where she was studying to be a radiologist. She was part of the intellectual circle to which Kinsella belonged, and the poet became increasingly attached to her while she was hospitalized for tuberculosis at St. Mary's Hospital in Phoenix Park between 1952 and 1954. The poems "A Lady of Quality" and "Phoenix Park" chronicle the visits he paid her in the hospital, and much of his early collection, *Poems* (1956), draws on incidents of their courtship. Eleanor came from a completely different background than Kinsella: she belonged to a well-to-do family from Wexford county, had been educated in a convent school, and had a Protestant mother.

Ill health plagued the young family and created severe problems. A crippling disease (*myasthenia gravis*) affected Eleanor in 1960, leaving her incapacitated for a number of years while her children were still young and her husband was facing the momentous decision of whether to leave his secure job with the government to launch a different career on a different continent. A bitter reflection of this period is to be found in *Wormwood* (1966), a cryptic poetical journal of the crisis, ending with a reaffirmation of the significance of the love relationship.

Notwithstanding several crises and strained periods, theirs has been a long-lasting, profound, and mutually enriching union, recorded movingly in a number of poems about different phases of Kinsella's life. Eleanor appears as a source of inspiration for her intuitive insight, which counterbalances the poet's more rational approach. Among the many tributes paid to his wife, is his avowal to Maurice Harmon that through her "vitality and brilliance under suffering," he detected "a possibility of order, suggestions for a (barely) positive dream."[8] The marriage was blessed with three children, and in recent years, a spate of grandchildren.

Literary and Academic Career

The 1950s and early 1960s were a period of frantic activity for Kinsella. Besides raising a young family on a rather restricted budget and coping with the practical problems related to his wife's disease, Kinsella had to juggle an increasingly successful poetic career, translations and editorial activities for Dolmen, and his responsibilities in the Department of Finance, where, among other things, he worked for a while as T. K. Whitaker's[9] private secretary. Indeed, says Kinsella, who remembers his civil servant days with some pride, it was the discipline and techniques of the civil service, especially the example of Whitaker's systematic behavior, which helped him acquire the work habits that allowed him to produce several collections of short poems, as well as such long poems as *A Country Walk, Downstream,* and *Nightwalker.*

The result of such determined and disciplined efforts was a consistent output of poetry, published in increasingly prestigious magazines, and then collected in volume after volume at a rate of, roughly, one every two years. Kinsella continued to write book reviews and began to make many public appearances, especially after the publication of *Another September* (1958), which won the Guinness Poetry Award. He participated in poetry readings, debates, and musical performances of his poems. These were exhilarating times.

The country too was going through a season of sanguine expectations. A sense of liberation from the past accompanied the Irish government's adoption in 1958 of Whitaker's economic program. This opened Ireland to the world and diverted it from an obsession with the inheritance of the civil war and the partition of the country. The outlook of *Another September, Moralities* (1960), and *Downstream* (1962), was cosmopolitan, matching the mood of the nation. Yet a tinge of bitterness about the country's social and political circumstances, due partly to Kinsella's natural predisposition and partly to his insider's knowledge of the situation, colored the poems of this period.

Kinsella's poetry was beginning to attract attention in the United States too. However, an American collection of his early work, *Poems and Translations* (1961), failed to confirm the reputation he had earned in that country. In spite of its cosmopolitan veneer, it was too rooted in Irish circumstances.

The stepped-up demands of his poetic career, together with the engrossing work on the translation of *The Táin,* made the civil service job harder and harder to bear. In 1963, Whitaker, who admired Kinsella's work and believed in the importance of the retrieval of a past literary tradition, was instrumental in obtaining a government grant for Kinsella to study in the United States and work full-time on his translation. Finally, in 1965, an invitation to be writer-in-residence at Southern Illinois University at Carbondale permitted him to abandon his government post and devote himself full-time to a literary career.

It was not an easy decision for Kinsella to uproot himself and abandon a secure job with twenty years seniority to travel abroad with a sick wife and three young children. This is reflected in such poems as "Ritual of Departure" and "Phoenix Park." Yet Kinsella says that he never hesitated: he wanted literature to be his life. Moreover, the salary was good and there was hope that proper treatment in the U.S. would bring an improvement in Eleanor's ailment; which, indeed, proved to be the case. The demands on a writer-in-residence at Carbondale were light. He had no duties except to give one lecture per annum for three years and to advise students. There was plenty of time for his other pursuits: writing, translating, and giving poetry readings. When a position became available in the English department in 1967, Kinsella accepted it, although it implied much more stringent obligations. In 1968 a Guggenheim fellowship allowed the family to spend the year in Ireland, where he supervised the publication of *The Táin* by Dolmen (1969) and Oxford University Press (1970). An important new collection of poems, *Nightwalker and Other Poems,* marked 1968 as an important year; a watershed between an old style and a new one which had been maturing during his American years.

After another year of teaching at Southern Illinois University, Kinsella accepted a post at Temple University in Philadelphia, a city which was more congenial to him than Carbondale. In September 1970 he started what was to be a twenty-year engagement at Temple with a seminar on Pound's *Cantos.* His ties with Ireland, however, were not severed. A second Guggenheim grant for the academic year 1971–72 brought the Kinsellas back to Ireland, where the family permanently relocated. At that time, Kinsella bought the fine Edwardian house, facing the canal on Percy Place, in Dublin, which along with the rest of the city center, forms the thematic core of several of the poetic sequences collected in *From Centre City* (1994).

Thus began a life of intercontinental commuting which was simplified and made official when, in 1975, Kinsella established Temple University's program in Irish studies, allowing him to divide his academic year between Philadelphia and Dublin. The program offered his American students, as he explained to John Deane, "a survey course in the Irish tradition, starting with prehistory, and ending with modern literature and politics."[10]

Kinsella's political conscience was profoundly touched by the events of 30 January 1972, "Bloody Sunday," when police in Derry, Northern Ireland shot thirteen peaceful demonstrators. What particularly incensed the poet, who had so far kept out of politics, was the official report affirming that the demonstrators were armed, although witnesses and documents proved the contrary. This spurred Kinsella on to write

Butcher's Dozen, a political pamphlet in verse, which, unlike most of his work, was produced in a very short time for quick publication. Although a minor work, the pamphlet spread his name among Nationalists and Loyalists alike, and many in Ireland know him only because of this poem.

It was in this circumstance that Kinsella put his Dolmen experience to use, setting and printing the booklet himself, and giving rise in 1972 to the Peppercanister Press (named after the nickname of a nearby church), which he operated from his home. Twelve Peppercanister booklets were published between 1972 and 1987. The chapbooks contained either a long poem (often an occasional one, such as the two elegies for Sean O Riada and one written on the assassination of President Kennedy) or a gathering of a few poems (*St. Catherine's Clock* being the most recent). Five more Peppercanisters have been published since 1987 by John Deane's Dedalus Press, bringing the total to seventeen.

The booklets were precious and elegant publications, lovingly set on good paper, and beautifully bound and illustrated by well-known artists. Signed limited-editions were marketed for book-lovers, while paperback editions were concomitantly issued at more accessible prices. The Peppercanister series of books "existed as an idea long before [*Butcher's Dozen*]," explained Kinsella in an interview with John Deane. It was Kinsella's response to his irritation at poetry being used in the journals as space-filler: "Peppercanister is primarily a substitute for magazine publication. It has a secondary effect in giving me another look at the work before publication—a final draft in published form" (Deane, 87). In the long run, this form of publication also influenced Kinsella's way of composition: "I have started writing books of poems as units" (Deane, 87). Although Kinsella had started composing sequences long before the Peppercanister experience, sequence-writing became his ruling mode of composition.

Meanwhile, Kinsella continued his work as an apologist for the lost tradition of Ireland, which had started with his translations and two seminal polemical papers: "The Irish Writer," first presented as a Modern Language Association address in 1968, and "The Divided Mind" (1972), which has been often revised and reprinted, and widely quoted. *The Dual Tradition* (1995), a book-length development of the same ideas, takes a more optimistic view of the question. Two extremely important contributions to the recovery of the lost patrimony of Gaelic literature were the anthologies he edited, especially *An Duanaire: Poetry of the Dispossessed 1600–1900* (1981), in which he revived through new translations a body of Irish poetry that was practically forgotten and inaccessible. The *New Oxford Book of Irish Verse* (1986), which superseded Yeats's and McDonagh's anthologies,[11] gave much space to Irish-language poetry, all in Kinsella's own translations, thus attracting a great deal of censure, because he had ignored the valuable work of other translators.

Because of his manifold activities in favor of the tradition, *The Irish Times* recognized that "few poets have done as much for their national poetry as Kinsella has."[12]

Move from Dublin

In 1988 Kinsella and his wife left Dublin and moved about two hours away to County Wicklow, near the historic site of Glendalough. In 1990 he retired from Temple and the Irish Studies program. These moves have increased the isolation of the poet and caused a further retreat into himself. He is rarely seen at public functions anymore and is no longer a public figure as other Irish poets have become through poetry readings, summer schools, and attendance at conferences. Poor health may play a role in this increased isolation, but temperament and the nature of his poetry are far more relevant. Kinsella does not believe that poetry should be a form of entertainment, nor could one imagine what form of enlightenment an audience sipping a cup of coffee or a pint of beer could derive from a difficult poetry which, in order to communicate, necessitates the most profound form of cooperation from the reader. Kinsella, in fact, "assume[s] that the act of reading is a dynamic one, the completion of an act of communication, not an inert listening to something sweet or interesting or even informative" (Deane, 88). More and more, this private style of living permeates Kinsella's poetry. Thus an aura of mystery and respect surrounds Kinsella, who is little known by the common reader, except for his anthologies and translations; but who is admired by the cognoscenti as a difficult, serious, and rewarding poet, perhaps the most important of his generation.

Chapter Two

The Phases of Kinsella's Poetic Career: Aims and Continuities

Works

Three major phases can be distinguished in Kinsella's career. His early phase, represented by various collections of poems (*Poems, Another September, Wormwood, Downstream, Nightwalker and Other Poems*), ended in 1968. It is a phase of apprenticeship in which Kinsella explores many genres and modes, often with great virtuosity. Although there are striking differences between the first two volumes and the next three, his respect for traditional forms (ranging from complex stanzaic and rhyming patterns to a loose blank verse) and for traditional subjects (love, self-reflexivity, subjective meditations on the passing of time, mutability and mortality) give the five volumes a sense of unity. The publication of a selection of Kinsella's poems in 1973 (*Selected Poems 1956–1968*), indicates that the poet himself considered the cosmopolitan, well-polished, and rather traditional production of these years a self-contained phase, now concluded. Successive selections made at later dates by Kinsella contained fewer and fewer of the early pieces, reflecting dissatisfaction with his early production, the "pointless elegance" of which he resents.[1]

Many readers who were enchanted by the self-control of that first phase were put off by the appearance of *Notes from the Land of the Dead* (1972) and the first Peppercanister volumes that followed it.[2] These works announced a new phase where the irrational and the incoherent seem to dominate. As of 1972, Kinsella started turning inwards to undertake a self-exploration along Jungian lines, which reached into the depths of the psyche and the mythical past of Ireland. The poems are apparently formless; the poet seems to dispense with rhythmic, structural, and syntactical modules and follows the free associations of mind and memory. Yet, thanks especially to the sequential form in which they are organized, lines of coherence appear even in these collections of poems; they are, in fact, an organic whole which shows close links to the concerns and thematic strains of the preceding phase.

There is no dramatic break in continuity between the second phase and the third, which is documented by the Peppercanister poems collected in *Blood and Family* (1988) and *From Centre City* (1994). The poems in these two collections are not as inward-looking as those of the preceding phase since the central persona is facing the social and cultural context rather than his or her psyche. Stylistically, Kinsella appears still to be engaged in his modernist search, although his poetry seems more accessible, even deceptively simple. But this is an illusion only: Kinsella does not return to formalist and traditional ways of expression, and he remains as elusive and demanding a poet as in the preceding phases.

Continuities

Kinsella's career is a complex yet coherent whole in spite of the plunge into the subconscious and the idiosyncratic style of the post-1968 phase. While the approach is different and the techniques more daring in his recent poetry, the content of his poems has always been, and still is, animated by a process of self-investigation and by the search for a point of stability in the face of erosion. A long meditation on what it means to be a poet and how poetry is elicited out of experience, constitutes the ruling continuity of his distinguished career. Similar situations, characters, and thematic concerns reappear in each phase, enriched each time by the significance they have acquired within the macro-text. Different imaginative contexts or stylistic approaches should not make us ignore the links and echoes between different works. A number of internal quotations from his own poems, in fact, underline their interdependency.

Repetition, indeed, is one of the features of Kinsella's poetry, and the poet himself alerts us to this by focusing on the use of repetition in Mahler's music: "the readiness . . . / to try anything ten times / if so excessive matter can be settled"(*B&F,* 44). To this day, Kinsella tries to make the "excessive matter" of his experience settle in poem after poem and sequence after sequence.

A Bare Possibility of Order

The main unifying factor in Kinsella's long poetic career can be found in his search for order. The artistic act, as Kinsella has declared at various moments of his career, is a tool for "eliciting order from experience," or from "significant data."[3] The ordering impulse dominates Kinsella's poetic venture; it is apparent both overtly, in the abstract patterns, ordered sequences, symmetries, and formal designs; and, covertly, and much more effectively, in the image patterns of his poems. These patterns, suggesting "a bare possibility of order," are in contrast to the equally idiosyncratic patterns of disorder, darkness, and decay linked to Kinsella's constant perception of "dislocation and loss" on both the personal and the national planes.[4]

In commenting on *Nightwalker and Other Poems,* Kinsella gave a blueprint for his poetic project:

> The first two sections of the book begin with certain private experiences under the ordeal, and follow with celebrations of the countermoves— love, the artistic act—which mitigate the ordeal and make it fruitful, and even promise a bare possibility of order.[5]

The constants of Kinsella's poetic oeuvre originate in these two alternative expressions of his concern for order: on one hand, the "ordeal of life" with its attendant images of disorder, waste, darkness, and decay; on the other hand, the "countermoves" of love and the artistic act with their patterns of positive images. The two poles affect both subject matter and textual strategies, and even more so the basic plot of Kinsella's individual poems and sequences of poems.

This concern for a patterned order, together with the images that most often convey it, emerges from the epigraph to *Downstream,* which describes a sort of prime moment in creation and human experience:

> Drifting to meet us on a darkening stage
> A pattern shivered: whorling in its place
> Another held us in a living cage
> Then broke to its reordered phase of grace.[6]

These lines provide the key to a coherent reading of the different volumes. An attempt to grasp the structure of order underlying apparent chaos, and to obtain a brief glimpse of understanding or a momentary sense of identity, is temporarily rewarded and then inevitably defeated by the spirals and destructive eddies of events. The anguished and frustrated poet, confronted with a new formlessness, is spurred to resume his search for that elusive "reordered phase of grace." It is this basic, unresolved cycle that the student of Kinsella's work must bear in mind when faced with the otherwise baffling diversity of the poems and their marked changes in style.

In the prologue to *Nightwalker* (1968), the author expressly declares that his poetry is dictated as much by "the shambles of the day" as by the "will that gropes for structure" (*SP,* 85). "Shambles" and "structure" are the two semantic cores around which consistent thematic and imagistic strains cluster. These provide a most impressive instance of continuity, and are to be recognized in the permanence of certain themes—the most obvious ones being "love, death and the artistic act" (Deane, 89)—and, more especially, in the recurrence of certain webs of images and certain metaphors, and in the similarities in the textual strategies adopted; as the present author has extensively demonstrated elsewhere.[7]

These instances are rooted in the dichotomies of order / waste or shambles / structure, and show Kinsella's oeuvre as an "ongoing project, with each installment offered to the public as a work-in-progress," as one reviewer wrote.[8] Each volume, in the eyes of another reviewer, constitutes an "accretion to an extraordinary enterprise."[9] To put the accent on continuity has become an axiom of criticism on Kinsella.

Subject Matter

Kinsella's poems display a great variety of poetic forms and a narrower range of subject matter, contained within the limits indicated by the poet as the "ordeal of life" and its "countermoves," and conveyed by repetitive patterns of images.

The way the human race, confronted with the many personal and public problems that beset it, arrives at "some kind of understanding" (be it through love, the artistic act, or a simple immersion into darkness) is the chief theme of Kinsella's poetry at all stages.[10] He perceives life as a process of continuous loss and waste, out of which the self must shape its identity; it is a "cup of ordeal" ("Phoenix Park," *SP,* 104) which must be drunk in order to find what lies at its bottom. The characteristic plot of Kinsella's poems is a confrontation with darkness, waste, or suffering followed by a brief moment of self-realization.

Autobiographical material   Autobiographical experiences are the mainstay of Kinsella's poetry since it is out of them that the poet extracts the instances of the ordeal, as well as the reasons for the countermoves on which his metaphysical constructs and his intimations of order rely. All through his career, Kinsella has made poetry out of the raw material of his personal life, responding to the various events with a continuous stream of writing although he admits that he cannot handle "day-to-day information" the way Pound handled "so satisfactorily what happened to him" (Fried, 6), and feels shy about mythicizing himself the way Yeats did. "I see poetry," says Kinsella, "as a form of responsible reaction to the predicament one finds oneself in. If a person has this impulse to record the important situation, I believe that is required. I've no idea what use it is. But I know it has something to do with continuity, with trying to compensate for the limited life span of the individual and things of that kind. It is essential to get the matter recorded and then disappear" (see appendix, p. 199).

Each of his volumes contains a number of poems on the development of self and on significant family or love relationships. Some compositions dealing with exemplary or monitory figures from his own entourage, or from his cultural and historical background, are also present in each of the main volumes of his production. Yet Kinsella never quite abandons himself to the full, documented, and factual song about himself. A natural reticence keeps him from a full revelation of personal circumstances and makes him choose oblique ways of confession: poetic personae, pathetic fallacies, metaphors, and even allegories. The factual data are sublimated out of recognition. Reticence, indeed, is the keynote of his personal poetry even when underpinned by naturalistic details.

Poetry, to Kinsella, is a continuous rumination on life rather than a revelation of circumstances. "I opt for poetry as an accompaniment [to life]," he says, "and work on significant memory, on data that refuse to go away, so as to make sense of relationships, including family relationships, in developing a sense of history and what history is for. And finally, using history as a device, an aid toward understanding" (Fried, 7).

The Irish context   History, myth, cultural tradition, and the public sphere are, however, also part of the poet's "significant memory," especially in what the poet calls their "private uses"; that is, the integration of the public within the fabric of the personal. The constant allusions to his cultural and historical context, and the presence of many Irish motifs, give the lie to the impression that Kinsella is only a personal or self-reflexive poet, who is detached from Irish concerns. The public sphere is a cause of dissatisfaction and invective in the many satirical poems of the early and late Kinsella, but love for Dublin and for the land transpires from many of the urban poems. History and myth are sources of subject matter in themselves or objective correlatives of personal modes of being.

The same two elements which characterize the personality of the poet—privacy and public commitment—are, in fact, also present in Kinsella's poetic career from its very beginning.

The ordeal of life   Both the personal and the public spheres are sources for instances of the "ordeal": harrowing experiences such as facing spiritual and physical suffering, being confronted with the death of someone one loves, or facing one's own mortality. What Kinsella, in a poem, calls "love's difficulty"[11]—misunderstandings, separation, disappointments—provides, predictably, another source of inspiration. At one stage the ordeal is that of plumbing one's psyche; at another, it is that of confronting public vexations, ranging from economic policies to political injustice and urban destruction. Kinsella's self-reflexive inclination makes him repeatedly dwell on the anguish of writing and on questions related to its purpose. Finally, traveling and exile are quintessential Irish themes which appear repeatedly.

Voyages   The paradigm of the voyage, indeed, is a time-honored allegorical device often adopted by Kinsella to represent the confrontation with the ordeal. Kinsella's voyage poems, which take the hero through many vicissitudes toward a single goal (the recognition of identity or of a pattern of order in reality), are shaped as Joycean peripatetic Odysseys or old Irish voyage poems (*imrams*). Among these are *A Country Walk, Downstream, Nightwalker,* and even, partially, *Phoenix Park*. At a later stage, the voyage takes the shape of a descent into the underworld, after the paradigm of Dante's *Inferno*. This underworld may be a psychic one (the subconscious world of the poems of Jungian exploration; for example, *Notes from the Land of the Dead, One,* and *Songs of the Psyche*) or, in the later poetry, an urban one (*From Centre City* and *Open Court*).

All the voyages imply a quest through ordeal and, in the more optimistic ones, a temporary reward, such as, in *Downstream,* the return to a "reordered phase of grace." A momentary sense of understanding, implied in the perception of a design or the achievement of some form of union, represents the climax of Kinsella's typical initiatic voyages.

Images of decay   While traveling is the arch-allegory for facing the ordeal of life, the landscapes traversed supply the imagery pervading Kinsella's poetry. The realistic landscapes of the early works and the archetypal or symbolic ones of mid-career, both yield recurring images related to waste. Rotting matter, excrement, dust, and ruins accompany the traveler toward the reward for Kinsella's typical initiatic quests. Although the aim of Kinsella's poetry is to catch a glimpse of order, the poems are dominated by its opposite. An amazing number of images—indeed entire poems—inspired by the themes of disintegration, disease, and waste are the counterparts to a fragmented sense of self and history.

Hardly a house stands upright and intact when Kinsella's imagination turns to the traces of man in urban and rural settings. "King John's Castle" is in ruins; chicken wire surrounds Coole Park razed to the ground ("Magnanimity,"*SP,* 80); royal Tara is reduced to dung-covered mounds ("Tara" *NOP,* 24). Kinsella's last look at Dublin, in "Phoenix Park," reveals a city where "dead men, / Half hindered by dead men, tear down dead beauty" (*SP,* 108). The frequency of such images reflects an obsession that goes well beyond the many ruins actually present in the Irish landscape.

These crumbling buildings may also be seen as oversimplistic synec-doches for the "broken tradition" and the mutilation due to "the death of a language," which are part of the significance of the past.

The awareness of decay, which is central to Kinsella's perception of the urban and natural worlds, also affects his view of man. The poet is particularly responsive to failing powers or to outright disease. His father is remembered "supine, jutjawed and / incommunicable, privately / sur-rendering his tissues and traps" ("The Messenger," *B&F,* 8); his wife, "brilliant with illness" ("Phoenix Park,"*SP,* 102); his dying grandmother is recognized through the "smell of disused / organs and sour kidney" (*NLD,* 20). Kinsella can rightly say of his world: "there's a fever now that eats everything" ("Phoenix Park," *SP,* 102).

Decay and death color Kinsella's relationship with both his familial and cultural forebears. A sense of waste and stark horror accompanies the commemoration of his literary and artistic masters, who are evoked as diseased or dying: the poet Egan O'Rahilly, with "red eyelids" and "the shrew his stomach" ("The Poet Egan O'Rahilly, Homesick in Old Age,"*SP,* 81); the musician Sean O Riada, associated in death with a rat killed during the excavation of his grave; Yeats abandoned to the inquis-itiveness of critics and biographers like a carcass abandoned to preying animals. Elegies dominated by horror rather than consolation, as a mat-ter of fact, abound at all stages.

The search for order must begin with its negation. The image of waste is but one of the poles between which Kinsella's poetry moves. An equally distinctive aspect of his poetry is the countermoves, and the positive images that accompany them, which represent the quester's reward. The two sets of images and themes are the carrying columns of the hidden architecture of his poems.

Countermoves   Epiphanies of order are conveyed either by positive sensorial images or, thematically, by such fruitful experiences as love and the artistic act. Both kinds of epiphanies are supposed to give access to understanding and a sense of identity, which are the two declared aims of Kinsella's poetic enterprise.

Love, termed in "Phoenix Park" as "the one positive dream" (*SP,* 102), appears in many poems as the only way to oppose waste. It is something through which human beings grow and "understanding may be gathered" ("Nightwalker," *SP,* 96). Yet, even from the beginning, love is not idealized; there is a continued awareness of "love's difficulty." Kinsella's love poetry, too, like his travels, revolves around two extremes.

Kinsella's first volume, *Poems* (1956), was an act of courtship to his future wife, who was made to appear both as a woman and as a muse. Later on she became the symbol of femininity, whose ability to trust her senses and intuition he hailed, exclaiming "Everything you know you know bodily" (*SP,* 102). In his Jungian phase, female qualities are the submerged element searched for in the quest for "individuation," which in Jungian psychology is the discovery of one's hidden, unique, and true self. Love understood as solidarity between man and woman animates the more recent poetry.

A distinctive aspect of Kinsella's poetry at various stages of his career has been its metapoetic nature. By returning repeatedly to the topos of the work of art—and by turning into subject matter the difficulty of expressing what is inexpressible—he has been conducting a long poetic reflection on the nature and function of poetry. Besides the many poems which discuss the artistic act directly, there are also several portraits of fellow artists who become specific masks through which Kinsella analyzes his commitment. Poetry, as he said to Peter Orr, is an instrument of "detection of the significant substance of the individual and common past."[12] Yet from the beginning of Kinsella's career, the "attempt to hold things in place," so earnestly maintained in his prose, is seen in an ironic light in his poems. Ironic self-images or self-deprecating poetic personae appear at all stages of his lifelong reflection on poetry. At times he chooses to represent the artist as a modest, methodical craftsman ordering his desk, in "Before Sleep"; or, in the prologue to *Downstream* ("I wonder whether one expects"), as a habitue of "the morning train, / The office lunch" (*SP,* 41); or as a clownish ringleader mustering his "bored menagerie" while "Futility flogs a tambourine" (*SP,* 41). In "Worker in Mirror" the artist has "the flashy coat, the flourished cuffs" and "floppy flower" of the stereotypical representations of artists.

In "Baggot Street Deserta," poetry is:

> Interpreting the old mistakes
> And discords in a work of Art
> For the One, a private masterpiece
> Of doctored recollections. (*SP,* 26)

Yet under the stance of self-deprecation, typical of the twentieth century, there are glimpses of the prototypical figure of the Orphic-inspired artist, as when he promises himself: "in the morning I will put on the cataract, / Give it veins, clutching hands, the short shriek of thought" ("Before Sleep," *SP,* 79).

Positive image patterns   The recurrence of clusters of words grouped around common semantic centers characterizes Kinsella's poetry and constitutes one of its elements of continuity. These patterns of images, both of a positive and a negative nature, present themselves in poems far apart from one another in everything else, and constitute one of the characteristic aspects of Kinsella's poetry.

In the many initiatic voyages of Kinsella's poems, the traveler goes through darkness, decay, confusion, and fragmentation—a whole register of undesirable situations—to be allowed a brief encounter with more desirable signals: tastes, perfumes, patterns of light, and organic tissues.

In the work of a poet who defines the desire for understanding in terms of that prime Irish metaphor, hunger, it is not surprising to find that sensations of taste play a major role. Vague or clearly defined tastes and smells signal visionary moments. "A tang of orchards" announces the apparition of the Muse in one of the first poems composed by Kinsella ("Night Songs," *SP,* 11). Images connected with taste are too numerous in each volume to be listed. "Brief tongues of movement / ravenous, burrowing and feeding," are rewarded, in "Ely Place," with "After lunch / A quarter of an hour at most / of empty understanding."[13] The group of images related to taste and eating is indeed a distinctive aspect of Kinsella's poetry.

Kinsella also uses his other senses—hearing, touch and sight—for evoking images of unity and the discovery of a structure. Music plays a fundamental role in signalling a harmonious unity, especially in the poems inspired by the musicians he admired. John Scotus Eriugena's concept of polyphony is the key fiction to which all of Kinsella's quests tend:

> that the world's parts,
> ill-fitted in their stresses and their pains,
> will combine at last in polyphonic sweet-breathing
> union.
> ("Out of Ireland," *B&F,* 61)

But it is sight that provides the most obvious group of images expressing an epiphany, as the Greek root of the word implies.[14] It is often nighttime in Kinsella's poetry; a nighttime replete with stars, moonlight reflections, lamps and lampposts, beams and lighthouses. Verbs such as "glitter," "glisten," "glare," "glow," and "flicker" are among the most frequently used words in Kinsella's vocabulary. A vision of constellations is the privileged way for conveying a pattern of order. As the search for identity and the search for individuation come together in Kinsella's Jungian phase, organic symbols of growth and completion such as eggs, embryos, crystals, or pearls announce that waste may reveal at its heart not only order but also an organic sense of accretion.

Recurring rhetorical devices   The search for order, which is at the origin of Kinsella's imagistic patterns and the dialectical structure of his poems and sequences, also determines his choice of rhetorical strategies. Often a poem is based on the description of an ordered sequence, or of routines and rituals which act as synecdoches to prove that laws of order are at work in the reality around him; even when shapelessness, chaos and decay seem to dominate. Such are the nighttime routines described in "Before Sleep," and the ritual of making tea in the opening poem of *Notes.* Both devices are a *mise en abyme* of the poetic act as an order-imposing one, tinged, however, with ironic skepticism as to the actual possibility of an artistic construct really inducing order.

A number of specific recurrent metaphors in Kinsella's poetry signify the search for identity. Tropes related to hunger, drinking, and eating are the central ones of Kinsella's middle years, closely linked to the "cup of ordeal" metaphor which appears in full force in "Phoenix Park":

> The ordeal-cup, set at each turn, so far
> We have welcomed, sour or sweet.
> . . . .
> Look into the cup: the tissues of order
> Form under your stare.
> . . . .
> Laws of order I find I have discovered
> Mainly at your hands . . .
> . . . .
> That life is hunger, hunger is for order,
> And hunger satisfied brings on new hunger
> . . . .
> And I taste a structure, ramshackle, ghostly,
> Vanishing on my tongue. (*SP,* 104–6)

Drinking and eating in an actual or metaphoric sense often lead to perceptions of self and pattern even if the result is partial and temporary.

A central figure in Kinsella's poetic world is that, suggested clearly in "Phoenix Park," of "A blind human face burrowing in the void / Eating new tissue down into existence," or of a snake sucking "at triple darkness" (*SP,* 105, 109). Many of the poems of *Notes from the Land of the Dead* and *One and Other Poems* are centered on a primordial, never-satisfied hunger. The reciprocal preying of creatures in the natural world (owls, serpents) represents the destructive process necessary to obtain a new identity through the integration of elements submerged in the unconscious. Asked about this in an interview, Kinsella commented:

> [T]he act of eating [is] an image of what goes on in the experience of reality. You are presented with the scraps, the disordered, and you absorb it, process it, and it is absorbed, with some relationship with an idea of order. That is eating and also digesting. (Fried, 16)

Mirrors also appear frequently in Kinsella's work—even in such titles as "Mirror in February" (1962) and "Worker in Mirror at his Bench" (1973)—as essential tools of the process of self-recognition, as well as of the self-reflexivity of the metapoetic exercises.

For much of Kinsella's career, allegory provides an ample structure of order; whereby a senseless, random experience acquires sense, point by point, through an implicit equivalence with the more ordered experience of the cultural model chosen. Kinsella's allegorizing habit goes back to Dante, Shelley, and, more recently, his acknowledged model, Auden, who often used this device, even while deflating it ironically. The author's elusiveness and reticence find a precious tool in allegory, which, in John Whitman's definition, is "an oblique way of writing" concealing "many of its secrets."[15] By favoring a technique that foregrounds its will to conceal, and dramatizes the opacity of language and its need for a key, Kinsella expresses an inherent pessimism in language.

Kinsella's poetry is repetitive, and it grows by accumulation and resonance. His poems follow the same itinerary, moving from waste and confusion to a brief moment of understanding, or a "provisional" structure of meaning. His material often generates such an enlightening vision, whether he deals with autobiographical material or elements outside himself, such as historical and mythical figures or ones from his personal entourage. Yet at times the pattern would hardly be recognizable unless one brought familiarity with his poetry to bear.

Often the positive moment becomes a celebration of the capacity of poetry to transform waste imaginatively into a positive linguistic construct. The "glory" of the modern poet, writes Kinsella in "Poetry since Yeats," lies in his "articulate, order-imposing" search, which is ultimately a search for a poetic language.[16] His quest for order and values is essentially linguistic. The tissue he has been trying to perceive is a fabric of words, rather than a transcendental or abstract tissue. He is seeking the ordering process of imagination. The web of images we have examined is capable of translating into words his vision of the desperate human condition, his concept of life as endurance, and, particularly, the relationship between the two. Writing poetry implies denying waste and disorder.

Textual Strategies

While Kinsella has remained faithful to his early themes and imagery, in the course of his career he has conspicuously altered the textual strategies he has used. These too are dictated by the two alternative expressions of his poetic concern—the disorder evoked by the "ordeal of life,"and the positive images corresponding to the "countermoves." Thus, when, as in the first phase, disorder and disintegration dominate his poetic universe, he is most concerned in creating a sense of stylistic order. But when he believes that a principle of abstract order is inherent in his apparently fragmented universe, the tissue of his poetry is at its most ragged.

The greatest change in Kinsella's poetry, which creates an impression of discontinuity, thus, lies in its diction, structure and prosodic aspects. In the 1956–1968 phase, Kinsella exorcised disorder by foregrounding external order through his use of traditional forms and regular prosodic patterns. In his early years, Kinsella was, indeed, quite a virtuoso in the use of external forms of order. The first voice Kinsella forged for himself was precious, elegant, and conservative in form. Yet even his early poetry shows a wide range of experimentation within traditional parameters, alternating from the predictable to the striking. From sonnets to ballads, from blank verse to rhymed and unrhymed terza rima, and, eventually, to free verse, Kinsella explores many forms; familiar or of his own design, cosmopolitan or Irish, in a show of bravura which he now rejects as "unnecessary." Even at his beginning, in fact, he was aware of the clash between the grace of forms and the ungracefulness of the experience. Increasingly, grating notes, odd rhymes, and indecorous images disturbed the decorum of his poetry, until he altogether discarded the external order of the "well-made poem," considering it insufficient to resolve the discontinuities and conjure up structure. In various interviews, he revealed that he felt "the strict forms were borrowed and imposed."[17]

By the time he came to write *Nightwalker and Other Poems,* Kinsella had mostly abandoned end-rhymes, and his versification was drifting towards more flexible semiformal solutions. He adopted not only free verse and "the open sequence," but also fragmentation and disorder used as expressive strategies. By the 1970s his experiments with free verse had become extravagantly untraditional. With *Notes from the Land of the Dead,* the formalist Kinsella seemed to have adopted formlessness as a device, and his poetry appeared shockingly free, even while still seeking musical effects through internal phonic associations. Starting with *Nightwalker and Other Poems* in 1968, and confirming the trend in *Notes from the Land of the Dead* in 1972, Kinsella reacted to waste in personal life, and to the dispossession of Ireland and the world, by refusing poetry as "music or mimesis for its own sake" (O'Driscoll, 65) and by foregrounding obscurity and lack of pattern (the negation itself of order) as significant devices—mimetic and ordering acts themselves, in a way, but of a more complex nature. The ordering function devolves on the reader since "communication that needs no completion," says Kinsella, "is a waste of time."[18]

More recently, the poetry of the late Peppercanister pamphlets has been characterized by composure and simplicity. There are no exhibitions of bravura as in the early phase, nor of daring avant-garde technique as in the poetry of the late 1960s and early 1970s. Kinsella, in short, has been steadily moving away from the running rhythms and regularities of his early attempts (the external patterns of order) and the syncopations of his middle phase, toward what G. M. Hopkins called "the rhythm of common speech."[19]

A refusal of a unitary poetic language and a heterogeneous mixture of different voices and stylistic levels, characterizes Kinsella's oeuvre and makes it an example of a Bakhtinian heteroglossic text. Rapid switches—sometimes within the same line—from Latinate to Anglo-Saxon lexis, or from a colloquial and demotic style to a more formal and literary diction, bring about an element of surprise and defamiliarization. In the 1970s and early 1980s, he alternates between high-flown bardic tones, or a language of trance, and a diction drawing on contemporary usage with many deflatory, bathetic terms. Even when his poetry was most structured, he tried to obtain contrapuntal effects by seeking the interplay of regularity and irregularity; of lyrical and musical effects against flat and grating sounds. An element of surprise has always been present in his poetry at both the aural and the semantic levels. This characteristic has been noted by Hugh Kenner, among others, who calls this "the Kinsella Effect: an irruption of darkness and violent enigmatic language" into "recognizable experience."[20]

All this makes for the complex musicality and notable difficulty of his texts. In spite of the many rhythmic and metric experiments in the early work, and the musical patterning of the longer poems of his later production, Kinsella's poetry does not appeal directly to the ear but rather to the mind or the eye.

The lack of musicality is one of the many elements which makes Kinsella's poetry challenging and daunting—a problem which the poet makes no bones about, as he expects total commitment from his readers. Kinsella's difficulty goes well beyond the modernist technique of loosely putting together his texts. His poetry presents a number of characteristic strategies which put high demands on the reader.

Difficulty

The chief causes of difficulty are a tendency to abstraction, the density and layering of his diction, the presence of defamiliarizing passages, the heteroglossia, and the intertextuality.

One specific device which distances the poems, by removing them from the personal to the general plane, is the absence of vital facts about the circumstances of the poem. The poems hint at precise events about which the poet gives little or no information. The reader is only offered fragments of episodes with no indication as to antecedents, or chronological and spatial location. Many of the portraits seem to refer to real people whose names, however, are withheld. Thus the reader is left guessing; unable to attach the poem with certainty to Kinsella's biography, or to actual political and cultural figures or events. This incompletion defamiliarizes the poems and adds to their power, creating a sense of puzzlement and mystery in the reader.[21]

Intertextuality is another strategy which puts high demands on Kinsella's audience, especially since he refers to other texts without giving any indication that he is doing so. Yet it is intertextuality which gives his poetry its peculiar stratification and allusiveness, allowing it to operate, to borrow George Steiner's words, "in an echo chamber of motifs." Steiner goes on to explain how essential intertextuality is for poets, but also how, paradoxically, it makes their work inaccessible to a modern public unable to understand the references. "Books . . . speak and sing inside books. . . . Thematic presences are, as in music, the instrument of economy. They shorthand the wealth and depth of adduced meaning."[22] Kinsella frequently recurs to this kind of shorthand, but often the complex resonances of his text are wasted on his public.

The allusions are not only to written texts, they are multimedial: music and musicians (i.e., Ó Riada, Mahler) are often evoked, and pictorial references are part of the subject matter. Illustrations and other visual elements become an essential part of the text. In "hesitate, cease to exist, glitter again," the poem's closure consists of a pen drawing of an oval open shape. The picture is part of the text and alludes synthetically, with a single line, to zero, a broken egg, and a snake figure biting its tail (the uroboros); all three of which are central symbols of the sequence of poems.

The graphic presentation of the poems has also been an instrument of economy from the very beginning. Kinsella has made extensive use of graphological patterning—such as the switch to italics and other fonts, the use of capital letters, and the alternation of poetry and prose—as a strategy of signification. Paratextual elements have great importance in Kinsella's shaping of longer poems and sequences. He turns to numbered divisions and subdivisions—mottoes, prefaces, epigraphs, illustrations, and even footnotes—to bring out the underlying structure to the eye. This is one more confirmation of the visual quality of Kinsella's poetry.

The above are just a few of the devices adopted by Kinsella in his texts. A passage by Giraldus Cambrensis on Irish music, chosen by Kinsella as the epigraph to *Out of Ireland*, reflects his lifelong search for effective technical strategies which become, in the course of his career, increasingly unobtrusive and all the more refined: "the perfection of their art seems to lie in their concealing it, as if 'it were the better for being hidden. An art revealed brings shame.'" (*B&F*, 58).

Conclusion

Kinsella has repeatedly dodged any questions of continuity in his poetry and has appeared embarrassed by much of what he wrote in his younger years. And yet the later work could not exist without the thematic and structural foundations laid in the early years. The work of Kinsella's first fifteen years constitutes a sort of fertile terrain out of which grow the roots of the major poems of the late-1960s (such as "Wormwood," "Nightwalker," and "Phoenix Park"), which in turn are the founding stone of *Notes*. Out of this major group grow the tendrils that feed into the various Peppercanister sequences; many late poems appear as "revisitations" or rewritings of earlier ones.[23] Moreover, phrases and symbols develop from book to book, and there is a mesh of recurring images that signal similar motifs and states of mind. This "system of living images,"[24] as Kinsella terms it in the poem "At the Head Table," provides signposts in an itinerary through the landscape of his poetry, which will guide the reader from phase to phase without making him lose sight of the poet's main concerns.

Becoming aware of these continuities, and keeping an eye on cross-references, provides an effective tool which helps in understanding both the single poems and Kinsella's lifelong aim in writing poetry. As we bridge the gap between one phase and another through a thematic approach, we are compelled to recognize, notwithstanding the idiosyncratic style of the post-1968 era, an inherent coherence and integrity in Kinsella's poetic career.

Finally, Kinsella does not contradict himself. Whether through a web of images or through intellectual patterns—but always through a mastery of language—he is still trying to confront and acknowledge the "madness without" and the "madness within."

Chapter Three
Early Poetry: 1956–1961

Publishing History of the Early Works

Kinsella's poetic career started casually, as he often likes to stress. He had at first intended to become a scientist, and then an economist. When his first volume of poems appeared, he was working as a civil servant. But a "slight feeling of curiosity" prompted him to write his first poem when he was eighteen: "It struck me as being an interesting experiment to see if I, personally, could produce anything which could pass for a poem. . . . It was quite sometime after that before the possibility of continuing to write verse entered my mind" (Orr, 105). Reflecting his double inclination toward public commitment and private rumination, Kinsella's first publications were a lyrical poem, "The Starlit Eye," and some translations from the Gaelic, "Three Legendary Sonnets" (both 1952).

Thanks to his enthusiastic collaboration with Liam Miller and his Dolmen Press, Kinsella had the unique opportunity, for a novice writer, of having access to a publisher and being able to bring his early work forth in elegant editions. *Poems,* his first cumulative and commercial volume, was published in 1956. In 1958, he produced *Another September,*[1] which was welcomed by favorable reviews in major papers and journals, and awarded the Guinness Poetry Award. 1960 saw the appearance of *Moralities* (part 12 of *The Dolmen Chapbook*). These three volumes have long been out of print and until the forthcoming *Collected Poems* appears, most of the poems contained in them are available to a general readership only through *Poems and Translations* (published in the United States in 1961), and the various selections made by the poet in different volumes. *Poems and Translations* contained most of the previously published poems and a few additional, new ones, and marked the close of a creative season, by the end of which Kinsella had confirmed himself as a poet and found his voice.

"Influenced by Literature More Than by Fact": *Poems* and *Another September*

Only a dozen of Kinsella's early poems passed the poet's scrutiny and found their way into *Selected Poems 1956–1968*. Kinsella considers his early ventures too technical and imitative, "not necessary"; and wonders "at what he could get away with," even while admitting he is sometimes "startled, in the other direction, by some of the things [he] managed to write" (see appendix, p. 195).

Yet many of these are the poems that made Kinsella popular and are still among the best known to the general public. It is true that some smack of deliberate literary exercise, being prompted by a desire to see "whether the thing could actually be done" (Orr, 105). Kinsella's early poetry is imitative, but it displays great virtuosity in the handling of traditional techniques of versification and the exploration of different genres. This very technical bravura, however, attracted some criticism. Calvin Bedient, for one, felt it acted as "a substitute for personality."[2] This excess of technique does not, on the contrary, denote lack of individuality: Kinsella reveals his characteristic enigmatic bent by hiding behind the accomplishments of the "well-made" poem. Reticence and obscurity are the trademarks of the early Kinsella.

In his first volumes, Kinsella pays lip service to the decorum of an older tradition, which he often adapts to his needs through imitation, pastiche, and outmoded rhetorical figures. His revisitations of traditional genres, often in an ironical key, favor the Middle Ages in both the subject matter and the devices adopted.

Kinsella relies heavily on allegory and personified abstractions, and tries his hand at conceits, heraldic poems and emblems of the Renaissance, balancing them with abrupt returns to reality which have a deflating effect. The contrast between tradition and the demands of a modern sensibility is the cause of the tortuous stylistic structure and the density of some of these poems. The result is an impenetrable poetry, in which concrete enough signifiers do not link up with a recognized signified.

For a young poet starting to write in the post–World War II period, and with the heavy Yeats heritage at his back, history, the past, and the public sphere were like quicksand—dangerous to explore—now that the old certainties had disappeared. Kinsella at this stage also eschewed the purely personal sphere or any clear referentiality. So he chose the metapoetic solution, writing poetry on poetry, and reflecting half-ironically on the tradition. As he admitted to Haffenden, at the beginning his poems "were influenced by literature more than by fact" (Haffenden, 104).

In a composition he soon rejected, "A Shout after Hard Work" (1956), Kinsella greeted the birth of a poem as that of "a bastard baby begotten in his head" through an intellectual act of artistic will; "No sin of pleasure got you, no marvelous fornication, / Nothing but the needle of art insemination."[3] The time-honored childbirth metaphor, modernized, is tantamount to a recognition of the cerebral nature of many of his early experiments, contained in *Poems* and, partly, *Another September.* The major themes of Kinsella's early volumes are, in fact, literary. In a large group of poems, he explores poetry as subject matter; dealing with inspiration, often under neo-classical trappings (muses abound at this stage), or trying his hand at the major genres, even while parodying them. The love poems, the majority of the group, also hide their impulse through imitation and irony. A diffidence towards the heroic phase of Irish poetry appears in many poems on Irish subjects, in which the poet questions the ideas of myth and nation.

Questioning of myth   Three poems in the 1956 collection, "Death of a Queen," "Test Case," and "The Traveling Companion," illustrate Kinsella's interest in pastiche and his poetic reflections on genres. All three poems have as their apparent subjects historical or mythological figures; however, it is hard to pinpoint the specific tradition to which they belong. A reader might be tempted to place those elusive figures within an Irish tradition, but Kinsella seems anxious to underline his distance from it. The "obvious desire to avoid the form of Irishism . . . so profitably exploited in the past," which Kinsella, in his introduction to *Dolmen Miscellany,* recognizes as fundamental for his generation, dictates the irony and indirectness of his treatment of mythological and heroic figures. Spoofs of a certain kind of rhetoric proclaim that for Kinsella and his generation, Romantic Ireland is indeed dead and gone.

"Death of a Queen" describes the death of an unnamed queen in abstract terms. The heroine is similar in spirit to Yeats's Deirdre, but specific references to a temporal sphere or a circumstantial world are irrelevant. The queen is torn from her Irish roots; all that remains is the hieratic pomp of her ritualized death:

> They sent counsellors and music
> Out across the promontory of her grief;
> And anger, after a while,
> Was released, shouldering like a bull;
>
> . . . .

> And she came with the step of a goddess,
> Hypocritical courageous,
> Wreathed with longing, out of the mast
> That crackled under her feet, not with pain
>
> But in pagan accompaniment of applause.
> Piece by piece, death was enticed
> Out of the hands that climbed about her. (*PT,* 2)

The poet has used abstraction and outmoded rhetorical figures as distancing strategies to underline the solitude and dignified despair of the dying queen as qualities per se separate from the actual person. By alienating the dying queen from the reader's sympathies, he also succeeds in eschewing all sentimentalism about death. In the end, dignity, despair, and a sense of void survive the literary exercise.

What dominates this poem is not the mythical figure but the inaccessibility of everything in her experience except her painful realization of decay and mortality—a favorite theme of the early and late Kinsella. The striking simile, whereby fading makeup on an aging face evokes both the physical realities of approaching death and the awareness of one's mortality, makes this early poem memorable:

> Yet it is not so much
> For disintegration of a lover or a kingdom
> Or burning of oak- and bronze-leaved
> Capitals that a queen grieves
> But that life, late or soon,
> Suddenly becomes, on the face, a jaded rouge. (*PT,* 3)

The crude realism of the final detail and the colloquial "late or soon" redeem the abstractions of the queen's ritual experience. This very private awareness gives a hint of a more inward-looking and pessimistic Kinsella, obsessed with physical disintegration and death. Notwithstanding its artificiality, "Death of a Queen" is a powerful poem.

"Test Case" is an ironic meditation on heroic diction and the rhetorical clichés of epic poetry and nationalist discourses. Expressions such as "rippling flags," "utter love," or "statuesque faith," and cliché situations such as dying for a belief or taking a "bleeding retreat to a stoic beloved," expose the empty rhetoric of a certain kind of poetic convention.

The subject of the poem is not a specific hero but the "heroic agenda" itself and the genres it inspires (elegiac, tragic, epic):

> Readier than flags rippling in the sun
> To turn tragic in elegiac weathers,
> More striking, forked and longer than lightning,
> Is the heroic agenda, full of frightening
> Things to kill or love or level down—
> A man's life, magnified with monumental bothers. (*PT,* 4)

The bathetic "monumental bothers" (and other incursions into colloquial diction) enhance the irony of the overblown heroic vocabulary. But the heroic figures hinted at fail to have concrete evidence, as in the following vague instance of a generic hero:

> In some kingdom his powers will be trapped
> Formally, his special innocence
> Quiver under his dilemma's vicious
> Tensions and be torn to pieces. (*PT,* 4)

The only direct portrait in the poem, of a Tarzan-like hero, presumably Cuchulain, clashes in its ironic robustness with the abstractions of the rest of the poem:

> Naked save for the skin of a preferably
> Ferocious beast, pulling down roofs
> Seriously to demonstrate some fact,
> His queer quality is noticed—direct
> Approach, statuesque faith—clearly he
> Is unforgettable. (*PT,* 4)

"The Travelling Companion" returns to the subject of heroism. A hybrid emblematic animal, foreshadowing one of the most potent symbols of Kinsella's later imaginary psychic world, acts as the hero of the narrative: "two starved jaws of the will, / Naturally ravenous . . . on claws. . . . [m]arched over murderous plains" to fight "with stern invaders. . . . Entirely happy in battle" (*PT,* 5).

Literary imitation in love poetry   The theme of love makes its appearance quite early; indeed, *Poems* is a sort of wedding gift for Eleanor. Some of the essential elements of Kinsella's love poetry can already be detected in these poems, such as the insistence on "love's difficulty" and the equivalence drawn between love, inspiration, and understanding. But the poems are far from being direct or personal; all personal references are carefully hidden under distancing devices and self-reflexive, parodic, or imitative elements are often present. Kinsella has pointed all this out himself: "Having remained inarticulate for most of my youth, I discovered more or less simultaneously the means of poetic expression and of honesty in love. For a time the two arts developed together so closely that only those poems succeeded which I wrote in the pursuit of love. Yet, while the matter of those poems was mine, much of their manner was drawn from other poets."[4]

The imitation of pastoral conventions, medieval bestiaries, and Renaissance moral emblems, for instance, creates a sort of screen to avoid overt revelation in Kinsella's early love poetry; as is the case in "Soft to Your Places" and "Midsummer." Love meetings between the poet and his wife-to-be in Dublin's Phoenix Park are thus transfigured and mythicized. "Soft to Your Places" plays on the dialectical presence of two voices: the first gives vent to an enraptured enjoyment, while the italicized refrain argues rationally against the first voice:

> Soft, to your places, animals,
> Your legendary duty calls.
>   It is, to be
> Lucky for my love and me.
> *And yet we have seen that all's*
> *A fiction that is heard of love's difficulty.* (SP, 14)

In "Midsummer" too there is a conjunction of the personal and the allegorical, as love announces itself through a metaphorical apparition of a deer, an animal which is present in great numbers in Phoenix Park, but which represents also a literary cliché:

> Something that for this long year
> Had hid and halted like a deer
>   Turned marvelous,

> Parted the tragic grasses, tame,
> Lifted its perfect head and came
> To welcome us. (*SP,* 12)

Both poems, however, are much more than literary exercises, although they do rely heavily on conventions. They achieve a fusion of personal feelings and elegant reticence which constitutes their originality.

Kinsella also avoids writing barefaced love poems by experimenting in various genres. "In the Ringwood," for instance, is a ballad combining the lilting rhythm of Rossetti's "The Blessed Damozel" with an "aisling" poem, the traditional Irish visionary composition. It relates how the speaker of the poem and his bride became estranged because of the woman's visionary premonition of the end of their love: "Love that is every miracle / Is torn apart and rent." The bride changed into "Sorrow's daughter" by a vision of the "ancient slaughter" at Vinegar Hill,⁵ has all the traditional attributes of the lady of a ballad (raven hair, red lips, white cheeks):

> 'Ravenhair what rending
> Set those red lips a-shriek,
> And dealt those locks in black lament
> Like blows on your white cheek,
> That in your looks outlandishly
> Both woe and fury speak?' (*SP,* 21)

The vision that has transfixed the lady is not only that of the ghosts of massacred Irish rebels, but a more cosmic vision of a general destructiveness in nature and human relationships. This is couched in Kinsella's customary abstractions and personifications, contrasting with the odd crude detail:

> 'Dread, a grey devourer,
> Stalks in the shade of love.
> The dark that dogs our feet
> Eats what is sickened of.
> The End that stalks Beginning
> Hurries home its drove.' (*SP,* 21)

Even the icy despair produced by the apparition of the ghosts is a literary echo, this time of Erlkönig and of Yeats:

> I kissed three times her shivering lips.
> I drank their naked chill.
> I watched the river shining
> Where the heron wiped his bill.
> I took my love in my icy arms
> In the Spring on Ringwood Hill. (*SP,* 21)

This is neither a nationalist nor a love ballad, notwithstanding the specific Irish theme. A protective display of Kinsella's craftsmanship in handling the conventions of the ballad mode make "In the Ringwood" yet another set piece, a ballad on ballads about love and war, rather than simply a ballad on love and war.

Muses and metapoetical exercises   "Night Songs," "First Light," "Who Is My Proper Art," and "An Ancient Ballet," all about moments of inspiration or their absence, represent another form of literary exercise. These and several other poems are based on narratives of how muse-like women make flighty apparitions in dreams or visions, and leave the persona of the poet either on the verge of some understanding or frustrated by the failure to seize it or put it into words. "Night Songs" presents such a situation with great musicality:

> Before I woke there entered in
> A woman with a golden skin
>   That tangled with the light.
> . . . .
>   Weakened with appetite
> Sleep broke like a dish wherein
> A woman lay with golden skin. (*SP,* 11)

In "First Light,"[6] all nature seems capable of expressing itself when, in a moonlit night, "two lips / were seen to break the crests of speech in fair order," and the sea let escape "one spoken / Shining syllable," and "a stylus, guided by the horizon, printed and mirrored." Unlike natural objects, the persona of the poet seems unable to respond with words or writing to such commotion: "For reply, I find I am left / with an unanswerable dawn upon my hands" (*PT,* 7).

Under his semi-serious musings on the nature of inspiration and the neo-classical trappings of muses and goddesses, Kinsella, in this group of poems, also gingerly broaches an important theme of his early poetry: the dichotomy between man and nature, or between rationality and instinct, which is often represented as a clash between male and female consciousness. The muse is as much an inspirer as a mistress, and the muse poems often double as love poems.

The muse of "Who Is My Proper Art," an object of fear as much as desire, illustrates the equivalence of love and inspiration:

> Much as calamities do, she took
> Her station near the heart; the crook
>   (That works the hand I steady
> This still-white leaf with) worked her voice
> To upper levels.
> . . . .
>   I kissed
> The effort in her wide
> Eyes and crowned the breasts where I
> Find order and sanguinity. (*PT,* 14)

So also does the muse-like moon of "An Ancient Ballet," which "draws our gazes thronging / Into the figured void," while the stars dance "until I loved" and "laid waste / This pillow with my tears, my joy" (*PT,* 16–17).

Altogether, whether Kinsella deals with the world of myth, or with inspiration or love, his first efforts are solipsistic reflections, often ironical, on various modes and genres.

New Themes and a Language of His Own

Kinsella evolved from the solipsistic stage of literary imitation in *Poems* to a more personal tone in *Another September.* Talking about the title poem, he commented: "In 'Another September,' love achieved its object, the vein of love poems came to an end, and new themes began to be freed in a language which, I believe, shows traces of being my own."[7] Many of the poems are written about specific and actual occasions, some inspired by his own life, others dealing with different people and places. Yet many of the elements pertaining to the first experimental phase remain, such as abstractions, distancing techniques, and sudden clashes. Even when using his own persona, or masks for himself, Kinsella hides self-revelation under imitations of Eliot's modernism or Auden's irony, coupled with late Romantic or Victorian ornateness. Poems dealing with personal subjects are defused by self-irony, although there are timid advances in the direction of confessionalism.

The acceptance of life's destructive forces is a major theme, whether in the impersonal forms of his earliest experiments or in the more personal poems. Kinsella himself described *Another September* as straining to "make real, in whatever terms, the passing of time, the frightening exposure of all relationships and feelings to erosion."[8] We can also detect the opposite movement, toward a search for something to set against time's eroding action and, therefore, justify the artistic function. Love and the poet's artistry are two interrelated forms of response to erosion, while the formal order of rhyme and stanza and the other complex stylistic patterns reflect his aspiration to find a design in reality. The search for a rigid form is almost an ontological necessity for Kinsella.

The Autobiographical Element

A few poems employ the poet's own persona to explore actual, rather than mythical, love relationships and his role as a poet.

"A Lady of Quality" (called "Dusk Music" in *Poems*), which dramatizes a hospital visit by the poet to his future wife, ill with tuberculosis, is an elegant musing on the theme of love and its difficulties. The fragile reality of the hospital world, and the tentative, artificial order that comes from the sickness, are successfully re-created in the poem through a succession of tropes ("airy architecture," "the air is like a laundered sheet," "to bless the room from present dread / Just for a brittle while"). The artificial atmosphere keeps at bay many preoccupations such as present illness and fear of death, but also acts as a lens through which other griefs are contemplated. Man's inability to be in touch with his own past is expressed by two metaphoric situations: the first, a rather clumsy one, tells of a mountain climber going back in vain to see the places he had tried to capture forever in a snapshot; the second, more evocative one, involves the flight of wild geese:

> The ever-present crack in time
> Forever sundering the lime-
>   Paths and the fragrant fountains,
> Photographed last summer, from
> The unknown memory we climb
>   To find in this year's mountains.
>
> 'Ended and done with' never ceases,
> Constantly the heart releases
>   Wild geese to the past.
> Look, how they circle poignant places,
> Falling to sorrow's fowling pieces
>   With soft plumage aghast. (*SP*, 16)

The conflict between the masculine and the feminine is a theme
which takes various forms and undergoes various developments in
Kinsella's poetry, and which converges with the ability of man and
woman to fuse through love.[9] In "A Lady of Quality," it appears as a love
relationship which can never be fully realized because of man's rational
and woman's instinctive attitudes:

> Our trophied love must now divide
>   Into its separate parts
>
> And you go down with womankind
> Who in her beauty has combined
>   And focused human hungers,
>
> . . . .
> And I communicate again
> Recovered order to my pen
>   To find a further answer. (*SP*, 16)

The successful re-creation of the "brittle while" of the hospital visit,
with its embarrassed silences and the avoidance of any worrisome subjects,
keeps in check heftier philosophical implications and offers a demonstra-
tion of "recovered order." An effect of ease is created by the iambic

tetrameters with doggerel cadences alternating with trimeters, and by the simple rhyme scheme with its many masculine rhymes. They "bless" not only the room "from present dread," but also the poem from too ponderous a tone. "A Lady of Quality" remains suspended between confessionalism, meditative poetry, and elegant exercise, and it reveals a light, yet pointed touch in the handling of narrative.

"Another September" presents the same male-female dichotomy as "A Lady of Quality." The sleeping woman, an "unspeaking daughter," is in perfect unison with nature; the garden drawing "long pitch black breaths" echoes the "black breathing that billows her sleep"; the "fragrant child," matches the "apple trees, / Ripe pear trees, brambles, windfall-sweetened soil," which "Exhale rough sweetness against the starry slates." The man, however, awake in a bedroom, "raw / With the touch of the dawn" from which the dreams have fled, confesses to a "half-tolerated consciousness, / Its own cold season never done."[10] In the light of his cold intellect, it seems as if her sleeping self "waned," leading, instead, to the apparition of menacing abstractions:

> bearing daggers
> And balances—down the lampless darkness they came,
> Moving like women: Justice, Truth, such figures. (SP, 23)

The grim personifications of moral concepts, perceived by a consciousness alienated from a life-giving nature, contrast with the other salient personification in the poem, that of a nature friendly and familiar to the woman:

> Domestic Autumn, like an animal
> Long used to handling by those countrymen,
> Rubs her kind hide against the bedroom wall. (SP, 16)

The rhetoric of the poem runs, however, counter to the trend of the discourse, which proves that the poet is not, as he claims, alienated from nature, but is in harmony with the slow rhythms of the autumn night. These rhythms are successfully conveyed in the poem by the luscious Keatsian imagery and the phonic structure, which creates an impression of sensuous slowness through a large number of anapests: "Dréams fled awáy, this cóuntry bédroom, ráw / With the tóuch of the dáwn, wrápped in a mínor péace."

Self-reflexive poems: "Baggot Street Deserta" Kinsella's distinctive voice can be heard especially in his meditative lyrics, the most famous of which, "Baggot Street Deserta," has made the central Dublin street as much a haunt for Kinsella's admirers as Eccles Street is for Joyce's. The poem is not about the street itself, nor about Kinsella's bachelor pad there, but about a youthful poet's reveries as he looks out the window at nighttime Dublin and beyond. The sounds of the river and the sight of the skies inspire his musings on time, decay, disorder, and, especially, the significance of art.

Literary and musical allusions abound. Taking a pause after "the spent attack" and "the strain of the rack" of inspired but strenuous literary composition, the speaker of the poem is half-ironically described in a romantic pose, sighing "a sigh / Of educated boredom," and adding to the natural sounds his "call of exile, half- / Buried longing, half-serious / Anger and rueful laugh." Indoors "[T]he mathematic / Passion of a cello suite" answers the imagined sounds of the river. The poet "reacts" to the regularity of the presumably baroque music through other auditory images: the "Adam's morse" of flashing images in dreamers' heads; the "curlew's lingering threadbare cry / Of common loss"; and, "The slow implosion of my pulse / In a wrist with poet's cramp"(*SP,* 26). The intellectualized music is not only a device of order that runs through the entire poem, it is also the auditory backbone itself of a poem that tries to frame the "main / Mystery, not to be understood" (*SP,* 28) through a fairly regular iambic rhythm and a strict rhyme scheme.

The musical metaphor underlines the artificiality of the poetic endeavor: "Versing, like an exile, makes / A virtuoso of the heart" (*SP,* 26). Unlike baroque music, modern poetry cannot provide a resolution for discords: the result will always be "doctored." The poem acknowledges the frustration of the poet at his impossible task, that of "eliciting order from experience," yet makes a plea for art as a human necessity.

The self-reflexive poem is an honest recognition of a young artist's doubts and pretensions, and an expression of his despair at failure. The main dilemma regards the source of inspiration, which is conveyed through elaborate figures of speech. Memories of the past, where an aspiring poet might look for a gleam of truth, are to the fury and passion of youth like a spray of dried flowers, or like a nightmarish "fairy bog." Two Irish body-snatchers of the eighteenth century, Burke and Hare, indicate the morbidity of dwelling on the past—both one's personal past and the past of tradition. He who looks back is like those sinister figures that haunt Kinsella's allegorical inferno of memory: owls, dogs, "shaven, serious-minded men," or the grotesque muse with "feet of dung," evoked out of a putrescent past.

Kinsella was to change his view about the past as a creative source. But at this point, the new imperative, the "risk" the poet has to take, is dictated by a voice from outside which commands, in the only unrhymed and italicized line of the poem: *"Endure and let the present punish"* (*SP,* 27). This stoic message invites a clear-eyed immersion into the present, and is validated by the confessionalism of some of the poems in *Another September, Wormwood,* and many of the poems that followed.

The final part of the poem is a statement of the speaker's present *ars poetica:* the aspiring poet must face "intracordal hurt" with "obsessed honesty," and bury all youthful illusions while recognizing their essential vanity. Most of all (and here we find the by now familiar theme of the contrast between instinct and reason), he must renounce intellectual and communicable knowledge, and trust "the alien / Garrison in my own blood" to keep instinctively "constant contact with the main / Mystery not to be understood" (*SP,* 28). The result may indeed be "spurious" and completely private, but it gives rise to lines which, in continuing the military metaphor introduced by the image of garrisons, stress the solitary role of the poet as a baffled sentinel, alone on the border of "the Real" to search and infiltrate a region alien to him:

> Out where imagination arches
> Chilly points of light transact
> The business of the border-marches
> Of the Real, and I—a fact
> That may be countered or may not—
> Find their privacy complete. (*SP,* 28)

The poem ends with a dejected yet defiant gesture: "My quarter-inch of cigarette / Goes flaring down to Baggot Street" (*SP,* 28).

Yet in the arch of light the cigarette traces in the darkness, we may see man's modest attempt to reproduce "the crawling arch of stars"; the chilly points out there "where imagination arches." While recognizing the privacy of the Real, the poet does not renounce his aspiration to draw "mathematical" order and design out of it.

Portrait poems   A move towards indirect self-revelation, concreteness, and a less impersonal style is also apparent in several portrait poems which make their appearance in *Another September* ("The Monk," "Clarence Mangan," "Thinking of Mr. D.") and constitute an important subgroup in *Downstream* ("The Laundress," "Portrait of an Engineer," "Dick King"), only to dwindle away in *Nightwalker and Other Poems* when there is a switch to a direct, confessional approach. Some of these poems are portraits of common people, others of literary people; both kinds are masks which allow Kinsella to muse on his usual themes: decay and death, the erosion of passing time, and which occasionally permit some self-revelation under the cover of impersonality. The literary portraits, moreover, open up the possibility for more personalized reflections on the poetic art than the previously discussed muse-poems. Both, however, are a first step in the direction of the confessional mode.

The stark and effective portrait of "The Monk," with its simple, regular, iambic rhythm, and sparse rhyming pattern, reflecting the contrived simplicity of the monk's lifestyle, introduces several themes which are close to Kinsella's heart. The foremost is the contrast between self-control and an intuitive, joyous communion with nature and the senses, which we have seen in the poems in which a male-female conflict is introduced. Two other collateral themes are the attempt to restrain passion and self-expression through a coherent system of language and form, and the masochistic fascination with mutilation:

> A sense of scrubbed flesh in the path
> A thought of washing in cold hours
> When dreams are scrubbed off
> In a chill room, huge flowers,
> Night blooms, accidentally plucked,
> Each dawn devours;
> Of a haggard taste in the mouth
> Savouring in death a tide of light,
> Harvest in all decay,
> Spring in February night. (*SP*, 25)

"Clarence Mangan" is a dramatic monologue spoken by the eccentric nineteenth-century Irish poet whose progress through the irrational is charted in the poem. Based on Mangan's own literary accounts of his misery due to loneliness, poverty, alcohol and drug addiction, each of the four stanzas of Kinsella's poem represents in a graphic way a different manifestation of Mangan's fears and hallucinations. Kinsella dazzles and surprises with his linguistic bravura as he describes the various phases of Mangan's madness, the bewilderment, the shout of fear, and his reaction to a crowd of "tumultuous talking faces":

> Sometimes, childishly watching a beetle, thrush or trout,
> Or charting the heroes and animals of night-time, sudden
>   unhappiness
> Would bewilder me, strayed in the long void of youth
> Where nothing is understood.
> Later locked in a frantic pose, all mankind calling,
> I being anxious to please, shouted my fear
> That something was wrong.
> . . . .
>   My heart was taken,
> Stretched with terror by only a word a mouth had uttered,
> Clipped to a different, faceless destroyer. (SP, 24)

The deviations from the norm in rhythm and lexis, along with the arresting coupling of terms ("fills with waiting," "surgical fingers," "naked meeting," "the long void of youth"), match the deviations of the subject. The poem closes with a surrealistic description of the schizoid poet probing himself as an impersonal yet healing torturer:

> Out of the shadows behind my laughter surgical fingers
> Come and I am strapped to a table.

> Ultimate, pitiless, again I ply the knife. (SP, 24)

Kinsella himself was soon to probe his own despair, out of necessity as much as masochism, and one of the main problems he was to encounter is manifest in this poem: how to be confessional without telling too much about his own "ordeal of life." For the language of "Clarence Mangan," with its imitation of both the ravings of a madman and the *poete maudit*'s own high Romantic ranting, hides as much as it reveals.

"Thinking of Mr. D." is a portrait of Austin Clarke, whose anger against Irish society he sees as alienating and damaging for his poetry. His criticism of the older poet's "rage barred in / By age" and of his "abstract wrecking humour," which make him "A barren Dante leaving us for hell," show Kinsella's concern for his own bitter satirical inclinations. Several portraits and self-portraits also appear in *Downstream,* and provide an interesting angle of comparison to illustrate Kinsella's new style.

Descriptive poems   Realistic descriptions are not relevant in *Poems* and *Another September,* in which Kinsella mostly depicts landscapes of the imagination; sophisticated allegorical or emblematic backdrops which have no reference in nature but only in literature (as, for instance, "In the Ringwood"). One purely descriptive poem about a crumbling castle ("King John's Castle"), however, establishes the quintessential Kinsellan scenario of ruin and decay, which dominates the 1956–1968 phase, and thus cannot be ignored.

> Now the man-rot of passages and broken window-casements,
> Vertical drops chuting through three storeys of masonry
> Draughty spiral stairways loosening in the depths,
> Are a labyrinth in the medieval dark . . .
>
> Life a vestigial chill, sighs along the tunnels
> Through the stone face. The great collapsed rooms, the mind
> Of the huge head, are dead. Views open inwards
> On empty silence, a chapel-shelf, moss-grown, unreachable.
>   (*SP,* 29)

The poem offers a vivid representation of one of the many crumbling buildings that dot Kinsella's poetic landscape—and indeed much of Irish poetry—and also works beyond literal signification as an emblem of a ruined and mutilated tradition.

Moralities   The apotheosis of Kinsella's abstract, allegorical style appears in the brief sequence *Moralities,* published in 1960 and later included in a revised form in *Poems and Translations* (1961), and again, as originally printed, in Kinsella's second volume of collected poems, *Downstream,* in 1962.

The collection has a medieval flavor. The eight-line compositions are dramatically structured around four abstract themes: Faith, Love, Death, and Song, which are themselves introduced in the untitled prologue as grotesque figures ("Flounced, scalloped, stuffed with hay, gay skin and bone") and set against the harmonious background of a church, almost to signify the loss of the certainties of traditional morality. The prologue provides a sort of outline for the brief satirical pieces that constitute the sequence, foreshadowing a technique Kinsella was to use extensively in later poetry. For each of the four themes, three short poems provide contrasting, fragmentary illustrations, as well as concrete situations to show how each of these universals can be experienced in the modern world. "Faith," for instance, presents three different attitudes: that of the skeptic, who finds nurture for his doubts in contemplating a polished seashell, a symbol of relentless erosion and decay; that of the unconditional believer, whose total abandonment to God's will is expressed through the metaphor of the diver soaring outstretched from the diving board "into the azure chasm"; and that of the opportunist, a Lucifer whose "puckish rump" is inscribed "Do good. / Some care and a simple faith will get you on" (*SP,* 33). Similar character sketches or vignettes illustrate the other themes; the brief poems are poised between the epigram and the enigmatic emblem. With its artificial conception, abstractions, and heavy reliance on all sorts of rhetorical devices, *Moralities* represents the culmination of Kinsella's abstract phase. Yet some of the vignettes give a foretaste of a poet more attentive to common human types. With its realistic setting at Euston Station, "Song," a poignant reflection on the humiliations of migration, has an unusual topicality: "Weight, / Person, race, the human, dwindle there" (*SP,* 37). It prepares us for a different Kinsella.

Conclusion

In Kinsella's poetic development, *Another September* marks the apex of the first stage of his career. While containing elements that were soon to disappear, such as a lyrical disposition, and a melodic and rhetorical elegance, it also establishes some longer-lived features such as a romantic inclination for self-searching, which, in *Wormwood,* would turn to confessionalism and a taste for long, often self-reflexive meditation (both present, for instance, in "Baggot Street Deserta"). Love, stern moralism, an obsession with time and decay, and an insistent search for order are common features of this and successive collections. Kinsella, moreover, appears as an isolated figure—an obscure poet, whose poems do not seem to be rooted in time and place.

Chapter Four
Nightwalker and Other Poems

Nightwalker and Other Poems (1968)—an anthology including poems from three preceding collections: *Downstream* (1962), *Wormwood* (1967), and *Nightwalker* (1967)—represents a major phase in Kinsella's development; the one to which he owes his reputation. *Downstream* was a transitional volume, suspended between the artificiality and literariness of the earlier collections, and the experimentation of his subsequent production. From his literary apprenticeship, Kinsella emerged with a personal, subdued poetic voice and a refined craftsmanship. This became evident in *Wormwood,* a sequence of love poems, and even more so in *Nightwalker,* in which the first indications of a new style became manifest.

Although *Nightwalker and Other Poems* presents many similarities in style and content with the earlier work, we can see in the poems selected from the three volumes that Kinsella is moving away from abstraction and impersonality towards what he defined at the time as "an expedition into the interior," and "an exploration of private miseries."[1] The poet dares to speak in his own persona, and several poems are in the confessional vein, notwithstanding his natural reticence. But the personal note is not the only one heard; many poems display Kinsella's public conscience and his sympathies for common humanity. Portraits, and descriptive and narrative sketches, provide a more concrete form of poetry than in the past. Yet the most characteristic form of the new collection is the long, partly narrative, partly meditative poem modeled on the Romantic or Victorian ode but organized according to modernist techniques.

The volume represents a refinement of old techniques and an opening up toward the new, within the framework of tradition. Together with *Notes from the Land of the Dead,* this, in Dillon Johnston's opinion, is "one of the least conventional volumes ever published in Ireland, and therefore one of the most difficult to characterize."[2] Even if Kinsella introduces freer, more conversational patterns and almost abandons rhyme and tightly controlled verse, a semblance of a formal structure remains. In several compositions, Kinsella works towards a bare, minimalist style; the language is often simple, almost flat, and the rhythms natural. In the longer compositions, Kinsella employs a loose blank verse or the

Dantean *terza rima*. Other stanzaic patterns can easily be recognized but we are a long way from the sophisticated formal patterning of his earlier work. By 1973, when Kinsella was well into a new phase of his poetic production, *Selected Poems 1956–1968,* which included many of his best-known poems, marked the close of one season and cleared the way for more experimental work.

Portraits

The link with the earlier volumes is provided by several portrait poems such as "The Laundress," "Dick King," "The Serving Maid," "Portrait of an Engineer," "Charlie" (the portrait of a bird), and "Scylla and Charybdis" (the portrait of a greengrocer and a fishmonger). Unlike the earlier portraits, however, these poems display an interest in the outer world rather than being an indirect way of self-representation. There are several self-portraits in the collection; in fact, Kinsella, at this stage, frequently uses his own persona, even if he does not yet delve into himself and dwells instead on general themes.

An example of the new social interest animating the portraits is "Dick King," a simple poem in which Kinsella reminisces about the repetitive, uneventful life of an old man he loved in his childhood:

> And season in, season out,
> He made his wintry bed.
> He took the path to the turnstile
> Morning and night till he was dead. (*SP,* 46)

The simplicity of the man's life is evoked, appropriately, by an Audenesque use of doggerel and by the folk rhythms of a ballad. While the poem shows a sincere concern for the old man, it also deals with more personal themes such as the acceptance of death and the importance love has in conferring value to a modest life. The two themes, indeed, are closely linked: in the "phantom vowels" of the dead man's name, the speaker realizes "That death roves our memories igniting / Love." Similarly the old man talking to the little boy had "named the dead . . . discovering / A gate to enter temperate ghosthood by" (*SP,* 45). Thus, in the name of love and death, a continuity is established between generations. "Dick King" is a poem of sadness and consolation in which a realistic portrait, childhood memories, and philosophical considerations blend harmoniously.

A companion piece to "Dick King" is "The Shoals Returning," a poem in memory of Gerry Flaherty, a fisherman from the Dingle peninsula.[3] Both poems compound elegy and portrait, and deal with simple people who have faced life and death with dignity and in harmony with natural rhythms, so that the horror of their deaths was erased. Gerry Flaherty is remembered through the specific actions which give their titles to the various sections of the poem: *"He comes from the sea,"* *"He sings,"* *"He returns,"* *"He disappears."* Unlike in many of Kinsella's other poems, death is not the central event in this life. The fisherman is remembered especially because he sang traditional Irish melodies to rapt audiences in the back of a shop:

> A voice rises flickering
> From palatal darkness, a thin yell
> Straining erect, checked
> In glottal silence. The song
> Articulates and pierces.[4]

The poem, commemorating the fisherman's song which "can prepare the spirit / To turn softly and be eaten," is also a celebration of the capacity of human creativity to overcome the erosion of the elements.

"The Laundress" could best be described as a painting in the Flemish style of a pregnant woman stitching a sheet, as she sits in her doorway and contemplates fields of maturing wheat. The poet creates an atmosphere of harmony and equilibrium, but on more careful reading, this appears to be only surface tranquillity. The central simile of the poem works in two directions. The flutter of the fetus (described through a ponderous metaphor as "the heels of ripeness") disturbs the woman's peace, "As a fish disturbs the pond / and sinks without a stain." The reader's first perception of harmony between subject and nature, however, is also disturbed by disquieting shadows created by the choice of diction. The fields are "harrowed"; meaning plowed, but also torn, lacerated, wounded. The luminous scenery is suddenly obscured by a shadow changing its stance. The stitching woman stares "At yellow fields unstitching / about the hoarded germ" (*SP*, 43); a presage of her own ripeness being undone as much in creation of new life as in possible destruction of it. The vision of the cold whiteness of winter that will accompany the end of her pregnancy reinforces the threatening presence of death. Moreover, the mention of Flanders cannot be innocent in poetry written in English. Echoes of Owen and the First World War poets interfere, and it is difficult not to read "The Laundress" in the perspective of those poems. The laundress's anxiety about the coming event—"Her heart grew strained and light / As the shell that shields the grain" (*SP,* 43)—is compounded by the reader's own anxious suspicions, ranging from more specific ones ("Is she a war widow?") to more general ones ("Is she breeding flesh for the cannons of war?").

Portraits of literary figures Poems about literary figures continue to be frequent, but rather than providing occasions for self-reflection, they are occasion for broaching on Kinsella's usual thematic concerns. "Death in Ilium," a poem written in Yeats's centenary year, reverts to Kinsella's usual obsession with waste and decay. The fate of the dead poet, abandoned to the inquisitiveness of critics and biographers, is compared to that of a carcass abandoned to preying animals:

> Hector among his books
> Drops dead in the dust.
>
> The tireless shadow eaters
> Close in with tough nose
> And pale fang to expose
> Fibre, weak flesh, speech organs.
>
> They eat but cannot eat.
> Dog faces in his bowels,
> Bitches at his face
> He grows whole and remote. (*SP,* 82)

The vision of the poet growing whole in spite of the tearing attacks does not totally dispel the horror of the physical and spiritual waste of death.

"The Poet Egan O'Rahilly, Homesick in Old Age" re-creates the feeling of disillusion of the eighteenth-century professional poet turned into an outcast by the disappearance of patronage. The poem is full of allusions and quotations from O'Rahilly's own "Cabhair ní ghairfead" (translated by Kinsella himself as "No help I'll call"). The old poet, making his "decrepit progress" along the stormy ocean, has visions of "aliens . . . / Breaking princely houses in their jaws" and of the "great houses like stopped hearts." Images of ruins are familiar to readers of Kinsella, as are those of the diseased body; such as "Bent with curses above the shrew his stomach," "incessant dying," or "winkle and dogfish persisting in the stomach . . . " (*SP,* 81). But there is more audacity in this portrait-poem than in similar ones in *Downstream* and *Another September;* the character of the old poet is represented more concretely than, for instance, that of Clarence Mangan. There are daring metaphors and a surprising use of adjective and verb, as is apparent from the preceding examples or in expressions such as "the cooling den of my craft," which gives a poignant measure of O'Rahilly's awareness of his own physical, social, and artistic decline.

"Magnanimity," dedicated to Austin Clarke on his seventieth birthday, also dwells on the passing of time and its effects on the physical world: "Helpless commonness encroaches, chews the soil, / Squats ignobly. . . . Houses shall pass away, and all give place / To signposts and chicken-wire"(*SP,* 80). Only verse and the memory of the poets can outlast their physical abodes, like the tree in Coole Park, commemorating Lady Gregory and Yeats, outlasted the big house. Kinsella's poem itself, incorporating Clarke's forgiving words about Yeats—"So I forgot / His enmity"[5]—makes the older poet's magnanimity survive the memory of the places where he lived.

Self-portraits

In *Nightwalker and Other Poems,* Kinsella often dares speak in his own person and draw a number of self-portraits. The preface to *Downstream,* "I wonder whether one expects," and "Mirror in February" are both self-portraits: the first is ironical in tone, the second is meditative and lyrical. The self-reflexive "I wonder whether one expects" ridicules stereotyped representations of poets ("flowing tie or expert sex") by using prosy language to describe the down-to-earth realities of the persona of the poet, who "can spare an evening drinking" or "lends / A hand about the house." But when it comes to talking of the flash of inspiration which turns the civil servant into a poet, Kinsella once more reverts to a language reflecting his romantic matrix: "The sunlight flickers once upon / The massive shafts of Babylon" (*SP,* 41). In the final part of the poem, in which personified abstractions and allegorical figures parade grotesquely, evoking "Another September," we may read an ironical farewell to this device, which he now mocks but which he had used extensively.

"Before Sleep," like the preceding poem, represents the poet at work and mixes self-deprecation with a romantic view of the poet inspired by

Orphic forces. Before unleashing "the cataract" of poetic creation—those thundering "Falls" carrying "love's detritus . . . . Into that insane / white roar"—the poet engages in a tidy nighttime routine; almost a propitiating act aimed at evoking a vision of order:

> It is time for bed. The cups and saucers are gathered
> And stacked in the kitchen, the tray settled
> With your tablets, a glass, a small jug of orange.
> Are the windows shut, and all the doors locked? (*SP,* 79)

The poem offers glimpses of "the poet at home"—a meticulous, fussy domestic animal—and then of "The Poet"—the prey of an uncontrollable force which he is, yet, capable of "putting on" at will.

"Mirror in February," another self-portrait, clearly marks a change from the old ways. Written in a spare, inward-looking style, and candidly revealing the intimate preoccupations of the speaker, it heralds the confessional poems. In this and other early personal work, there is a correspondence between a disintegrating landscape and visions of failing, diseased man. As the persona of the poet contemplates himself in the mirror while he shaves, he abandons himself to considerations of human and natural decay, prompted by the photographic observation of his face. The mirror in "a crumbling place of growth" reflects images of a "dark exhausted eye, / A dry downturning mouth." The external context of this is equally dismal:

> The day dawns with scent of must and rain,
> Of opened soil, dark trees dry bedroom air.
> . . . .
> Below my window the awakening trees,
> Hacked clean for better bearing, stand defaced
> Suffering their brute necessities,
> And how should the flesh not quail that span for span
> Is mutilated more? (*SP,* 61)

The final consideration expresses a quiet stoicism:

> In slow distaste
> I fold my towel with what grace I can,
> Not young and not renewable, but man. (*SP,* 61)

Other poems partake of this semi-confessional vein, and rely on pathetic fallacies and objective correlatives to confront personal states of being. In "Soft Toy," a battered teddy bear, or some similar soft toy, becomes a fitting persona for the poet—a "soiled," "crumpled," "beaten," "ragged," "heaped" thing, "limp with use and re-use" "with a cold pitted grey face" (*SP*, 83).

An awareness of decay, central to Kinsella's view of man, makes him particularly responsive to failing powers or outright disease in his many portraits and self-portraits. For a relatively young man, at that time, Kinsella seemed morbidly obsessed with deteriorating physical forms and loss of power.

Concern with Mortality

Kinsella's "awareness of the passing of time, of mutability and mortality,"[6] inspires the poems of all this early season. A sense of horror at the destructiveness of death, and, as usual, at the decay that awaits mankind, transpires from the many elegies and poems about death in *Nightwalker and Other Poems,* but concern with mortality takes a more direct form than in the past. Instead of the cold and abstruse allegory of "Death of a Queen," in *Nightwalker* we have a series of poems centered on specific deaths; vignettes about real enough people with their anguish of dying or watching someone die. The elegies "Dick King" and "The Shoals Returning" could belong to this category, but they pay more attention to the personality of the protagonist than to the waste inherent in death, while the other poems seem obsessed with the theme of mortality.

Two poems deal with the death of the speaker's mother. "Our Mother" displays the poet's usual reticence; the speaker can only deal with the death that concerns him through analogues. Only one stanza of the poem turns on the dying mother, who, through the plural possessive adjective "our," becomes a general mother, the mother of all mankind. In spite of the realistic description—she "Turns on us an emptiness / Of open mouth and damp eyes" (*SP*, 71)—the pain remains impersonal. There is much more feeling in the description of two other women in the ward: a young woman under anesthetic, sleeping "on her new knowledge, a bride / with bowels burning and disarrayed" (*SP*, 71); and her mother watching her daughter suffer. All three women represent for the speaker the common fate of humanity: "Living, dying." The sense of death in life, in other words the process of decay and suffering, is what concerns the poet more than specific deaths.

"Office for the Dead" hinges on two images: the "grief-chewers" in the funeral service, and the memory of the dying mother, graphically recalled as in the preceding poem, through the most painful physical details of her agony ("eyes boring out of the dusk— / Wistful mis-shapenness—a stripped, dazzling mouth"). The consolation of church people is unable to reach those who suffer, as their "Church / Latin chews our different losses into one." The incense pot, in the final simile of the poem, is like "An animal of metal, dragging itself and breathing" (SP, 73), underlining the feeling of alienation the sufferers experience.

"Cover Her Face" also concentrates on the uncomprehending grief of the bereaved, and on the distance death establishes between the quick and the dead. To her relatives, the young woman who has died suddenly in Dublin is more of a stranger than "the black official giving discipline / To shapeless sorrow" (SP, 47). Grieving and religious ritual are, indeed, acts of life, attempts to give shape to death, which is a mystery: "who understands / The sheet pulled white and Maura's locked blue hands?" She "whose blood and feature, like a sleepy host, / Agreed a while with theirs," is now severed from them. The poem evokes with poignancy the fading away of all physical attributes; those ties which anchored her to the living:

> Soon her few glories will be shut from sight:
> her slightness, the fine metal of her hair spread out,
>
> Her cracked sweet laugh such gossamers as hold
> Friends, family—all fortuitous conjunction—
> Sever with bitter whispers; with untold
> Peace shrivel to their anchors in extinction. (SP, 48)

Maura's life was one of unfulfillment, "unmarriage"; her own brief affair with the narrator was bled "to a diagram," a "scrap of memory." Negativity and absence dominate this poem rather than the customary sense of horror or waste. Even peace in death, wished to the girl's relatives, is "out of all likelihood."

Another poem that also deals with the concept of mortality under-stood in a wider sense, is "Chrysalides." This is a short narrative poem interleaved with meditation (as many poems of this collection are), establishing, like "The Laundress," an atmosphere of peace and ecstasy, only to disrupt it with an intimation of death. The poem nostalgically

evokes a bicycle holiday "on our last free summer," with its simple pleasures and its innocence:

> Sleeping too little or too much, we awoke at noon
> And were received with womanly mockery into the
> kitchen,
> Like calves poking our faces in with enormous hunger.
> (*SP,* 60)

The idyllic scene appears even more worthy of nostalgia because the protagonists were then insensitive both to "The unique succession of our
youthful midnights," and to the horror of the discovery that death is
inherent in the moment of birth. The realization comes to the uncomprehending young people at the sight of "a wedding flight of ants /
Spawning to its death, a mute perspiration / glistening like drops of cop-
per in our path" (*SP,* 60). The mature narrator has now, sadly, the full
capacity to assess and explore such horror, hence his smiling delight at
his younger self's perplexity.

Other poems, such as "Downstream," which concerns a boy's first discovery of what Kinsella calls the "lasting horror" of mortality, constitute
a much more ambitious attempt to deal with the theme. In his later
poetry, Kinsella would attempt to justify and integrate the awareness of
death in his *Weltanschaung.*

Visions of Order

The fact that poems in this period of Kinsella's production are so dis-
tinctly dominated by waste, death, and ruins, is all part of a wider plot.
"We're surrounded and penetrated by squalor, disorder and the insignif
icant, and I believe the artistic impulse has a great deal to do with our
trying to make sense out of that," said Kinsella in an interview from
roughly that period (Haffenden, 101). Several poems, thus, are totally
devoted to eliciting order from waste, but, at the same time, to viewing
ironically the attempts to hold things in place.

In a 1968 poem, the trope of the museum is used to meditate ironically on the poetic act as an act of order:

> Webs of corridors and numbered rooms
> Catch the onward turbulence of forms

> Against museum technique: flux disperses
> In order everywhere, in glass cases
> Or draped or towering in enormous gloom. (*NOP,* 17)

Kinsella's volumes of poetry are also "webs" and "numbered rooms" in which "the turbulence of life is caught."

The pathetic attempt made to oppose a regular pattern or an orderly sequence to waste, pain, and confusion is also reflected in another portrait poem, "The Serving Maid." In her desperate task, the maid appears as a *persona* for the artist:

> I come, I come, in decent skirt and jumper
> And flat-heeled shoes, with flowers and prayer book
> All in order to remember you;
> To kneel by the grave's gravel and pluck the weeds
> And replace the withered things—and if I could
> Even death's eery filth, tidying your substance. (*NOP,* 20)

One of the supreme examples of Kinsella's musings on the theme of the imposition of order is "Ballydavid Pier." This is one of his best-known poems and the poet himself chose it to represent his work in *Choice,* an anthology of pieces picked by their own authors. Kinsella writes, it was "[c]hosen not necessarily as the best I think I have written, but as the one of best-directed anger—anger at the continuum of waste, injustice, etc., in which we are apparently expected to survive."[7] The waste in question is a misbirth brought in by the "luminous tide," "a bag of flesh, / Foetus of goat or sheep" floating with "the film of scum." The observation of the phenomenon lends itself to an attempt to generalize it, and to link it to evolutionary notions:

> Allegory forms of itself:
> The line of life creeps upward
> Replacing one world with another,
> The welter of its advance
> Sinks down into clarity,
> Slowly the more foul
> Monsters of loss digest. . . . (*SP,* 74)

The progress the observer has watched in the harbor from the advancing life-bearing scum, to the temporary clarity, and finally to the "small monster of true flesh"—a new evidence of waste—is an obvious allegory of the cycles of the evolutionary process, but even more so of Kinsella's poetic process. His characteristic itinerary is also that of moving from waste to clarity, and to the ordering principle of allegory, only to be confronted with new waste. With skepticism, the poet asks the fetus and himself: "Does that structure satisfy?" Try as one may, the remains of a wasted life-process are difficult to justify. The fetus, represented in such attentive detail, is also, allegorically, the poet's budding (and aborted) attempt to impose order whenever confronted with waste. The vision of the fetus lost in self-search indicates the dubiousness of the attempt to solve the problem through allegory or art:

> The ghost tissue hangs unresisting
> In allegorical waters,
> Lost in self-search
> —A swollen blind brow
> Humbly crumpled over
> Budding limbs, unshaken
> By the spasms of birth or death. (*SP*, 75)

The Angelus bells ringing over the vacant harbor provide a contrast between a world of faith which can make sense of waste, and the post-Darwinian world in which the poet must find ways of justifying waste rationally. In spite of the failure of reason, however, there is a sense of purpose: the misbirth touching the surface "glistens like quicksilver" and becomes for an instant a vital symbol. The aesthetic moment succeeds where allegory-forming reason has failed.

Wormwood

Wormwood, a seven-poem sequence with an epigraph from the Apocalypse of John justifying the title, and a dedication to a "beloved," was first published by Dolmen as a limited-edition in 1966, and was included, in a heavily revised form, in *Nightwalker and Other Poems.* *Wormwood* is a landmark in the poet's production, since in it Kinsella perfects the sequence form (first explored in *Moralities*) and timidly explores the confessional mode, employing the poet's own persona rather than projecting himself though portraits and indirect representations.

The opening prose poem (titled "Prologue" in *Nightwalker*) introduces two central themes: ordeal and love. Combined or appearing independently, these themes animate Kinsella's production to this day. In his essay "The Divided Mind," Kinsella indicates how the two are linked: "In the private context, as the ordeal bears down on us one by one, the weight may be lightened by the experience or the ideal of love."[8]

In "Prologue," Kinsella affirms his belief that we go through life in a cycle of ordeals and new beginnings, and that the cup we must drink is as bitter as wormwood. "It is certain that maturity and peace are to be sought through ordeal after ordeal, and it seems that the search continues until we fail . . . . But if we drink the bitterness and can transmute it and continue, we resume in candour and doubt the only individual joy— the restored necessity to learn" (*NOP,* 28). In *Wormwood,* love and marriage themselves are the bitter cup from which eventually comes also the force to endure the ordeal. The vicissitudes of love relationships ("each torturing each . . . . Pigs in a slaughter-yard that turn and savage each other in a common desperation and disorder." [*NOP,* 28]) are described in pitiless terms in the dedication and developed in the seven poems. But "the individual plight," the specific cases, should not make us forget "the common plight." In a general sense, love becomes a positive force: "Love also, it seems, will continue until we fail: in the sensing of the wider scope, in the growth toward it, in the swallowing and absorption of bitterness, in the resumed innocence . . . " (*NOP,* 28). The words are a tribute to conjugal love in spite of its difficulties.

"Prologue" also suggests a plot for the sequence, and each individual poem can be linked to parts of the introductory prose-poem. The direct, intimate opening address—"Beloved, A little of what we have found"— promises a personal note instead of the previous abstractions. The expected confessionalism, however, is much toned-down in the individual poems. The conjugal crisis, in fact, is signified by recurrent dreams and nightmares, and there are only opaque references to the actual events. Emblematic trees, a distorted mask, and a child's ugly wail are so many ways of concealing the actual crisis and depersonalizing it. The revisions on the first draft eliminate the personal note completely, making the poems published in *Nightwalker* impersonal. Redshaw, in his conflation of the two versions, demonstrates this very convincingly.[9]

The first poem, an invitation to open the book and see the picture inside, is in the form of an emblem, or a riddle. The speaker represents himself as "a nearly naked tree" in autumn, shaken by a tempest of "self-punishment"—an oblique and overdramatic projection of a tormented self. The studied simplicity of language and form—regular tetrasyllabic verse with simple masculine rhymes; the key word "bare" being repeated twice, and rhyming with "air" and "tear"—give this poem a childish, innocent tone, belying the anguished self-portrait, and also casting some doubt on the sincerity of the account.

The emblem of the tree also reappears in the second poem, which relates a recurrent nightmare, but this time it is "A black tree with a double trunk—Two trees / Grown into one" (*NOP*, 30)—an all too transparent allusion to the couple. The fusion of the two trees is represented as painful. The shared life, an "infinitesimal dance of growth," has made them turn "completely about one another," leaving "a slowly twisted scar" in the place where they are joined; the branches have "blurred" individualities. Different phonic devices slow down the rhythm and underline this long-drawn hanging on to each other. A quickening iambic rhythm announces the nightmarish ending: a heavy blade separates the two trunks, projecting at the same time the speaker's fear and his desire.

In "Mask of Love," abstractions, again, frame the illustrations of the misunderstandings and difficulties besetting the couple. The poem starts and ends with a vision of a nightmarish mask of love, abstract and concrete at the same time, bearing the lover's face and symbolizing the masquerades of love; as, for instance, the sexual act—"the nocturnal dance"—which fails to bring peace and bridge the abyss. A "narrow abyss," a "silent abyss," and, finally, a "fuming abyss" separate the lovers. Within this frame of illusory love and actual separation, the poem examines some more concrete instances of the difficulties besetting the lovers. Physical ailments such as "skin angrily flam[ing]" and "Nerve grop[ing] for muscle" torment them. The woman's pragmatic approach ("She, bent on some tiny mote") is in contrast to the man's more idealistic stance ("I . . . clasping my paunch in grief / For the world in a speck of dust"). The resulting irritations lead to a "nocturnal / Suicidal dance" [*NOP*, 31]), an oxymoron which echoes the suffocating "dance of growth" of "Wormwood." The occasional rhymes—or, actually, false rhymes (face-abyss)—and, mostly, the absence of rhyme, mime the illusion of being a pair and the actual absence of a real correspondence.

"Secret Garden" uses a much more direct approach. An overgrown garden, with a lawn full of "flails of bramble," "toughened branches," and "leaves and thorns" on which, however, "glitter" drops of dew, is the analogue for the speaker's "secret garden"—his inner life, itself hardened, thorny and difficult. The poem is structured around an implied equation: as "glittering, toughened branches drink their dew. / Tiny worlds, drop by drop, tremble / On thorns and leaves," so the dried-up life of the speaker of the poem receives energy through the closeness to his child—"I touch my hand to his pearl flesh, taking strength" (*NOP*, 32). Both the dew and the child are "glittering," and both evoke the perfection of a round shape: the drop, the tiny world; the pearl, the "immaculate kernel" of the child's brain. The child's purity will be "tainted" by growth in the same way "the dew dries to dust" when the sun climbs. The branch and the speaker's inner life both receive nourishment: the branch from drinking the lifegiving force, and the father from smelling the energy in his child's mouth.

In a sentence that merges the literal with the symbolic plane, the poet can say "I cultivate my garden for the dew" (*NOP*, 32). The poem, which had opened with a description of the thorny garden, contains in its central part the revitalizing contact with the dew and the child, and closes chiastically with a return to the garden and a sense of death. "A rasping boredom" suggests dryness and illness, and the father-gardener is left with one "sick leaf" in his hand.

"First Light" is the most accomplished and poignant poem in the sequence. In the bleak light of dawn—the same "raw" time, in "Another September," when the first disquieting differences between the lovers had emerged—an empty kitchen makes the alienation of the couple evident, even spatially:

> an empty
> Kitchen takes form, tidied and swept,
> Blank with marriage—where shrill
> Lover and beloved have kept
> Another vigil far
> Into the night, and raved and wept (*NOP*, 33)

A child "enduring a dream" gives expression to the pain caused by the rift; from "a whimper or sigh," his cry "lengthens to an ugly wail," which becomes, like the dream, "Unendurable." The light of dawn ascending "like a pale gas," the empty kitchen, and the wailing child are indirect ways to express the pain of ordeal; but the poem also represents an escape from the solipsistic obsession of the couple and an opening up toward the growth mentioned in the Prologue.

In "Remembering Old Wars," the condition of the two lovers, exhausted by their fights and their endurance, is well-represented by the image of their bodies "leaking / Limp as the dead" (*NOP,* 34). Analogy with the stuffed animal, "limp with use and reuse," of "Soft Toy," suggests that the leakage of the substance—the sawdust—which gave them body, has turned them into objects, useless toys. Verbs such as "clamped," "prodded," "laboured," which semantically belong to the field of hard, imposed labor, indicate a mechanical union and a painful imposition of life together. On the other hand, the repeated appeal to the sense of smell ("we lay down / In the smell of decay and slept . . . breathing that smell all night" *NOP,* 34) stresses the instinctive, animal-like bond which keeps the couple together. The quasi-homophony between "smell" and "smile," the last word of the poem, underlines the passage from bestiality to humanity—man, after all, is the only "smiling ape." Even if smile is qualified by the adjective "savage," reminding us of the pigs of the Prologue savaging each other, the picture is not totally bleak. In the end, the lovers are able to "renew each other" through their destructive union, even if they do it with "a savage smile." This guarded optimism is confirmed by the short concluding poem, "Je t'adore," in which, however, the use of a French title makes the love declaration oblique and artificial. As in the preceding poem, "props" and "iron arms" semantically belong to a hard, mechanical world, but the poem ends with praise to "Love the limiter" (*NOP,* 35).

The sequence follows a progression from the indignities of "the individual plight"—the pitilessness of the conjugal relationship—to the faith that "the common plight" is not "only hideous," but that love offers the bases for growth and understanding. This will be the central theme of the volume *Nightwalker and Other Poems.*

Poems of Quest

Starting with "Downstream," a new brand of poems appears for the first time in Kinsella's canon. They are the long meditative poems in which the poet confronts the "mess" of private as well as public experience, and develops a spacious and flexible form able to encompass the multiplicity of experiences and modes the new genre entails. Public events, often with their private repercussions, play a large role; for instance, World War II in "Downstream," Hiroshima and the role of Truman in the nuclear war in "Old Harry," and local history and politics in "A Country Walk."

Many of these longer poems are shaped by the tentative plot of a lonely quest for patterns of vital order and structured by the convention of a walk or journey. They could be seen as modern versions of the great meditative odes or travel poems of the past, like Wordsworth's "Tintern Abbey," Gray's "Eton Ode," and Matthew Arnold's "Dover Beach."

"A Country Walk"   "A Country Walk" records the narrator's complex response to the environment he traverses. "Sick of the piercing company of women," he takes a walk along the river in the outskirts of Dublin, first finding peace in the contemplation of the immediate details of country and city scenery, and then in their mythical and historical resonances. The excursion is taken not only through the countryside but also, and especially, through the country's history; the two levels intermingle.

In this poem Kinsella turns his back on emblematic or literary landscapes; the poem is spatially structured around clearly defined and recognizable landmarks: "a path / [Leading] to the holy stillness of a well"; "an ivied corner"; "[a] ruined aqueduct in delicate rigor / Clenched cat-backed, rooted to one horizon." But these physical details are, at times, also charged with metaphysical significance. The town, perceived in its outline, for instance, represents endurance through change and destruction. For a poet preoccupied by decay and a ruined civilization, this is a potent symbol:

> Mated, like a fall of rock, with time,
> The place endured its burden: as a froth
> Locked in a swirl of turbulence, a shape
> That forms and fructifies and dies, a wisp
> That hugs the bridge, an omphalos of scraps. (*SP,* 52)

The peaceful rural setting and the "resilient stability of the town 'enduring' its place in spite of its ruined aqueduct," and its "crumbled barracks, castle and brewery," provide the pathetic fallacy on which the poem is built. For in both the personal and the historical accounts, there is a progress from violence to peace reflected in the natural background. As the speaker walks, his mood changes from exasperation to peace: "I walked their hushed stations, passion dying / Each slow footfall a drop of peace returning" (*SP,* 51).

Similarly, the "speckled ford" on the river brings back memories of past violence, which, in turn, give way to peace. In chronological order, the poet evokes the saga of Cuchulain and Ferdia ("Brothers armed in hate . . . mingling their bowels at the saga's end"); the Norman massacre of his forefathers; "Cromwell and his fervent sword / Despatch[ing] a convent shrieking to their Lover"; and the 1798 uprising, when "a rebel host / . . . piked in groups of three / Cromwell's puritan brood" (*SP,* 53). The peace which follows, however, is not so much harmony as shallow compromise: "Pulses calmed; / The racked heroic nerved itself for peace; / Then came harsh winters, motionless waterbirds, / And generations that let welcome fail" (*SP,* 53). In a scathingly ironic rewriting of Yeats' "Easter 1916," Kinsella lambasts the middle-class mediocrity of contemporary Ireland. The heroes of 1916, canonized by Yeats, are indeed "Changed, changed utterly," but no "terrible beauty is born"[10]:

> Around the corner, in an open square,
> I came upon the sombre monuments
> That bear their names: McDonagh & McBride
> Merchants: Connolly's Commercial Arms. . . . (*SP,* 54)

Ireland is now a land of shopkeepers and moneylenders. Pearse's death has been followed by the materialistic Free State, "when freedom burned his comrades' itchy palms," and by the cruelties of the Anglo-Irish and Civil Wars. Yeats' prophetic verse, "Now and in time to be, wherever green is worn" ("Easter 1916," Yeats, 179), is answered by Kinsella's commemoration: There is still a perfunctory gathering around the grave, but the elders "chatting they return / To take their town again, that have exchanged / A trenchcoat playground for a gombeen jungle" (*SP,* 54). Images of a degraded present and a sordid town ("a lamp switched on above the urinal") are finally left behind in the climactic ending, which is quintessentially Kinsellan. The persona of the poet, in a sort of baptismal rite, receives from the dripping sycamores "a single / Word upon my upturned face" (*SP,* 54). This signals a return of vitality and faith in self and poetry. The final contemplation of the river concedes the vision of a temporary pattern at the end of his quest, where physical and metaphysical come together for a brief instant:

> Under a darkening and clearing heaven
> The hastening river streamed in a slate sheen,
> Its face a-swarm.

. . . .
a thousand currents broke,
Kissing, dismembering, in threads of foam
. . . .
their shallow, shifting world
Slid on in troubled union, forging together
Surfaces that gave and swallowed light. (*SP*, 54–55)

The pattern is soon decomposed, as the flood "grimly" divides. But the poet has had a moment of recognition, and song or poetry can ensue in the wake of Virgil's tenth eclogue:

Venit Hesperus;
In green and golden light; bringing sweet trade.
The inert stirred. Heart and tongue were loosed:
'The waters hurtle through the flooded night. . . .' (*SP,* 55)

The river with its eddies—an emblem of dynamic order—allows the walker to grasp a luminous and shifting design, as opposed to the stupidity, destructiveness, and decay he has been contemplating so far in "the piercing company of women," in the historical mementoes of past violence, or in "the gombeen jungle" of the town.

"Downstream"   "Downstream," Kinsella's best-known peripatetic poem, presents a characteristic itinerary from darkness to light and back; with the river offering, as in the preceding poem, a symbolic structure for the ordeal of quest. The poem, written ambitiously in Dante's *terza rima,* and representing the apotheosis of Kinsella's prosodic achievement, went through several versions. The fifty-six stanza poem originally published in the homonymous volume was revised and abridged drastically to twenty-six stanzas.[11]

The occasion for both versions is a rowboat journey down a river at dusk. The earlier version is spatially and temporally more circumstantial and, on the whole, less intense and somber. It begins at the beginning of the trip with the two travelers trusting "their frail skiff to the hungry stream," fighting the current, rowing vigorously, and discussing poetry in a relaxed mood. Only as the landscape and time of day change, does the mood of the journey also turn disquieting with the gathering shadows. The second version of *Downstream* starts in media res; there is a change from the narrative to the meditative mode, so the details of the trip, its destination, and the gradual changes are glossed over. A four-line quotation from the preceding poem establishes the mood and gives a hint of the outcome of this and many other Kinsellan quests: the encounter with a pattern of order.

Downstream starts with a sense of uneasiness as the boat slides between "ghostly banks," through "dark woods," and under "a matted arch." The same details were also present in the earlier poem but were more diluted. The two poems, however, converge for the central episode: as it gets darker and the channel shrinks, the travelers are gripped by a sense of anguish. Childhood memories of the narrator's first traumatic awareness of war and holocaust in Europe blend with his recollection of a body found dead and half-eaten on those very shores. From that moment, the young adult had learned that he could not shirk "the actual mess," but "taste [he] must." The poem consists of reliving this first confrontation with violence and mortality in all its crude horror, and in assessing its continuing importance for the grown man. "Downstream," in short, is a Wordsworthian ode in reverse: The Ode on Intimations of Mortality.

The semantic registers Kinsella employs reveal the change in consciousness from a sentimental view of death to a mature one. The decorative qualifiers "silver," "starlit," and "velvet" of the sentimental childhood view of death, are replaced by the harsher terms and grotesque details of the boy's nightmarish vision of the world at war. Like Dante's *Inferno,* which Kinsella takes as a model here and for many other poems recording stages of his descent into fear, the trip down the river is an archetypal journey into an underworld peopled by all sorts of devils and monsters:

> each day a spit
>
> That, turning, sweated war, each night a fall
>   Back to the evil dream where rodents ply,
>   Man-rumped, sow-headed, busy with whip and maul
>
> Among nude herds of the damned . . . It seemed that I,
>   Coming to conscience on that lip of dread,
>   Still dreamed, impervious to calamity,

> Imagining a formal rift of the dead
>   Stretched calm as effigies on velvet dust,
>   Scattered on starlit slopes with arms outspread
>
> And eyes of silver—when that story thrust
>   Pungent horror and an actual mess
>   Into my very face, and taste I must. (*SP,* 57)

As the adult paddles down the frightening river, however, he can discern a pattern in the horror. Two vital images emerge out of the darkness: the ghost of the dead man "[c]almly encountering the starry host, / Meeting their silver eyes with silver eye" (*SP,* 58); and a white bird, "A soul of white with darkness for a nest" (*SP,* 58). The oxymora of this section of the poem signify that all oppositions are reconciled in the brief moment of acceptance.

In the final part of the poem, the unfathomable ghastliness of death and the mystery of evil are annulled by the pattern of stars; a principle of cosmic order able to appease the speaker's horror and his sense of waste:

> I lifted up my eyes. There without rest
>
> The phantoms of the overhanging sky
>   Occupied their stations and descended;
>   Another moment, to the starlit eye,
>
> The slow, downstreaming dead, it seemed, were blended
>   One with those silver hordes, and briefly shared
>   Their order, glittering. (*SP,* 59)

This burst of clarity has, for a pathetically brief instant, stayed and even justified the sense of desolation fostered by images of darkness and recollections of past horror. For a moment, death has been relegated to its place in the structure of the universe. But, as the poem proceeds, a "barrier of rock" blots out the sight of the heavens and again plunges the poet into bewilderment.

"Nightwalker"   Kinsella's most important poem of quest, and also the most perplexing one, is "Nightwalker," which lends its title to the volume. Using the figure of a solitary walker as the organizing central consciousness—a figure familiar to the reader of this central stage of

Kinsella's production—the part narrative, part meditative poem explores the "madness without" in Irish society, and the "madness within" (*SP,* 85) of the speaker's own sense of alienation from contemporary Ireland and reality. Political and social discontent play a large role in "Nightwalker," Kinsella's most public poem, in which he turns his civil-servant experience into poetry. The poem for this reason is often marred by an excess of topicality, but Kinsella overcomes the narrowness of his grievances through the dominant theme of the poem: the quest for a pattern of order, which, as in "Downstream," takes the form of "searching the darkness" for a vision of light. The walker's quest and bitter musing on the decay of modern Ireland take place "within the light and gravity of the moon," and the transformations of the moon reflect his changing moods while also providing him with a vehicle to express his rare visions of order. The moon is the constant to which the wanderer returns. Descriptions of its shape and luminosity provide occasions for many remarkable lyrical moments and constitute an element of unity.

Mostly, as the narrator on his night walk through the Dublin suburbs looks up at the skies, the moon is seen as a malignant feminine presence controlling the tides and human lives; a "fat skull" and "a mask of grey dismay" (*SP,* 86). It is also the center of grotesque constellations of the Irish zodiac, such as "The Twins, / Bruder und Schwester," "The Wedding Group," or "the "Foxhunter." In the final part of the poem, however, the speaker, inspired by love, can see the moon momentarily transformed into a muse and a wife-like figure, giving sense and shape to his moments of rebellion and nausea:

> Virgin most pure, bright
> In the dregs of the harbour: moon of my dismay,
> Quiet as oil, enormous in her shaggy pool.
> Her brightness, reflected on earth, in heaven,
> Consumes my sight. (*SP,* 96)

The poem finds its conclusion on the moon, to which the walker is transported, only to find a landscape of cruel desolation. The moon, then, is the thematic core around which various fragments, adding up to a narrative line, coalesce.

"Nightwalker" is divided into three main sections and starts with an epigraph establishing the general mood of discontent at the common human lot: *"The greater part must be content to be as though they had not been* (*SP,* 85). A preamble states the main oppositions around which the poem is constructed: "the shambles of the day" contrasted to "will that gropes for structure," "madness without" to "madness within," and reason to unreason (*SP,* 85). Echoing the ritual language of prayers in its rhythmic accents and alliterative repetitions of key words (*m*indful, *m*adness, sla*mm*ed), the speaker, like a priest inviting the congregation to recite the prayer "Our Father" ("we presume to say," *SP,* 85), initiates his meditation with a flat statement of pessimism: "I only know things seem and are not good" (*SP,* 86).

The next three sections provide ample illustrations for this statement of pessimism. The first section is structured in several satirical vignettes of increasing violence, and held together by the figure of the wandering narrator with his eyes lifted to the sky to encounter increasingly grotesque constellations. Discontent rules over the opening lines of the poem. The wanderer, himself "a vagabond tethered" to his shadow, looks, like Joyce's Stephen, into suburban houses and sees a spectacle of modern paralysis: shadows "slumped in the corner / Of a living-room, in blue trance, buried / Alive" watching television; a humanity of insect-like figures (*SP,* 87). Nor do the skies to which he lifts his eyes yield a much more reassuring pattern. The moon evokes childhood memories of meteors, confused with half-understood visions of a war-torn world:

> —Bone-splinters, silvery slivers of screams,
> Blood-splinters rattling, like crimson flint.
>   There it hangs,
> A mask of grey dismay sagging open
> In the depths of torture, moron voiceless moon. (*SP,* 86)

A brief interlude prepares us for the change of voice. The embittered walker, now in his suburban home, describes his everyday routine in the flat, ironic tone of the Prologue to *Downstream:*

> We'll come scratching in our waistcoats
> Down to the kitchen for a cup of tea;
> Then with our briefcases, through wind or rain,
> Past our neighbours' gardens—Melrose, Bloomfield—
> To wait at the station. (*SP,* 88)

The transition from the meditative walker to the civil servant is accomplished and the voice of a government official—a voice senior officer Kinsella knew well—rattles off platitudes and cant about Ireland's economic policy of encouraging foreign investment. In the large-scale polyphonic experiment Kinsella is conducting in "Nightwalker," he extends the semantic field of his poetry to include the language of his everyday office activities. In a parody of the words inscribed on a tablet at the foot of the Statue of Liberty, the statue of "Productive Investment"—a debased symbol of the new Ireland—invokes foreigners, "Lend me your wealth, your cunning and your drive, / Your arrogant refuse," while the official brags to foreign investors about "our labour pool, / The tax concessions to foreign capital, / How to get a nice estate though German" (SP, 88). The irony becomes even more scathing when the speaker relates one of his business encounters with a couple of German investors and transfigures them surrealistically into a new constellation in the Irish zodiac: "The wakeful Twins / Bruder und Schwester" (SP, 89).

Another change of voice from officialese to the personal permits an outburst of indignation at having to deal with the heirs of Nazi Germany:

> I cannot take
> My eyes from their pallor. A red glare
> Plays on their faces, livid with little splashes
> Of blazing fat. The oven door closes. (SP, 89)

The outburst may sound embarrassing both because it is out of place in the Irish setting, and because its violent intensity contrasts with the mocking tone of the rest of the poem. The poem is made of such violent shifts of tone and speaking voice.

The next satirical vignette focuses on former political heroes, now government officials: "The ministers / Are working, with a sureness of touch found early / In the nation's birth—the blood of enemies / And brothers dried on their hide long ago" (SP, 89). The "Dragon old men," like the German investors, are part of the Irish zodiac, a constellation of violence, "Linked into constellations with their death." The ironical description of this new constellation, "The Wedding Group," is one of the weakest parts of the poem because of the dense allegory, and the obscure political and literary allusions. Without Maurice Harmon's explanation that behind the savage fable of cunning and betrayal lay a real wedding group, photographed at Kevin O'Higgins's marriage, the

fable would be incomprehensible (Harmon, 64). The historical characters too ended up savaging one another with the same animality as transpires from this cruel fable.

Like the first section, the second opens with a description (one of
Kinsella's best), which places the narrator spatially and establishes the
mood. The setting is the seawall rising near the Forty Foot Pool close to
Joyce's Martello tower. The section, indeed the whole poem, is under the
sign of Joyce, who is invoked as "Watcher in the tower" (*SP,* 92) and, further on, as "Father of Authors," and asked "to be with [him]," turning
"his milky spectacles on the sea." The passage alludes both to the still
beauty of the moment and to the disappointment and pettiness it contains; following Joyce's example, both can be translated into art. Instead
of the angrily described moon, a more serene yellow lamplight, and the
ebb and flow of the tide, create a dreamy atmosphere:

> The tide is drawing back
> From the promenade, far as the lamplight can reach,
> Trickling under the weed, into night's cave.
> Note the silence.
> Light never strays there. Nothing has a shadow there.
> When a wind blows there . . . . (*SP,* 91)

Yet the dreamy mood yields another surrealistic vision of Ireland's
political debasement. A picture of "our new young minister . . . / On
horseback, in hunting pinks" (*SP,* 91), glimpsed by the walker in a newspaper scrap in a gutter, comes to life as a grotesque figure emerging
from the waters and finding himself a place among the constellations, "a
new sign: Foxhunter" (*SP,* 92). Joyce is invoked again to help with the
description of this foppish creature, surrounded by curs which "Mill and
yelp at your heel, backsnapping and grinning . . . . A pack of lickspittles
running as one" (*SP,* 93). Kinsella turns to the Joyce of *Finnegans Wake*
for the pun through which the new star in the constellation is ridiculed:
"The sonhusband / Coming in his power: mounting to glory / On his big
white harse" (*SP,* 92). Newspaper headlines extend the satire to other
facets of Irish society, such as the Church's backward attitudes or nationalist feelings about the language question:

> The newspaper settles down in the gutter again:
> THE ARCHBISHOP ON MARRIAGE

NEW MOVES TO RESTORE THE LANGUAGE
THE NEW IRELAND . . . (SP, 93)

A brief description of the moon and the stars—the leitmotif of the poem—leads to a long passage about the language questions. In this ironic piece, a montage of various voices and styles, the tone and codes shift continuously and different functions of language succeed each other with a kaleidoscopic effect. Childhood memories of the Christian Brothers school, where the teaching was in Irish, mingle with a teacher's own speech full of nationalist cliches and smug, subservient cant about the school's alumni, and the role of the schools on behalf of the "Irish national language":

> And you will be called
> In your different ways—to work for the native language,
> To show your love by working for your country.
> Today there are Christian Brothers' boys
> Everywhere in the Government—the present Taoiseach
> Sat where one of you is sitting now. (SP, 94)

Several other shifts in voice from the adult walker's to the naive school-boy's finally take us to the narrator's own poetic synthesis of the questions of language and tradition. The song of a passing sea mew evokes that of Amergin, the first mythical Irish poet, who, on touching the soil of Ireland, broke out in a great mystical speech claiming to be at one with the whole environment. The sea mew's song in "Nightwalker" incorporates snatches of Amergin's song[12]: *"I will become a wind on the sea / Or a wave of the sea again, or a sea sound"* (SP, 95). But the sea mew also laments what the first poet could not have imagined: the loss of the language and audience. Its invocation, *"Eire, Eire . . . is there none / To hear? Is all lost?"* (SP, 95) indicates Kinsella's own despairing views on the subject, so distant from the pat nationalist solutions of politicians and Christian Brothers.

"Nightwalker" is the first poem in which the poet reaches down to the traditional and mythical fund of Irish tradition, and incorporates the "mutilated" past into his own poetry, thus giving it new life and healing it more effectively than by imposing a dead language on the nation. The sea mew's song is one of the few passages in which irony is set aside and there is fusion between the speaker's and that other voice. Johnston (109) points out the similarity and the opposition between this passage

and the close of *A Portrait of the Artist as a Young Man,* in which gulls cry
to Stephen, "Come . . . and the air is thick with their company, as they
call to me, their kinsman, making ready to go. . . . "[13] The section ends
with the speaker accepting the call to go backward and downward to
repossess home and family, not unlike Stephen:

> A dying language echoes
> Across a century's silence.
> It is time,
> Lost soul, I turned for home.
> Sad music steals
> Over the scene.
> Hesitant, cogitating, exit.
>
> (*SP,* 95)

The reminder of Joyce's influence (even in the insistence on the HCE ini-
tials so important in *Finnegans Wake*) is appropriate at this point because
he had been capable of fusing myth, national history, personal history,
and everyday Dublin life. This will also become Kinsella's project in his
next volume, and "Nightwalker" indicates the transition to the new
introspective and mythical stage.

In the third section, the poet takes a subjective turn and the narrative
line, caught between introspection and hallucination, becomes less easy
to follow. The walk has ended and the lost soul is returning home to conjugal bliss:

> Home and beauty.
>   Her dear shadow on the blind,
> The breadknife . . . she was slicing and buttering
> A loaf of bread. My heart stopped. I starved for speech.
>
> (*SP,* 96)

The speaker of the poem has come home to his two certainties, the
power of love and the power of speech, both contained in the trope of
the loaf of bread, source of physical and spiritual nourishment—as in
Communion, when the Word is made bread. The dispenser of bread is at
the same time wifely muse, lunar goddess, virgin Mary, and even Queen
Victoria. Fed by such a composite female figure, the poet becomes rec-

onciled to the moon, under whose influence he can begin to compose his book. In a metapoetic passage, Kinsella enacts the fragmentary conception of the poem; its most characteristic details—the wedding photograph, the newspaper cutting in the gutter—coming together in the pool of light:

> Gradually, as my brain
> At a great distance swims in the steady light,
> Scattered notes, scraps of newspaper, photographs,
> Begin to flow unevenly toward the pool
> And gather into a book before her stare.
> Her mask darken as she reads, to my faint terror,
> But she soon brightens a little, and smiles wanly. (*SP,* 96)

Similarly, the ruins of a country, Ireland, come together in the simplistic mind of Queen Victoria, who, in her person, represents colonial power. The next segment of the poem is spoken by the queen herself, who had commented about Ireland, "It was a terrible time."[14] Frivolously and unemotionally, the queen then observes, "We came to take the waters. The sun shone brightly, / Which was very pleasant" (*SP,* 96). The same superficiality (and flat grammar) appears in the assessment of the Irish situation after the Famine:

> From time to time it seems that everything
> Is breaking down; but we must never despair.
> There are times it is all part of a meaningful drama
> That begins in the grey mists of antiquity
> And reaches through the years to unknown goals
> In the consciousness of man, which is very soothing. (*SP,* 96)

The fact that waste and the breaking down of order may reach "to unknown goals" through the evolutionary process, is something Kinsella himself has sustained in many of his poems. Here, however, it appears as a shallow message of optimism contrasting with the reality of violence and suffering the queen and the walker have witnessed. The flat concluding remark "Which is very soothing," paralleling "Which was very pleasant," sounds ironical and deprives the statement of any depth and credibility.

In a series of phantasmagoric transformations, the British queen is identified with several figures of power and the poem focuses again on the moon, "Our mother [who] / rules on high, queenlike, pale with control. / Hatcher of peoples!" (*SP,* 97). As in the first part of the poem, Kinsella affirms through the queen/moon couple that authority cannot be dissociated from violence. When the walker is transported to the moon, he finds it a place bristling with sharp, wounding asperities: "Rock needles stand up from the plain; the horizon / a ring of sharp mountains like broken spikes" (*SP,* 97).

Neither is life on the moon any different from what goes on in the "laboratory / Near Necropolis" of nighttime Dublin:

> Hard bluish light beats down, to kill
> Any bodily thing—but a million dead voices hide
> From it in the dust, without hope of peace.
>
> . . . .
> The shadows are alive:
> They scuttle and flicker among the rock needles,
> Squat and suck the dry juice, inspect
> The eggs of shadow beneath the surface, twitching
> Madly in their cells. (*SP*, 97)

The myriad insect-like shadows inhabiting the moon remind us of the TV-watchers who "in blue trance, buried alive . . . snuggle in their cells / faintly luminous, like grubs—abdominal / Body-juices and paper-thin shells, in their thousands" (*SP,* 87). The analogies don't stop with these two examples, but they are sufficient to prove that the apparently free-floating poem is tightly organized, and that the random walks and meditations have one explanation, foreshadowed repeatedly in the poem.

The spiky, dead world of the lunar surface, is the same as the human world the nightwalker was trying to escape by lifting his eyes to the skies. The "ghost sea" he finds on its desert surface has "a human taste, but sterile; odourless" (*SP,* 98). The poet, who not much earlier had expressed his belief in the possibility of reaching understanding through love, has to confess to another belief: "I think this is the Sea of Disappointment" (*SP,* 98). The nightwalker's walks have led him to this.

The narrative line of "Nightwalker" is hard to follow, as Kinsella leaves many gaps in the exposition, slackly links the larger units of the poem, and creates a difficult order in his appropriation of the lessons of modernism. But order there is, and it is offered by recurring thematic and topological signposts.

Many voices and many influences are heard in the poem, an excellent example of Bakhtinian heteroglossia, but the most important of all is that of Joyce, invoked as "Watcher in the tower" and often alluded to. The spirit itself of the poem, turning urban discontent and the "filthy modern tide"(*IW,* 63) into poetry, is Joycean, and the speaker ends one of his "morose condemnations" (*SP,* 88) by admitting: "Clean bricks / Are made of mud; we need them for our tower"(*SP,* 88). Many mud-bricks compose "Nightwalker," Kinsella's Joycean tower, which is deliberately fragmented, but essentially unitarian in its structure.

Turning Inward

The final two selections of *Nightwalker and Other Poems,* "Ritual of Departure" and "Phoenix Park," mark a transition from what Kinsella in "Nightwalker" called "a will that gropes for structure" (*SP,* 85), to a recognition that the structure must be sought in one's psyche rather than at large in the natural or social world. The theme of the internal quest, and its reward, which is also experienced intimately, will then develop into the major Jungian phase of *Notes from the Land of the Dead.* Both poems hinge on love, memory, and exile as components of the "cup of ordeal," and mix autobiographical elements with the more abstract theme of the search for order, which is nowhere more explicitly expressed than in "Phoenix Park."

"Ritual of Departure"   "Ritual of Departure" is a poem of farewell. The speaker, about to leave his city and his former life (as indeed Kinsella did when he moved to the United States), contemplates his past life, the city, and the countryside, focusing on a few objects and sights. First, the speaker detaches himself from his personal belongings, symbolized by the lovingly described silver spoons with the stag crest. The spoons, however, have long since lost "brilliance in use" and the stag becomes a symbol for the unsettled owner: its heart "stumbles. / He rears at bay . . . ; rattles / A trophied head among my gothic rocks" (*SP,* 99).

The traveler then bids farewell to Dublin—the Georgian Dublin the poet loved and celebrated—described in the poem as if seen in a print. The pleasure of contemplating its harmonious proportions, the "Domes, pillared, in the afterglow, / A portico," cannot be dissociated from the

beggars and the horserider "locked in soundless greeting," nor, especially
from the fact that its beauty was tied to a time of dispossession:

> Dublin under the Georges . . .
>   stripped of Parliament,
> Lying powerless in sweet-breathing death ease
>   after forced Union. (*SP,* 99)

Another vision is of the countryside itself represented by its most distinctive feature—the potato fields:

> The ground opens. Pale wet potatoes
> Break into light. The black soil falls from their flesh,
> From the hands that tear them up and spread them out
> In fresh disorder, perishable roots to eat. (*SP,* 100)

The mind's eye then spreads to the formalized vista of a " landscape
with ancestral figures" (*SP,* 100). In this case, too, its quiet beauty reveals
its social blight: the famine and the ensuing diaspora:

> The seed in slow retreat, through time and blood,
> Into bestial silence.
>   Faces sharpen and grow blank,
> With eyes for nothing.
>   And their children's children
> Venturing to disperse, some come to Dublin
> To vanish in the city lanes. (*SP,* 100)

Each of the objects the speaker has contemplated in his farewell bears
in its heart the causes that led to that same farewell. At the end of the
poem, the narrator identifies himself with the primordial Irish exile, the
victim of the famine. In the ease of his house with grey floorboard and
plush, he becomes one with his less fortunate forebears: "I scoop at the
earth, and sense famine, a first / Sourness in the clay. The roots tear
softly" (*SP,* 100).

"Phoenix Park"   While famine in "Ritual of Departure" has principally a social and political meaning, making the poem one of the many

in *Nightwalker* which show concern for public and Irish matters, the same metaphor of hunger is extended in the key poem, "Phoenix Park," to include the characteristic Kinsellan search for order and understanding. Accepting the diversity of life, which includes also waste and bitterness, is called metaphorically "drinking the cup of ordeal," and the nourishment contained in the cup is the rich "tissue" of "undying love."

The title of the poem indicates a double perspective, biographical and symbolic; there is a vast park of that name at the center of Dublin which is the backdrop of the peregrinations of this poem's speaker. Moreover, the phoenix is also an emblem of Ireland. But the epigraph, *"The Phoenix builds the Phoenix' nest. / Love's architecture is his own"* (*SP*, 101), a quotation from Crashaw,[15] points to the mythical dimension of the poem's central trope: love, like the phoenix, renews itself and is reborn out of its own ashes, and the cycle of ordeals and discovery of structure is never-ending. Tissues form under the lover's stare, fade, and take shape again in a perpetual alternation of chaos and "slowly forming laws . . . of order" (*SP*, 104), soon to be lost again through some other form of decay until "order dulls and dies in love's death" (*SP*, 107).

Although, like "Ritual of Departure," the poem deals with the sadness of leaving and the weight of memory, all these negative elements take on a profounder significance as part of the "cup of ordeal" which must be tasted if the positive dream is to be found. It is, indeed, in terms of taste that the structure is first recognized: "I taste a structure, ramshackle, ghostly, / Vanishing on my tongue, given and taken, / Distinct" (*SP*, 106). The knowledge is acquired instinctively, through the senses. This form of immediate revelation is "love's own architecture," contrasted in the epigraph with "building," the workaday, deliberate search.

"Phoenix Park" is a great love poem but also a philosophical one in which Kinsella, through the persona of a narrator, states his thoughts on the cyclical nature of experience, on its ultimate significance, and on instinctive versus rational knowledge.

The organic process of crystal formation rules the pattern of order which is formed inside the cup of ordeal; past experiences, even suffering and disappointment, coalesce kaleidoscopically. In an apotheosis of abstractions and oppositions solved, Kinsella represents his vision thus:

> Look into the cup: the tissues of order
> Form under your stare. The living surfaces
> Mirror each other, gather everything

Into their crystalline world. Figure echoes
Figure faintly in the saturated depths;

Revealed by faint flashes of each other
They light the whole confines. (*SP,* 104)

The crystalline structure, which symbolizes the way experience and ordeals are combined into the positive tissue by symmetrical aggregation, also operates structurally in the formation of the poem. The passage (as the one in "Nightwalker") is a blueprint for the composition process of this particular poem. The poem has a cyclical pattern: it returns to words and figures used before which echo and mirror one another. Individual words, grammatical patterns, whole sentences, and thematic elements recur, thus miming the repetitive order in the structure of crystals. Intertextuality is particularly important in "Phoenix Park." It is indeed an "echo chamber"[16] in which a mosaic of citations from different parts of the poem, from the earlier poetry, and from Crashaw and other poets creates refractions and symmetries. The poem, like the crystal of experience, grows by slow accumulation. It gathers power and weight, in spite of an impression of repetitiveness, and reflects a new affirmative attitude: "And the crystal so increases, / Eliciting in its substance from the dark / The slowly forming laws it increases by" (*SP,* 104).

The long poem is divided into four parts, each starting with an accurate description of locale and mood. It has as its setting Phoenix Park, through which the speaker and his wife take a last drive before their departure. Actual occasions along the drive (seeing a special place, drinking a glass of beer) set off the various reveries, many of them leading to a vision of order. The main differences between this poem and the many preceding ones based on the same leitmotif are that the search does not take place in the outer world but inwardly, and that the structure of the poem itself mimics the process of search and discovery.

"Phoenix Park" opens with a description of a broken twig falling on the car—a symbol of nature's participation in the central theme of biological fracturing and regeneration. Instinctively, the woman recognizes the analogy with the fracture taking place in their own lives—the departure, their cooling love, the husband's lagging inspiration:

—You start at the suddenness, as though it were
Your own delicate distinct flesh that had snapped.

> What was in your thoughts . . . saying, after a while,
> I write you nothing, no love songs, any more?
> *Fragility echoing fragilities.* . . . (*SP,* 101)

Passing St. Mary's Hospital in the Park, where the poet's wife had been hospitalized for tuberculosis in the days he was courting her, the narrator compares those times to the present, when illness and fever seem to have extended to all life, consuming all. And yet, through the destructive fever, the lover had achieved a moment of fusion evoked as an experience of taste:

> I stooped and tasted your life until you woke,
> And your body's fever leaped out at my mind.
> There's a fever now that eats everything,
> Everything but the one positive dream.
>
> That dream . . . it is something I might offer you,
> Sorry it is not anything for singing.
> Your body would know that it is positive
> —Everything you know you know bodily. (*SP,* 102)

The affirmation, against all proof to the contrary offered by life and nature, that there is a dream surviving the fever—recuperation and healing, new energy in a broken tradition, order in waste—can be accepted intuitively. As in "A Lady of Quality" or "Another September," masculine rationality is contrasted to feminine intuitiveness and the female companion is encouraged to recognize "the dream" of their love as positive, although it emerges out of ordeal.

Much of the poem is dedicated to love, seen as an abstract force in some parts, but also celebrated in its actual manifestations. The poet remembers the exaltation of the early days of love, the lover in darkness whispering, *"Take me, / I am nothing."* He remembers when the stars seemed in his grasp for being in love, but also contradictions inherent in the discourse of love: "But the words hovered, their sense / Revealing opposite within opposite" (*SP,* 102).

The other main theme of the poem, in point of fact, is that of contradictions resolved, as suggested by the death of the phoenix, which is also its rebirth. The positive dream of love prompts several negative instances

in the poem. Thus, on his way towards his beloved, the young wooer had
seen a vision of famine and death: "A child stooped to the grass, picking
and peeling / And devouring mushrooms straight out of the ground: /
Death-pallor in their dry flesh, the taste of death" (*SP,* 102). The same
hunger that leads to the revelation of love can be poisonous as well. An
encounter with a prostitute also prompts thoughts on biological hunger
and physical desire. Finally, the knowledge of the paradoxical nature of
love applies to the narrator's own life:

> Midsummer, and I had tasted your knowledge,
> My flesh blazing in yours; Autumn, I had learned
> Giving without tearing is not possible. (*SP,* 103)

Part II, in a circular way, comes back to the notion of the dream offered
as positive in part I. Taking the cue from an actual glass of beer drunk in a
pub, the sad leave-taker muses over his symbolic cup, expressing faith in
the future in spite of the tearing apart represented by their departure:

> The ordeal-cup, set at each turn, so far
> We have welcomed, sour or sweet. What matter where
> It waits for us next, if we will take and drink? (*SP,* 104)

Looking into the cup reveals the crystal-like pattern of life. All multifarious experience (in this case indicated by the images in the first part of
the poem, such as the child and the woman, "all gathered") coalesces
into an organic whole which can be recognized intuitively. Thanks to his
wife, the speaker can affirm that he has discovered the laws that rule the
chaotic process of life:

> Laws of order I find I have discovered
> Mainly at your hands . . . of failure and increase,
> The stagger and recovery of the spirit:
> That life is hunger, hunger is for order
> And hunger satisfied brings on new hunger
>
> Till there's nothing to come. (*SP,* 104–5)

Even when the crystal cracks, its heart "accepts the flaw, adjusts on it /
Taking new strength—given the positive dream; / Given, with your per-

mission, . . . Undying love . . . " (*SP*, 105). The miracle worked by love cannot even be destroyed by death, represented here as a lewd allegorical figure out of a medieval dance of death, "aching to plant one kiss / In the live crystal." In spite of the affirmative tone, part II ends with the speaker restating the discovered principle but admitting his tentativeness; to him it is a mere abstraction, an idea, not something he can feel bodily as women can:

> I give them back not as your body knows them
> —That flesh is finite, so in love we persist;
> That love is to clasp simply, question fiercely;
> That getting life we eat pain in each other—
> But mental, in my fever—mere idea. (*SP*, 106)

Part III starts with a tribute to the poet's wife, Eleanor, here greeted with Percy's words, as "Fair Ellinor. O Christ thee save,"[17] and admired not only for her intuitiveness but also for her "thoughtless delicate completeness." The emotion at seeing her in the autumnal atmosphere makes the husband actually "taste" what he knew only as an idea: "I taste a structure, ramshackle, ghostly, / Vanishing on my tongue, given and taken, / distinct" (*SP*, 106). At the same time, however, contradicting himself, he shivers in realization of her mortality. Belief in undying love is threatened by the possible end of the dream through the refusal of the cup or actual death:

> Love, it is certain, continues till we fail,
> Whenever (with your forgiveness) that may be
> —At any time, now, totally, ordeal
> Succeeding ordeal till we find some death,
>
> Hoarding bitterness, or refusing the cup;
> Then the vivifying eye clouds, and the thin
> Mathematic tissues loosen, and the cup
> Thickens, and order dulls and dies in love's death
> And melts away in a hungerless no dream. (*SP*, 107)

Working Crashaw's lines into his own, Kinsella composes a metaphysical love poem (the section in italics) to the beloved who has

accepted "inner immolation" peacefully and with "ghostly gaiety," and
who is teaching her companion to accept the ordeal. Renouncing his
designs and the structures he used to impose on reality, the speaker can
declare: "I consign my designing will stonily to your flames" (*SP,* 107)
and accept being instructed by his female counterpart.

The climax of the poem is a description of the fire in which the
Phoenix burns. Love, too, is a consuming fire and the woman knows how
to *"approach the center by its own sweet light"* and let herself be *"wrapped in
that rosy fleece,"* achieving the union of opposites so the two distinct individualities are destroyed and a new single one emerges—*"two lives / Burn
down around one love"* (*SP,* 107). The intertextual references add a dimension of mystical carnality: "the rosy fleece of fire"—the Phoenix' nest—
representing Mary's womb, as George W. Williams points out, was a
symbol of carnality Crashaw rejected,[18] but Kinsella accepted as a way of
access to total union. Crashaw, moreover, with his accumulation of
oxymora—"Sommer in winter. Day in Night. Heauen in earth, & GOD
in MAN"—seems to be the source of Kinsella's particular delight in this
figure of speech underlying the coincidence of opposites.

Part IV opens with a touch of the satirical Kinsella. As the speaker of
the poem leaves the Park, he addresses Dublin, seen in the distance as
"the umpteenth city of confusion," where "dead men, / Half hindered by
dead men, tear down dead beauty" (*SP,* 108). Yet each of those distant
vistas of the city brings back a different memory of their love relationship, "past visages of memory / Set at every turn" (*SP,* 108). A room and
a time "Before you came," when "shapes of tiredness" drew near, was the
occasion for the writing of "Baggot Street Deserta," a moment of order
different but premonitory of the present one:

> One midnight at the starlit sill I let them
> Draw near. Loneliness drew into order:
> A thought of fires in the hearts of darknesses
> A darkness at the heart of every fire,
> Darkness, fire, darkness, threaded on each other
>
> The orders of stars fixed in abstract darkness,
> Darknesses of worlds sheltering in their light;
> World darkness harbouring orders of cities,
> Whose light at midnight harbours human darkness. (*SP,* 109)

The poet is thus describing the process of searching the darkness, which animated his poetry till then as an obsessive recurrence of order and chaos, darkness and fire. In the new approach, explored in this poem for the first time, the searcher is represented as an eater: "A blind human face burrowing in the void / Eating new tissue down into existence." His tongue is like a snake: "A snake out of void moves in my mouth, sucks / At triple darkness" (SP, 110). The source from which nourishment is drawn is the world of shadows, on which rules the triple goddess Hecate. In the poems immediately following, this world will be called the land of the dead.

Using his senses rather than his reason, the searcher will delve into himself and let new patterns emerge out of his subconscious, no longer trying to find patterns in the external world, as one who would watch the skies trying to recognize the constellations. This kind of search will no longer yield symmetries but only "Certain half-dissolved—half formed—beings . . . " As he looks deeper, in fact, "A few ancient faces / Detach and begin to circle. Deeper still, / Delicate distinct tissue begins to form," (SP, 110). The comma at the end of the lines concluding "Phoenix Park" highlights the continuity of Kinsella's "hunger," which is not satisfied by the order found in this volume. The same words are repeated as a prologue to the poem opening his new book, *Notes from the Land of the Dead,* which begins in mid-sentence with the words "hesitate, cease to exist, glitter again," and thus completes the sense of the final vision.

The secure recognition of an order out there, temporary though it may be, will be replaced by hesitation and depth. The new vision will have to emerge out of the self.

Chapter Five
The Jungian Phase

Notes from the Land of the Dead, first published in 1972 by Cuala Press, announced a turning point in Kinsella's career.[1] The new phase had been heralded by the publication of a few isolated poems in the new style— "Tear," "Finistere," "A Selected Life"—and was confirmed by the innovations developed in several Peppercanister sequences later collected in *One and Other Poems* and *Fifteen Dead,* both of 1979.[2]

The three volumes, in the opinion of many critics, represent the major phase of Kinsella's career. But the new, more daring literary experimentation, and the turn inward and backward, lost him the favor of his audience, which was turned off by the difficulty of the enterprise. Faithful to the blueprint presented by the final lines in "Phoenix Park," Kinsella in these poems turns his explorations "deeper still," into his psyche and backward to a primordial past in which "ancient faces" circle. The search has the aim of getting in touch with the origins of the creative self, the "delicate distinct tissue" which begins to form in the depth. In his exploration of the individual and collective subconscious, early personal and family memories often merge with figures and stories from the country's earliest, mythical era.

The poet in these sequences abandons the "designing will" to impose a pattern, choosing instead to let early childhood, and even prenatal memories come to the surface and mingle with other, racial memories, to dictate their own patterns. By so doing, the poet puts reason aside, merging with his feminine counterpart, hailed in "Phoenix Park" as knowing everything bodily. Following Jung's directives that the chaotic life of the unconscious should be given the chance of having its way too, he accepts sensory and extrasensory experiences.

The obsession with beginnings and with the flux of becoming, and the acceptance of the irrational, determine the shape (or rather shapelessness) of many of these pieces, which give the impression of being fragmentary and intentionally chaotic. This is helped by Kinsella's adoption, on a larger scale than in "Nightwalker," of typical devices of modernism such as fragmentation, collage, ellipse, and incomplete syntax. Although individual passages are clear, the way they are assembled creates an impression of lack of cohesion. The extraordinary clarity of his vignettes of family life, in the style of hyperrealistic or naive painting, gives way to "the chaotic" or the surrealistic. A bardic and innovative voice alternates with the realistic narrative style through which the child's point of view is expressed. The two voices keep changing within the same poem and also in the macrostructure of the sequence, with some poems being exclusively written in one of the two voices.

The discrete units of the poems (for they cannot be called stanzas) are loosely connected by ties determined by emotion rather than craft. Kinsella abandons all prosodic and formal patterning, moving from blank verse to free verse. The diction is at times, especially in the childhood pieces, deliberately flat and colloquial, yet evocative; at other times, it is compressed and associative, a trance-like language. The poems lack closure and there is apparently no progression, at least within the individual poems. In spite of this first impression, however, the careful reader can find what Kinsella called "sideways progression"[3] and sequential structuring.

Paratextual elements, for instance, play a large role in indicating the shape of the poems and especially the sequences. Bold and italic characters used in alternation indicate the different functions of the various parts. There are prefatory poems, epigraphs, introductory and in-text quotations, subtitles, asterisks and other marks indicating structural subdivisions, and, at least in the Peppercanister editions, illustrations providing further guidance.

This external organization of material, different from the rhythmic and stanzaic patterning of the earlier poetry, indicates that the production of the 1970s is as much animated by a belief in structure and a search for patterns of order as Kinsella's earlier poetry had been. A design is also evident in the relationships of the various parts of the sequence to one another; some poems, for instance, having a framing function.

The sequence amplifies the plot of quest and reward already apparent in "Nightwalker" and "Phoenix Park," but now based on Jung's extended explorations of the psyche through dreams and symbols. The aim of the quest is to integrate several figures of the unconscious into conscious life, thus achieving what Jung called "the process of individuation": the psychological transformation in which the patient gradually abandons the stereotyped expectations of conventional society (which Jung termed the persona, or mask) in order to discover his or her hidden, unique, and true self. Individuation does not proceed by conscious willing and thinking, but by bringing the unconscious to the conscious level.

The peregrinations, as a consequence, are not spatial but temporal, and take the form of a descent or fall into the past and the depths of the psyche; what Jung called "the mythic land of the dead."[4] The final result of such a search is the achievement of a new wholeness and the cancellation of gender differences. Arthur Guinness, who has explored the Jungian component of Kinsella's poetry quite exhaustively, recognizes Jungian individuation—the encounter with the female within—as "an intimation of inner order" to which Kinsella often recurs.[5]

Kinsella also employs a numerical scheme ordering the stages through which the subject repossesses his personal (and parallelly his racial) past to obtain a sense of identity. As Kinsella explained in an interview with Philip Fried in *The Manhattan Review,* the numerical approach makes some synthesis out of reality: "Zero, I was not there. One, I exist. Two, I am aware. Three, I am involved. Four, it exists. Five, it is over. But before it vanishes we are back with Zero again" (Fried, 18). Even if it failed to explain life, this numeric scheme became an organizing device for holding together a group of poems in a sequence. *Notes,* as the section titles of the first editions underline, is about phase zero, while a great deal of *One,* "occurs at the very beginning, at the stroke of one, and has to do with infant memory" (Fried, 7). Moreover, the invasions of Ireland (numbered 0 to 5) duplicate the pattern on a racial level.

An even more arcane and transcendental principle of unity is the symbol of the quincunx, a cosmic structure based on the number five (as expressed by the disposition of the dots on a die). "The center of the quincunx is (a) Zero and (b) One," explains Kinsella, who adds that he is aiming toward the idea of middle, the point of balance between being and not being, death and rebirth. The idea of middle, toward which he is aiming, is also present in Irish myth as that of a center joining and integrating all the diverse and divergent elements. Kinsella, who had been struggling to find, as Seamus Deane indicates, "a more comprehensive system of order in which the disorder will be subsumed,"[6] was quite ready to adopt the emblem of the quincunx. For a while Kinsella was able to achieve, through the imposition of the quincunx pattern on reality, a sense of coherence out of the very lacerating pulls he was aware of both in the cosmos and in his physical and mental makeup. The charts he elaborated show the correspondences which tie the individual story, myth, and national history together.[7]

Kinsella's need for order and meaning, which in the earlier phases had expressed itself in the search for concrete patterns, and in the late-1960s through abstractions such as love and tissues, is at this stage satisfied by a syncretism of esoteric approaches and mystical symbols of unity in diversity. These allow him to contemplate and even immerse himself in all the disruptive and random elements of his poetic world, without feeling obliged to order them in a manner that "makes sense."

Notes from the Land of the Dead

Notes from the Land of the Dead, in spite of appearances, has a tight organization: an epigraph (the final four lines of "Phoenix Park") is followed by a prefatory poem and three groups of five interdependent poems, each clustered around major themes which, at least in one of the editions, also bear sectional titles. The words "hesitate, cease to exist, glitter again" function as yet another structuring device. Each part of the sequence, in fact, loosely illustrates the concepts expressed by the three verbs.

Paratextual elements, indeed, are very important in this as in other sequences, and the prefatory poem ends with a symbolic drawing which encloses the major symbols of the sequence: the zero, the (broken) egg, and the snake, or actually, in this case, the uroboros; that is, the snake biting its tail. Moreover, the subtitles of the first ("an egg of being"), second ("a single drop"), and third ("nightnothing") sections evoke, semantically or graphically, the zero-phase of psychic development. Section titles were dropped by Kinsella in later editions as, "facetious journalism. A display of smartness" (appendix, p. 198), leaving the recurring images to reveal the theme and establish a link with the first line of the prefatory poem.

The prefatory poem spoken by the persona of a poet/magus connects the new series with "Phoenix Park." Starting in mid-sentence, the text completes the description of the tissue which could be seen at the bottom of the cup in the previous poem. The tissue "begins to form" in "Phoenix Park," and in the new sequence proceeds to "hesitate, cease to exist, glitter again / dither in and out of a mother liquid / on the turn, welling up from God knows what hole" (*NLD,* 3).

The introductory poem also connects with the distinctive Kinsella "hunger": images of drinking and eating persist in a dialectical process of destruction and replenishment. The cup of ordeal which must be emptied is no longer that of "present miseries" (illnesses, death, conjugal unhappiness) but rather of a prenatal, family, or ancestral past. Indeed it is no longer a cup but a cauldron, which, with the "mother liquid" it contains, signals that we are now in a magical and psychoanalytical domain.

The persona of the poet describes in a half-ironical, half-serious tone, the poetic and psychoanalytical process of "getting quietly ready / to go down quietly out of my mind" (*NLD*, 3) in order to achieve the Jungian goal of individuation and to bring to surface the contents of the unconscious—the memories and archetypes boiling in the cauldron. Two different but parallel metaphorical contexts convey the fall into self: the descent underground, accomplished through magic by a Faust-like figure, and the drop of a hungry snake on its prey.

The momentousness of the search, which is "far and deep," "long and cruel," is offset by irreverent language and a mock-magic atmosphere. Like Goethe's Faust, the poet is among his books, "cooped up / with the junk of centuries," and engages in the propitiatory ritual of preparing a snack and a cup of tea. Apparently this is not too different from the writing rituals described elsewhere, as for instance in "Before Sleep." But a few words, such as "abstracted hunger," alert us to a different level of significance: It is not only scrambled eggs the poet is eating, it is the primordial tissue of existence itself, which indeed eggs represent in myth and in Kinsella's poetry, in which he burrows his face and searches with a snake-like tongue. This is no less than an initiatic journey to the land of the dead turning "to things not right nor reasonable," and made possible, as for Faust, by the esoteric symbol of the key. The voyager, like "the snake sucking at triple darkness," will explore an underworld ruled over by the three-headed goddess, Hecate, or by the triple goddess Brigid of Irish mythology.

The second part of the preface switches to the new elliptical and syncopated style to describe the voyager's fall into the netherworld of his subconscious:

> The key, though I hardly knew it,
>   already in my fist.
> Falling. Mind darkening.
>   Toward a ring of mouths.
> Flushed.
>   Time, distance,
>   meaning nothing.
>   No matter. (*NLD*, 4)

The third section of the poem describes the fall from the point of view of an egg. The origin of the image of the falling egg is explained in "Hen

Woman," the next poem in the sequence. The narrator as a child had seen an old woman pick up a hen as it was laying an egg. In spite of her fumbling, the egg had fallen through the air, smashed against a grating, and gone down a cistern or sewer. This gives a hint of how the preface and the various poems in the body of the sequence are connected by cross-references and anticipations. Strands of images in the preface allow an understanding of the other poems in the series at a deeper level, while subsequent poems in the series throw light on the prefatory poem.

While "Hen Woman" retells the story from the point of view of the now grown child, in this section of the prefatory poem, the narrator is the egg itself falling "in terror of the uprushing floor / in my shell of solitude," and breaking "in a distress of gilt and silver, / scattered in a million droplets of / fright and loneliness" (*NLD*, 4). The terror of the fall and the scenery through which the fall takes place—"A thick tunnel stench rose to meet me. Frightful. Dark nutrient waves" (*NLD*, 4)—lend themselves to various interpretations. We recognize the terrors of the fetus falling down the birth canal, or even of an ovum falling down the Fallopian tube to be fecundated. Individuation must start with vertiginous falling into a void and "breaking the shell" of the persona's mask of conventionality, as well as breaking the shell of formal and coherent composition, if we want to examine the metapoetic dimension of the poem. At the bottom of the pit, in fact, is a cauldron in which the various images coalesce:

> ceaselessly over its lip a vapour of forms
> curdled, glittered and vanished. Soon I made out
> a ring of mountainous beings, staring upward
> with open mouths   naked ancient women. (*NLD*, 5)

The menacing women, who had first revealed themselves in the cup of ordeal, prefigure the grandmother figures who play an important role in the section, "an egg of being." For Kinsella, the women of his childhood represent that "imprint or 'archetype' of all the ancestral experiences of the female," which males carry within themselves, and which Jung calls the anima.[8] In Jung's psychology, the initial struggle of a male's urge toward wholeness is with the archetype of the feminine or the feminine element of his masculine psyche. This may be threatening if repressed, but is essential to one's "individuation" if acknowledged and integrated into one's psyche.

The egg-hero, like the archetypal protagonists of those Jungian journeys described as privileged myths by Joseph Campbell, must return (through the "unattainable grill" covering the sewer) "carrying [his] prize" (NLD, 5).

The final section of the poem describes the return with the prize; in other words one step of the individuation process brought to the conscious level and partially understood or interpreted. Since analysis and the creative process go together in this phase, they are also re-created and projected by the artist for his readers: "How it was done—that the pot should now / be boiling before you . . . I remember only snatches" (NLD, 5).

The magic cauldron, which Faust had touched with the key Mephistopheles had given him so that he could descend to the netherworld to seek Helen, is now mockingly termed a boiling pot, but it preserves all its portentousness. The poet promises other snatches from the land of the dead and suggests for the first time a numerical pattern of order based on the number five—like the poems in each section of the sequence, the stages of one's psychic career, and the points of the emblem of the quincunx:

> Yet by the five wounds of Christ
> I struggled toward, by the five digits
> of this raised hand, by this key
> they hold now, glowing, and reach out with
> to touch . . . you shall have . . .
>
> —what shall we not begin
>   to have, on the
>   count of. (NLD, 6)

Although the poet seems to hesitate about what principle of order will be revealed by the mystical key, the poem ends with the line drawing of an incomplete oval, a broken zero or egg, suggesting it has been fecundated into a new self. The figure can also be interpreted as a broken uroboros; in other words, a snake ready to uncoil and reach a higher level of existence than the ever-recurring cycles implied by the figure of the snake eating its tail. The affirmative drawing, and the two positive concepts it suggests, seem to be in contrast with the hesitating tone, the fragmented syntax and rhythm, and the frightening imagery of the poem.

The metaphorical contexts of the prefatory poem clarify and deepen the understanding of the individual poems in the three sections of the sequence. As Harmon has aptly remarked, "*Notes* is a sequence of poems in the strict sense, because each poem therein gains in significance from its relationship to and interaction with other poems in the book, and any poem, taken by itself, loses much of its force" (Harmon, 90).

The first phase, also suggested graphically at the end of the preface, deals with "an egg of being," the zero stage of identity out of which hatches the self. All five poems focus on early childhood experiences which have some autobiographical grounding. Four out of five are about "ancient women," the poet's own grandmothers fused into one threatening figure also closely linked to the *cailleach,* the hag, of Irish mythology. Moreover, the five poems illustrate the verb "hesitate" of the opening section, as they show the hero on the brink of a recognition of self, but beset by fears, especially regarding the threatening feminine figures.

"Hen Woman" describes the episode of the accidental laying of an egg into a sewer already alluded to in the prefatory poem. A woman presides over the event; she is at the same time a familiar neighbor and a mysterious female emerging out of the cave-like "black hole" of her cottage. The meticulous, hyperrealistic description of the event, the egg emerging out of the black hole of the hen's sphincter, is experienced in slow motion (while "time stood still" and "Nothing moved") and narrated by the speaking voice of a child (section one). The tale is interrupted by a meditation and explanation of the significance of the event for the mature speaker (section two). In this section, the egg symbol is given its polyvalent significations: The egg's emergence out of "the black zero of the orifice" teaches the surprised child the mystery of origins and the secret of birth. As the mature narrator comments, "something that had—clenched / in its cave—not been / now was: an egg of being" (*NLD,* 11). The egg is also imagined as the receptacle of the germ from which life develops through the division and multiplication of its fertilized cells:

> there to undergo its (quite animal) growth,
> dividing blindly,
> twitching, packed with will,
> searching in its own tissue

>   for the structure
>   in which it may wake. (*NLD,* 11)

It is also the first nucleus of identity forming subconsciously:

>   that which,
>   not understood, may yet be noted
>   and hoarded in the imagination,
>   in the yolk of one's being, so to speak. (*NLD,* 11)

Understanding, individuation, and poetry all derive from such early experiences, so that the persona of the poet may say "I feed upon it still, as you see," and he expects "it will continue / to fall, probably, until I die, / through the vast indifferent spaces / with which I am empty" (*NLD,* 11).

The third part of the poem briefly reintroduces the old woman and her words of wisdom: "It's all the one / There's plenty more where that came from!" The poem ends with a pun: "Hen to pan! / It was a simple world" (*NLD,* 11), in which Kinsella cannot resist using the ancient homonymous alchemical formula meaning one in all.

"A Hand of Solo" deals with another experience obtained through the influence of an ancient woman, here identified as a shopkeeping grand-mother presented through a few homely yet symbol-laden details:

>   Strings of jet beads wreathed her neck
>   and hissed on the black taffeta
>   and crept on my hair.
>
>   " . . . You'd think I had three heads!"
>   My eyes were squeezed shut against the key
>   in the pocket of her apron. Her stale abyss . . . .
>   (*NLD,* 14–15)

The child is reluctant to embrace this frightening figure, who is hissing like a serpent. We may remember at this point the hissing in the cistern where the egg had fallen in the prefatory poem, and the threat of destruction to the new forming life of the egg of being. The grand-mother's black clothes and her allusion "to the three heads," make her indeed a guardian, like Hecate, of "the stale abyss" to which she holds a key in the pocket of her apron. But the child, who has been sent by the cardplayers he was watching (and whose game is described impressionistically in the central part of the poem) to call his grandmother, has been given "a bright penny," a "satiny, dream-new disk of light," his own *obolus* to descend into the netherworld. This fall (or "drop") will be achieved once more by yielding to one's hunger and tasting a "drop" of knowledge. The child in "A Hand of Solo" buys with his new penny an Indian apple or pomegranate; the fruit, as Kinsella told Haffenden, "of life and death: it is full of seed and blood" (Haffenden, 108) but is also mythologically related to the underworld. Through the metaphoric experience of eating it, the child has a double initiation to sexuality and death. Libido and the killing instinct are both aroused as the child tastes the blood-like red juice.

> [I] went at it with little bites,
> peeling off bits of skin
> and tasting the first traces of the blood.
>
> When it was half peeled,
> with the glassy pulp exposed like cells,
> I sank my teeth in it
>
> loosening the packed mass of dryish beads
> from their indigo darkness.
> I drove my tongue among them
>
> and took a mouthful, and slowly
> bolted them. My throat filled
> with a rank, Arab bloodstain. (*NLD*, 15)

Having faced the dark grandmother and experienced his primitive, animal urges, the speaker is in the position to invoke the image of a sweet singing woman with whom he aspires to merge: "Woman throat song / help my head / back to you sweet" (*NLD*, 13).

The figure of the menacing grandmother is also present in the next three poems: "The High Road," "Ancestor," and "Tear." "The High Road," like the preceding poem, blends Jungian allusions with a realistic description of childhood experiences in the Liberties area of Dublin, where the poet's grandparents lived. The topographical precision and the use of reassuring proper names (Aunty Josie, Granny and Granda) should not obscure the hints to another dimension. The narrator's awe at certain sights is certainly childish but also reminiscent of the narrator's fear of "hesitate, cease to exist . . . ." In the opening poem, the narrator had stated clearly the difficulties of the process of quest: "if I had known how far and deep, / how long and cruel, / I think my being / would have blanched: appalled" (*NLD,* 3). "The High Road" enacts the fear of the descent. The scene is a naive, colorful painting of magic childhood moments—the gift of the silvery mandolin-shaped candy, the exploration of the Robber's Den, and many other similar events—but the symbolic elements are also there: bird-like, dark women, as well as threatening actual birds, and, especially, abysses, which the protagonist, however, dares not plumb. There are suggestions of the abyss in the view from the bridge of the river Camac (which runs most of its course underground), down where "the brown water poured and gurgled / over the stones and tin cans" (*NLD,* 16). When the child peers into Guinness's he sees an unsettling sight: "a mob of shadows / mill in silence" and "spectres huddle everywhere" (*NLD,* 17); and when he looks down from the embankment of the High Road he feels "pulled downward by a queer feeling. Down there" (*NLD,* 17). Finally, he kneels with expectation at the mouth of the big hole, the Robber's Den, and finding in it only "a dusty piece of man's dung / and a few papers in a corner / and bluebottles," he drops the silvery mandolin, his shiny *obolus.* In his aborted descent underground, the *obolus* has not helped carry him beyond darkness and frustration: " (Not even in my mind / has one silvery string picked / a single sound. And it will never.)" (*NLD,* 18). The Robbers' Den has not revealed itself to be like the tunnels and caves of the earlier poems, yet the sibilants in the description of the final drop evoke somehow the threatening and healing hissing in the dark womb-like places where the voyager meets his anima and begins to be born to his identity:

> the breeze gave a sigh: a sin happening . . .
>
> . . . .
>
>   and let it fall
> for ever into empty space
> toward a stone shed, and saw it turn
> over with a tiny flash,
> silvery shivering with loss. (*NLD,* 18)

"Ancestor" blends most successfully the archetypal subtext with the realistic portrait of an old woman seen from the child's point of view. With "her black heart" and her "faint smell, musky and queer"—the smell of whisky and old age—she appears as a typical Irish grandmother, hiding "a small bottle under her aprons." The key she bears is to her desk, but we must not forget that in these poems all the figures that give access to the netherworld bear a key. She "perches on the high stool," her profile "dark like a hunting bird's"; a homely grandmother evoking, however, the many birds of prey of the succeeding poems, psychopomps (i.e., conductors of souls), or symbols of the souls of the dead. As she moves "brushing by me in the shadows / with her heaped aprons," (*NLD,* 19), the child hears a sigh, another instance of the hissing presences in the poems and the prologue of the sequence. "Ancestor" does not only depict an intimidating old woman, but also a creature of darkness. As Kinsella said of another old lady in one of his poems ("St Catherine's Clock"), she is "an actual case," but at the same time she is "the cailleach, the female, potent woman" (Fried, 8) who must be faced in order to attain the self. Like the snake and bird to which she is likened, she is an archetype buried in the subconscious. On the other hand, the poet admits that often in driving down the mythical past, he finds "the actual people I grew up with" (Fried, 12).

In "Tear," the link between the figure of the grandmother and the underworld is even more obvious. The poem deals principally with a child's first understanding of death. It contains a re-creation of a child's fear and repulsion in front of a dying person, and the memory, tinged with envy, of his infant sister's death. At another level, it is also, like all the others, a poem about an initiatic voyage offering, however, an intimation of a less frightening femininity than the one which confronted the hero in his descents towards the "ancient women with open mouths." The child is sent in to kiss his dying grandmother and he has to pass through "a fringe of jet drops," be "swallowed" in "chambery dusk," and met by "the smell of disused organs and sour kidney" and the sight of "her mouth, / that the lines of ill-temper still / marked" (*NLD,* 20). Terror grabs the child as it grabs any voyager embarking on a downward exploration:

> I couldn't stir at first, nor wished to,
> for fear she might turn and tempt me
> (my own father's mother)
> with open mouth

> —with some fierce wheedling whisper—
> to hide myself one last time
> against her, and bury my
> self in her drying mud. (*NLD*, 21)

Yet he had to kiss, sinking his "face in the chill / and smell of her black aprons," and was carried into "a derelict place / smelling of ash." From that derelict place, however, he did carry back a prize, "a single drop," the tear of the title. This is the memory of his grandmother's relenting for the grief of his little sister's death; her voice, "soft, talking to someone" offers a fleeting vision of anima, the more emotional aspect of femininity, which is also revealed by his father's shedding "big tears . . . bright drops on the wooden lid for / my infant sister." At that time, the child, instead, was still locked in his primitive, animal-like stage of development and could only emit a "wail of child-animal grief." But the experience of kissing the dying woman represents a first confrontation with the uses of pain and waste, which comes to him with the immediacy of drinking or eating: "How I tasted it now— / her heart beating in my mouth!" (*NLD*, 22). It is, as Kinsella told Fried, "a cannibalistic world" (Fried, 18). The epiphanic moment, as Brian John points out, has been brought about "through contact with the grandmother-*cailleach*, just as in Irish myth union with the *cailleach* brings illumination and, in certain instances, sovereignty."[9]

In "Irwin Street," the speaker goes over the moment when he first acknowledged his identity. In Kinsella's numerical scheme this is degree One. On his way to school, the child sees his father, "my maker, in a white jacket, and with my face." This first narcissistic experience is relived on awakening by an onanistic search of self:

> Wakening again, upstairs,
> to the same wooden sourness . . .
>
> I sat on the edge of the bed,
> my hand in my pyjama trousers,
> my bare feet on the bare boards. (*NLD*, 24)

The second section of the sequence, titled "a single drop" in the Knopf edition, is still about the zero-phase of development. The five poems, however, deal with the collective subconscious and use a mythical context to explore the first steps of individuation in their spatial and temporal dimension. The poems focus on the time when not being becomes being, which is conveyed by the stories about Ireland when it was still empty and without form. In keeping with the motto "cease to exist" of the opening poem, death and sleep are the ruling modes of existence of this section. Several of the poems hinge on wordplay around the two meanings of the term "drop," signifying a fall (often through chasms or caves), as well as a round, zero-like particle of liquid, which in turn generates water and river imagery.

"Nuchal: (*a fragment*)" is a very free translation or adaptation of the sixth poem of *Lebor Gabala Erinn* (or *Book of Invasions*).[10] A definite stylistic change can be perceived in comparison with the other poems; a partial return to rhyme signals a highly crafted and refined composition of an incantatory, Keatsian richness of detail. The poem describes the mythological four rivers of Eden (Gen. 2:8–17) flowing from the fingers of a reclining woman—a Great Mother archetype. The exploration of one of the myths an Irishman carries in his cultural baggage, as well as in his subconscious, yields this feminine image—a headspring of life—at the core of the pattern of a quincunx drawn by the four rivers.

"Endymion" uses the Greek myth of the moon goddess, Semele, falling in love with a shepherd sleeping in a cave. The focal moment is that of the conjunction with the other through a kiss, which is conveyed, as in the earlier poetry, by luminosity:

> I stole nearer and bent down; the light grew brighter,
> and I saw it came from the interplay of our two beings.
> It blazed in silence as I kissed his eyelids. (*NLD,* 29)

When the goddess straightens up (and the moon wanes), the cave falls under the dark rule of Hecate and her owl:

> and the ruddy walls with their fleshy thickenings
> —great raw wings, curled—a huge owlet stare—
> as a single drop echoed in the depths. (*NLD,* 29)

The benign and threatening influence of Selene reflects the two aspects of femininity. The poem starts with the words, "At first there was nothing"; it is the beginning of individual and mythical time, the brink between zero and one. The union achieved through a kiss brings about the beginning of existence. In Endymion's cave, reminiscent of the womb, but also of the "curled" wings of the owlet, this comes about as "a single drop echoed in the depth"—the drop of semen, but also the predatory drop of the owl in a coincidence of birth and death.

The zero-world of womb-life and the time before Ireland was settled is the theater of "Survivor." The poem initiates the fruitful marriage in Kinsella between his experience of the psyche and Irish myth,[11] drawing inspiration from the account of the first invasion of Ireland by Cessair.[12] In Kinsella's eyes, the story of Fintan's flight from the sexual appetites of Cessair and fifty female invaders lends itself to Jungian interpretations, and is indeed archetypal as representing the flight from the other sex's image in oneself. The fear of women and the apathy of Kinsella's Fintan are keys to the psychic interpretation of his story. As Fintan lies still in the cave, "curled in self hate," and fails to move his lips "to let out / the offence simmering / weakly / as possible / within" (NLD, 31), he misses his chance to achieve consciousness and begin to exist.

Yet the mythical Fintan who, in Kinsella's poem, refuses to move his lips and exclaims, "What is there to remember?" is also considered the first Irish poet. After going through several incarnations and living through all the invasions of Ireland, he becomes the living memory of all that has happened. In the second part of "Survivor," Kinsella will show Fintan winning over his reticence and seeking the right words to tell his story of origins. Fintan's experiences are emblematic of Kinsella's own psychic and linguistic exploration of the land of the dead, and demonstrate the origins of poetic language itself. What Fintan retells is the zero moment of the existence of Ireland, when it was settled only to have the Flood wash away all traces of the invaders. Appropriately, this invasion is not numbered in Lebor Gabala Erinn, being the story of a taking of the country which did not really bring it into existence.

Kinsella's poem dwells principally on the survivor's sensations and memories while he is in his womb-like "first home." His halting account of life in the cave (where he lies "the head huddled close / into the knees and belly") is also of prenatal life—the zero-stage of human existence—and of life before language. Fintan struggles to preserve consciousness by remembering and putting into words the journey westward, the discovery of a new paradise ("an entire new world / floating on the ocean like a cloud"), and the pristine state of the country, "a land with no sins," where there are "No serpents. / No lions. No toads" (NLD, 32). But he also puts into words the sickness brought about by the presence of "the she-wolf" and by the great rock, "The Hag: squatting on the water / her muzzle staring up at nothing" (*NLD*, 32). Instead of confronting the malignant female figures, as a mythical hero would have done (and as indeed do the protagonists of some of Kinsella's other poems of this period), Fintan flinches back. The final image is of his flight from the sexual appetites of the women:

> A final struggle up rocks and heather,
> heart and lungs aching,
> and thin voices in the valley
> faintly calling, and dissolving one
> by one in the blood. (*NLD*, 33)

In the end, Fintan escapes from Cessair's womb to the womb of the cave, incapable of achieving his creative consciousness, and is left spelling out stutteringly his bleak vision of a feminine predatory world. Through Fintan, Kinsella also reconstructs the beginnings of poetic language. The final words, evoking a place of origins haunted by clawed women (indeed a land of the dead), are bare nouns, adjectives, and verbs not yet organized into sentences, but barely coalescing fragments:

> There is nothing here for sustenance.
> Unbroken sleep were best.
> Hair. Claws. Grey.
> Naked. Wretch. Wither. (*NLD*, 33)

"At the Crossroads" is also dominated by fear, the fear of being swallowed if one does not turn into an eater. The condition described in the opening poem of *Notes*—"Falling. Mind darkening. Toward a ring of mouths"—is here enacted inversely; the victim is threatened by open mouths above him, menacing to drop on him. There is the moon, as it must have appeared to supine Endymion: "A white face / stared from the / void, tilted over, / her mouth ready" (*NLD*, 35).

And then there is Hecate's bird, the owl, dropping down on its prey. The owl's hunger is seen as a cosmic force, the eater and its victim, reduced, respectively, to a mouth and meat in a stomach. The roles are interchangeable:

> And all mouths everywhere so
> in their need, turning on each furious
> other. Flux of forms
> in a great stomach: living meat torn off,
> enduring in one mess of terror
> every pang it sent through every thing
> it ever, in shudders of pleasure, tore. (*NLD*, 35)

Appropriately, the speaker of the poem, terrified by the obscure men-
aces at the crossroads, does not know "whether the care was for myself /
or some other hungry spirit"; he is both the owl, who must drop into the
underworld of his dreams and memories, and the owl's victim, who must
allow himself to be swallowed. It is an unending process of never-satisfied hunger and ever-recurring cycles of destructive search and assimilation, the only way through which integration may be reached. This is
the most terrifying aspect of the process:

> The choice—
> the drop with deadened wing-beats; some creature
> torn and swallowed; her brain afterward,
> staring among the rafters in the dark
> until hunger returns. (*NLD*, 35)

"Sacrifice" transforms the destructive search into an ecstatic experience.
Images of open-heart surgery and lovemaking blend in the enactment of a
sacrificial killing of a female victim, described from the point of view first
of an observer and then of the victim herself. The victim submits to the
tearing of tissues, described in realistic and symbolic terms at one time:

> onto her back on the washed bricks
> with breasts held apart
> and midriff fluttering in the sun.
> . . . .
> it is done in a shivering flash.
> The vivid pale solid of the breast
> dissolves in a crimson flood.
> the heart flops in its sty. (*NLD*, 36)

Seen from the victim's point of view, however, this is accepted with joy:

> Never mind the hurt. I've never felt
> so terribly alive, so ready, so gripped
> by love—gloved fingers slippery
> next the heart! (*NLD*, 36)

Allowing herself to be totally possessed by another, to have her heart "in another's clutches," she attains love and knowledge:

> We are each other's knowledge. It is peace that counts,
> and knowledge brings peace, even thrust crackling
> into the skull and bursting with tongues of fire. (*NLD*, 37)

In spite of the hieratical diction, fitting for the high tone and slow pace of the poem, with its polysyllabic and cultivated lexis, this, like the other more abrupt poems, is about the satisfaction of the primary passion of hunger. The metaphors of surgery and lovemaking imply, like eating, the tearing apart of one tissue to allow the formation or preservation of another. The onlooker with "wisps of hunger / hovering above the table," evokes the owl ready for its "murderous drop." But here the victim has accepted her owl-like surgeon / lover, and addresses him lovingly as he rises from their union:

> I love your tender triumph, straightening up,
> lifting your reddened sleeves. The stain spreads downward
> through your great flushed pinions.
> You are a real angel.
> My heart is in your hands: mind it well. (*NLD*, 37)

The process of assimilation of male and female is well on its way in this well-rounded poem with a traditional closure.

After the orderly, almost traditional tone of "Sacrifice," the third section of the sequence, formerly "nightnothing," surprises the reader by its use of language. Its novelty is apparent even in the morphology of the subtitle, and the five poems are characterized by an exploded form. By admitting the irrational as a channel of understanding, Kinsella breaks apart traditional language and structure, and the brief moments of clarity are so slight that language itself cannot complete the communication. Yet a sense of identity is wrenched out of the darkness. The poems are a fitting illustration of the "glitter again" stage of the prefatory poem.

"All Is Emptiness and I Must Spin" presents the usual situation: the speaker is enclosed in "a vaulted place," "a vacancy in which apparently / I hang / with severed senses." There are intimations of torture and imprisonment, as well as of the primeval cave. As the title suggests, the hero must spin in this emptiness "with drunken pleasure," and be "hurled Onward! / inward!" The poem hints at several "flickers" of positive experiences: the encounter with a female, the drop of sperm teeming with "Fantastic millions of / fragile / in every single," (*NLD*, 42), the dew of a tear, the echo of voices, a hand touching lightly. The whole section will insist on the provisional status of such brief revelations, and on the cycles of hunger and appeasement, descent and stasis, symbolized by the coils of the serpent.

"Ely Place" is a complex poem, reenacting how imagination perceives various events simultaneously and reprocesses them. Walking in Ely Place, still haunted by memories of George Moore (a literary ancestor who lived there), the walker hears a gull, ready to dive onto its prey and carry it away in ravenous hunger. Impressions of the place and its associations are interleaved with the gull's cry "I. I. I." asserting its identity, and with expressions of violent sexual desire aroused by the sight of a girl dressed in white. This turns into "a blood vision"—digging a penknife "in her throat, / her spirting gullet!" (*NLD*, 44).

The gull's hunger, as well as the speaker's amorous passion and the writer's search for expression, are destructive impulses conveyed by images reminiscent of "A Hand of Solo." The lines apply to all three situations:

> (and they are on it in a flash
> brief tongues of movement
> ravenous, burrowing and feeding,
> invisible in blind savagery,
> upstreaming through the sunlight with it
> until it disappears buried
> in heaven, faint, far off). (*NLD*, 44)

Yet such violent destructiveness holds in itself the promise of the revelation of some glimpse of identity. The descent and tearing hunger are rewarded with:

> A few beginnings, a few
> tentative endings over
> and over . . .
> > Memoirs, maggots.
> > > After lunch
> A quarter of an hour at most
> of empty understanding. (*NLD*, 44)

The experience, so masterfully communicated through the sense of taste, is typical of the poems of this section, when understanding comes to the poet with the trappings of revelation but turns out to be elusive, opaque, a harbinger of further chaos.

The sepia-colored picture of a woman trailing her fingers "in the stopped brown waters" of "Touching the River," expresses visually the fact that the search yields no illumination at all. Two suspended concessive clauses communicate syntactically the discouragement of the poet's fruitless search inside the most fruitful environments—the current of a river, and a nest of lark's eggs:

> Though we kneel on the brink and drive our stare
> down—*now*—into the current.
> Though everywhere in the wet fields—listen—
> the reeds are shivering (one clump of them
> nestling a lark's eggs, I know, in a hoof-print. (*NLD*, 45)

The last two poems of the section go back to childhood memories. The first one, "The Liffey Hill," returns to the motif of the search for order in purely naturalistic terms. The boy walking along a path among garbage ("papers and bottles scattered everywhere / and lodging in the roots"), discovers patterns of pure beauty on a snowy Christmas morning: "the rabbit tracks / dotted along light and powdery everywhere" or "Snow powdery pure / on the wool glove, detailed and soft." As usual this is a momentary revelation, soon "the magical-bright first print" is gone; the

wool of the gloves "got dark and wet and smelled of cold." But a sense
of wonder and pleasure remains, enacted by the language of the poem,
which is guardedly experimental with such new exploratory coinages as
"Flatsour? Raw . . . Notsour," through which the boy tries to define the
smell of his wet gloves. More often a formal search for harmony reflects
the poet's linguistic delight. We find it in the wide use of assonances,
consonances, alliteration—"*whe*re the rabbit *we*nt / *whe*re? / *whi*rring
past / a bird"—and in such devices as stanza design.

"Good Night," the final poem in the sequence, represents the successful completion of the first part of the voyage with the voyager bringing
back his prize. Although the poem admits "we won't / find truths, or
any certainties," it keeps the promise contained in the epigraph to *Notes,*
that "out of the void," deeper than "triple darkness," "delicate distinct
tissue begins to form." The poem presents the same semantic choices as
the final lines of "Phoenix Park," indicating the continuity of the process.
Stylistically, however, with its open-ended syntax, lack of punctuation,
and languorous, dreamy tone, it is less affirmative:

> What essences, disturbed from what
> *profound*er *nothingness* . . .
> flickering, *delicate*
> *and distinct,* fondled
> blindly and drawn down
> into what sense or languor. (*NLD,* 49)[13]

The poem recreates the dreamy impressions of the little boy going to
sleep. Sounds and memories merge as he sinks into the well of his sleep
and lets himself finally be "swallowed" without posing any resistance:

> and the sounds of the house are all
> flowing into one another and turning
> in one soft-booming, slowly swallowing
> vertige most soothing and pleasant
> down this suddenly live
> brinegullet
>   to a drowned pit
> clasping the astonished spectre of
> the psyche in its sweet wet. (*NLD,* 48)

The "live brinegullet" no longer holds any threat and the images of eating are shorn of their former violence. The many sibilants of the passage do not evoke the snakes hissing in the cistern but rather the sweet flux of the "mother liquid" of the prefatory poem, in which the searcher may recognize the first germs of his identity, "the psyche in its sweet wet" (*NLD*, 48). The poem enacts both the opening up of consciousness in childhood and the getting in touch with one's earliest memory, the memory of one's beginnings. The poet's imagination at work is well-represented by the metaphorical situation of the child, who, unlike the reclining figure of "Touching the River," has all his senses "unstopped":

> Attached into the darkness by every sense
> —the ear pounding—
> peering eye-apples, unseeing—
> fingers and tongue
> > outstretched—
> into a nothingness
> inhabited by a vague animal light
> from the walls and floor. (*NLD*, 49)

The readiness of the senses is rewarded by an image of tissues forming, which becomes particularly felicitous by virtue of the definiteness acquired through the metaphor of the embryo:

> Out of the glassy rock,
> like tentacles moving on each other
> near their soft roots, human thighs
> are growing; if you look closely
> you can see the tender undermost
> muscle actually forming
> from the rock, and the living veins
> continuing inward, just visible
> under the skin, and (faintly lit from within)
> clusters of soft arms gathering down
> tiny open eyes, finger-tips, pursed
> mouths from the gloom, minute
> drifting corruscations of light, glistening
> little gnat-crescents of hair! (*NLD*, 49)

The poem concludes with a comment on the workings of the imagination, how the irrational becomes part of the rational and vice versa, in
a continuous process of feeding, which is like the coils of a serpent. The
disappearance and reappearance of Dublin's underground river Camac,
its sounds running into each other, as in the palindrome
"Camacamacamac," is another figura of the snake biting its tail.

> daylit, we are the monsters of our night,
> and somewhere the monsters of our night are . . .
> here . . . in daylight that our nightnothing
> feeds in and feeds, wandering
> out of the cavern, a low cry
> echoing—Camacamacamac . . .
>
> that we need as we don't need truth . . .
>
> and ungulfs a Good Night, smiling. (*NLD,* 50)

Out of "nightnothing" and the land of the dead, the voyager brings back
a prize, a "Good Night," which puts an end to phase zero of the numerological plot.

Other Poems

After his inward journey, Kinsella returned to a more deliberate self-
reflexive mood, to explore poetically, as he had at various stages of his
career, the functions and meaning of his craft, and assess the results
achieved in writing the preceding sequence. The persona of the artist in
"Worker in Mirror, at His Bench" utters both the positive faith in the
ability of a work of art to elicit some structure and understanding, and
the doubts that beset him as to its final value.

The artist voices Kinsella's own public poetic creed in a sort of dramatic monologue addressed to some visitors in his workshop. A few
asides, however, bring out the hypocrisy of the show he is putting on:

> No, it has no practical application.
> I am simply trying to understand something
> —states of peace nursed out of wreckage.

. . . .
Take, for example this work in hand:
out of its waste matter it should emerge light and
                                            solid.

. . . .
Often, the more I simplify,
the more a few simplicities go
burrowing into their own depths,
until the guardian structure is aroused . . .
. . . .
Here the passion is in the putting together. (*NLD*, 56–57)

These affirmations, however, cannot be accepted at face value. Once the visitors are gone, the artist looks at himself in the mirror-like "bright assembly" he has been working on, and the mirror (the epitome of self-reflexive devices) casts back a reflection of his face as different masks. As Kinsella points out, in his interview with O'Hara, the heads of "gold, silver, bronze, iron" suggest "the ancient Greek 'Ages.'"[14] The last mask, as layers of civilization have been stripped off, is a dark "wolf-muzzle" lapping "brother's thick blood" (*NLD*, 59), a reminder of Cain, Romulus, and the savagery inherent in human history.

An even more threatening "outline" lies behind these masks, "in the silt of the sea floor": " a marble carcase," "The calm smile of a half- / buried face: eyeball / blank, the stare inward" (*NLD*, 59). The work of art may indeed induce understanding and reveal truth, but, as Kinsella explains, "This is the truth towards which we are pushed: the face that is waiting, in fact, for the first, innocent face . . . . The act of understanding initiated by the worker, as observer when he looks into the construct, ends in an understanding of what lies in wait for unreasonable hope" (O'Hara, 14). In the conclusion of the poem, the worker suggests there may be a more threatening pattern emerging out of waste and darkness:

blackness—all matter
in one light-devouring
polished cliff-face
hurtling rigid
from zenith to pit
through dead. (*NLD*, 59)

The same pessimism about the kind of understanding that may be reached through a lifelong search appears in two of the "Other Poems." The route of the Táin, in the homonymous poem, is discovered by chance after a tiring search by a group of hikers seeking to retrace the steps of the epic heroes and plunge into the nation's childhood.

The poem, an extended metaphor of the lifelong search for understanding, insists on the alternating states of disappointment rather than on a feeling of elation on discovering the route in a flash of light:

> . . . Flux brought to fullness
> —saturated—the clouding over—dissatisfaction
> spreading slowly like an ache: something
> reduced shivering suddenly into meaning. (*NLD,* 54)

"Death Bed," drawing upon Thomas Mann's account of the death of Jacob, also acknowledges the futility of a lifelong focus on disintegration and death in search of a woven pattern, a sign, which instead "might / have coursed across the heavens" and gone unnoticed as "we had spared no one to watch."

> And it is those among us
> who most make the heavens their business
> who go most deeply into this death-weaving.
>
> As if the star might
> spring from the dying mouth
> or shoot from the agony of the eyes. (*NLD,* 66)

Once Kinsella's deep-rooted hope of weaving a tissue of unity out of disorder is abandoned ("we / can weave nothing but our ragged / routes across the desert), the poet places the ordering principle outside the poem, leaving his images as the title of one of his poem suggests, to "spin in emptiness."

In the remaining compositions, Kinsella relies on intertextual references to give a less personal scope to the theme of the presence of violence at the very origins of life. "Drowsing Over the Arabian Nights" summarizes its conclusions with the support of other authors as well: "We are elaborate beasts, / If we concur it is only / in our hunger—the soiled gullet" (*NLD,* 61). Even in paradisal lands, the "soiled gullet" rules, as Darwin and Renan have convincingly demonstrated to Kinsella, who bases some of his poems on their thinking. "St Paul's Rocks: 16 February 1832," based on an entry in Darwin's journal of the voyage of the *Beagle*, describes a virgin land where life takes its first hold "in squalor and killing and parasitic things," and the seeds of vegetation might bob into an inlet "like a matted skull" (*NLD*, 63). "The Clearing" presents the instinct of survival in man, which transforms him into a beast whose "eyes grow sharper—and the teeth" (*NLD*, 62), after he has killed a stalking animal. In the part of the poem which is in diary form, the protagonist describes as "ease" his holding by the fur the cutoff head, "the blood dropping hot / the eye-muscles star-bright to my jaws!" (*NLD*, 62).

"The Dispossessed," based on Renan's *Vie de Jésus*, shows how the "long pastoral" of early Christians was interrupted when John the Baptist turned up on their threshold, "a mangled corpse," leaving a mark of violence on what had been a dream of peace.

After so much violence, the collection ends with a gloss freely imitating the sort of annotations medieval monks would inscribe in the margins of their manuscripts. This one, named "Wyncote, Pennsylvania: A Gloss," indicates the direction Kinsella's writing was to take in the future, in spite of the successive waves of ordeal. The allusion in the title to Ezra Pound's residence is itself a stylistic and intertextual gloss indicating Kinsella's intention to follow the poet he often declared to admire:

> Another storm coming.
> Under that copper light
> my papers seem luminous.
> And over them I will take
> ever more painstaking care. (*NLD*, 71)

One

One keeps the promise of Kinsella's final gloss to *Notes*. The new collection is characterized by a "luminous" tone. After the threat of nihilism in the preceding collection, we find in *One* that past waste and violence have been effectively assimilated into the poet's imagination, and constitute a "nutrient inheritance" permitting the achievement of identity. Within Kinsella's numerological plot, the sequence represents step one in the psychic and mythic voyage of exploration. The poems are about beginnings and self—I and one (at least in roman numerals) using the same graphic sign which, also, symbolizes the phallus. A great deal of *One,* as Kinsella explained to Philip Fried, "occurs at the very beginning, at the stroke of one, and has to do with infant memory. All that is as a given. But the more I pushed it, the more I found that it offered a primordial or other, almost legendary, reality. So that my own memories and *The Book of Invasions* made a lot of sense together" (Fried, 7). Hence the mixture of personal and racial myth in the poems that make up *One.*

Like *Notes,* the sequence of *One* is structured around a central core of interdependent poems about the narrator's and the country's earliest years, connected to the central poems and to the preceding sequence by a strand of iterated motifs. The central core is framed by a prologue and an epilogue both in a more searching and symbolic style than that in the central poems; it is also connected to the preceding sequence and the central, narrative poems through the imagery of the erect snake satisfying its hunger, and, in a more general way, through a series of phallic symbols linked to the graphic representation of the digit 1. There is, thus, an evolution from the womb-like zero and the female figures of *Notes* toward the successive step in the psyche's evolutionary progress in experience and understanding. The sequence is dominated by male figures—fathers and grandfathers in the personal poems, and ancestral figures of wisdom and creativity in the poems about Celtic antecedents.

In the preamble to the series, the poet identifies with the traditional storyteller, or *seanchai,* who, sitting by the fire and drawing from his memorized repertoire,[15] prepares to retell his stories about "the Voyage of the First Kindred"—the other-world voyage in reverse, which in Alwyn and Brinley Rees' study of Celtic tales and sagas, *Celtic Heritage,* is interpreted as "a coming into existence, a change from infinite possibility to actual manifestation."[16] The narration of the voyages in *Lebor Gabala Erinn,* as a matter of fact, merges with cosmogonic myths—Genesis and the story of Cessair's father, Bith, whose name means world.

The prologue of *One,* a poem about a snake driven by its hunger ("Up and awake"), coiling and uncoiling, renewing itself and going through different transformations, is connected to the process of creation and destruction from the preamble, and with the other poems of the sequence which explore the first signs of identity. It is also about the self's voyage back to its origins, which parallels the mythological account of the First People. The description of the snake's momentary satisfaction of hunger by its attacks on "little hearts beating in their / furry feathery bundles, transfixed," is a cosmic image for personal evolutionary progress, implying destruction for survival, and for the "patterns of invasion and absorption, violence and recovery" which constitute, according to Seamus Deane, the essence of *The Book of Invasions.*[17]

The poem is told from the point of view of the snake and thus forms a telling counterpart to the prologue of *Notes,* which was told from the point of view of the egg falling towards the open mouths of hissing snakes. The two sequences are dominated by the motif of eating, but while in the first sequence we find the fear of being eaten, "One" represents hunger and eating as positive forces. The erect, masculine snake absorbing with delight its victim, the little bird—"Snapdelicious . . . Throbflutter. Swallowed. / And another. The ache . . . The ease!"—(*One,* 9), represents the psychic process of the male integrating the power of his anima. A dream signals the positive vision of identity achieved:

> I saw
> —I was—two discs of light in the heavens
> trembling in momentary balance.
> They started to part . . . There would be a pang, I knew.
> I associate this with the return of hunger. (*One,* 10)

As the snake rises from its coiled position, its zero stage, to combat, it also "in a final spasm" leaves its "decrepit skin" and, like the Phoenix, renews itself.

"The Entire Fabric" is yet another self-reflexive poem recapitulating in self-mockery the structure and leading motifs of *Notes.* On a shabby theatrical set which contains, among other things, "a metal grating set in the floor" (but see, "hesitate" and "Hen Woman") and a "round pot" bubbling on a stand (but see, the cauldron of "hesitate . . ."), a mechanism brings up on stage "a man, sporting a striped Jacket, / posed in confident quackery, bearded" and "a woman, drawn up like a queen, / rouged and spangled." Like the poet / alchemist of "hesitate, cease to exist, glitter again," this masculine figure also has a magical key: "Something flashed / in his right hand as he reached out / to touch the vessel's rim once."

As the actor, "a hand cupped behind an ear / out at the waiting dark," wrests his moment of vision, "the entire fabric sang softly," reminding us of the "delicate, distinct tissue" forming in "Phoenix Park." The obtrusive stage mechanisms reproposing parodistically some of the features of the prologue (the grate "creaking open," the "contrived fumes," etc.) imply that the poet's first voyage into the land of the dead is a fabrication, a mere theatrical trope.

Amergin, the first Irish poet, and the first of the Sons of Mil to touch the soil of Ireland, is the narrator of "Finistere," an account of the mythical voyage of the first Kindred. The Milesians are the Gaelic ancestors of the Irish, who occupied the country after five more or less abortive invasions by their predecessors, and inaugurated a new era. The poem contains many mythical elements from *The Book of Invasions,* such as the sighting of Ireland from across the sea, the storm getting hold of the ships as they come into the harbor, and the invaders' repeated attempts at landing. It also incorporates a loose translation and adaptation of Amergin's song, the *rosc* (rhetoric) pronounced by the mythical hero on setting his right foot on the soil of Ireland.

The search for his own origins brings the poet back to one of the earliest accounts of emerging Irish identity. The poem begins with the pun on "one" and "I" announcing that the leading motif, subjacent to the motif of the taking of the land, is that of the conquest of identity. The trope of the uncoiled snake with its urge to devour creatures, conveys the idea that the search for identity has to go through ordeal and a confrontation with waste and death.

All these elements are present in the account Amergin gives of how he "spied out the horizon" and "sensed that minute imperfection again." The challenge awakens his emerging creative self, represented as a maggot or an embryonic snake (or as Kundalini, the snake of sexual energy, which, in Indian mythology, lies coiled at the base of the spine ready for erection): "A maggot of the possible / wriggled out of the spine / into the brain" (*One,* 12).

The impulse of the voyagers to explore is also connected with that of the earlier invaders, whose traces (menhirs and passage graves) left on the territory are also marked in the consciousness of each successive generation ready to relive their exploits:

> Whose ghostly hunger
> tunnelling out thoughts full of passages
> smelling of death and clay and faint metals
> and great stones in the darkness? (*One,* 13)

The primordial "ghostly hunger" is the psychic energy which has driven Kinsella's personae from "Nightwalker" onward to descend into self, past, and racial memory in search for the prize of integration and illumination. This time, however, as the preamble confirms, the voyage is to the new land, the land of the living, and it ends with Amergin's triumphant affirmation of the primeval unity of all things; a song "in the nature of creation incantations," which, as is pointed out in *Celtic Heritage,* on "the ocean of non-existence . . . has the power to bring a new world into being" (Rees, 99).

The narration weaves the facts of the invasion with passages that lend themselves to a more personal interpretation. Amergin, like Cessair's people and all those heroes who like him "turned inward," must face the terrible mother. It is a sign of his mature identity that he can address the goddess as "mild mother" in a prayer which includes in its structure a series of resolved contradictions, and which assimilates the Irish spiral stone markings as its central symbol. Moreover, by using the typical devices of Irish poetry—alliterations, assonances and internal rhyme—Kinsella suggests unity not only through imagery, but also through repetitions of sound:

> —Ill wind end well
> mild mother
> on wild water pour peace
>
> . . . .
>
>   whose goggle gaze
> and holy howl we have scraped
> speechless on slabs of stone
> poolspirals opening on
> closing spiralpools
> and dances drilled in the rock
> in coil zigzag angle and curl
> river ripple earth ramp
> suncircle moonloop. (*One,* 13–14)

Thus, through the absorption of old poetic formulae and graphic signs into a modern linguistic creation, Kinsella demonstrates the process of assimilation and transformation of his broken tradition. The song, telescoping the mythical story and the psychic one in a series of images which work at both levels, leads to the peace of the waters and, we might also add, a psyche which has yielded to the liquid and feminine elements. Made strong by this, the hero can resist the "she-hiss" of the waves "plucking at my heels," and allow the snake of his own creativity and sexuality to rise erect:

> At the solid shock
> a dreamy power loosened at the base of my spine
> and uncoiled and slid up through the marrow. (*One*, 15)

As in earlier poems such as "Up and awake," and "hesitate, cease to exist, glitter again," the reward is an entrance into light: the "glitter." At the conclusion of his song, Amergin can affirm he is "the jack of all light" and can "finger the sun's sink hole."

The speaker of the poem, exclaiming "I had felt all this before," or "I chose the old words once more," shows his awareness of rehearsing an old scenario. "The Oldest Place" insists even more on collective memory and repetition. The poem, told in the first person plural by a narrator who gathers all the other narrators in one voice, starts by dwelling on the motif of "repeated memory":

> We approached the shore. Once more.
>   Repeated memory
> shifted among the green-necked confused waves.
> The sea wind and spray tugged and refreshed us,
> but the stale reminder of our sin still clung. (*One*, 16)

The story moves back from the Sons of Mil to the First People, the invaders preceding them, and elements of different invasions (the fashioning and naming of the land, the eruption of a lake, the erection of a "standing stone" in a nightmarish landscape) are fused into one story, which also integrates the quest of the poet. The memory of all the former conquests and sea-crossings is inscribed in the consciousness of the voyagers, and of the island-dwellers after them, as part of a poet's inheritance. Wholeness can be obtained only by a reverse journey towards the first father and the first drop:

> We would need to dislodge
> the flesh itself, to dislodge that

> —shrivel back to the first drop
> and be spat back shivering into
> the dark beyond our first father. (*One*, 16)

Not only is each invasion a reliving of the former ones, and each poem a retelling of a former one, but whenever a human being succeeds in integrating into conscious life the figures of the unconscious and the ancestral experiences which he or she carries within the self, he/she also retraces the steps of the first explorers and conquerors.

The next three poems examine Kinsella's own biographical experience and that of his family, and are more straightforward than the mythical poems. "38 Phoenix Street" is made up of four recollections from childhood regarding the narrator's relationship with a little neighbor next-door, a mirror image of his male self. Like the First People, the child explores his territory and seeks words to name it. In this poem, Kinsella tries to repossess not only memories but also infant vision. The experiences are relived indirectly through minute details, such as a child would note, and retold in childish language. As in "Survivor," the beginnings of self coincide with the beginnings of language. He remembers himself and the other baby being lifted by their "mammies" to look at each other. "A bit of dirt" and a "wiry redgolden thing," although named imprecisely, are remembered with extreme clarity. The needle of a gramophone "liftfalling, liftfalling," and a picture of the Sacred Heart, holding "out the Heart / with his women's fingers like a toy," are two more epiphanies. Even the name of the street, although autobiographically correct, adds significance to the poem by suggesting a return from the land of the dead, exemplified by the war story of Jimmy's dad being rescued from under a hill of dead by the trickle of blood on his forehead. The child too, through these first revelations of self, emerges from his land of the dead and acquires a sense of self.

"Minstrel," as the title suggests, is about artistic response and style. A child writes in a kitchen on a dark night full of threats until his father's face looks in from the window, dispelling his terrors and indicating the direction his writing is to take. The poem enacts the progress, both in consciousness and style, of the persona of the young poet, moving from the impressionism of the description of a literary object (the minstrel), to stark naturalism ("a dry teacup stained the oilcloth") in the description of the kitchen.

As the young poet is shown writing "bent like a feeding thing / over my own source," and then stretched out towards the threatening cosmic space, his style becomes more searching and laden with symbolism. Verses such as "A shadow, or the chill of night, advanced out of the corner" or "a starless diaphragm / missing an enormous black beat," evoke the early Kinsella of "Baggot Street Deserta." As the consciousness of darkness advances, a landscape of primeval murderous instincts is conveyed in the language of the land of the dead:

> Little directionless instincts
> uncoiled from the wet mud-cracks
> . . . .
> leaving momentary trace
> of claw marks, breasts,
> ribs, feathery prints,
> eyes shutting and opening
> all over the surface. (*One*, 22)

But the sight of his father's face in the pane frees him from "fantasy fright" and allows him to reach the psychic and stylistic maturity which goes with the recognition of his identity in the adult male, and which is reflected in the simplicity and depth of the two final lines: "My father looked in from the dark, / my face black-mirrored beside his" (*One*, 23). Turning his back on the dark recesses of the psyche and the night, the young poet seems to choose sources of inspiration such as his own masculine mature identity, the family, and others. The transparent style of those final lines is a paradigm of development.

"His Father's Hands" is in the form of a conversation between the narrator and his father about the narrator's grandfather, a man who knew how to use his hands for cutting tobacco for his pipe, cobbling, or playing the fiddle. Then comes the turn of the forebears and their involvement in the 1798 Rebellion, and, finally, the regression takes the narrating persona back to a primeval place he dislikes, the place of the "First Kindred":

> I do not like this place.
> I do not think the people who lived here
> were ever happy. It feels evil.
> Terrible things happened. (*One*, 26)

The poem is connected to the prologue of *One* by the theme of transformation and renewal (the Phoenix motif or the snake shedding its old skin). From that past violence through his grandfather's "blocked gentleness," the poet has been brought to his own repressed impulses:

> The blood advancing
> —gorging vessel after vessel—
> and altering in them
> one by one.
>
> Behold, that gentleness already
> modulated twice, in others.
> to earnestness and iteration;
> to an offhandedness, repressing various impulses. (*One,* 26)

The initial violence has been integrated, evolving into this ancestral model of peace and craftsmanship, and giving nourishment to the growing embryo. The final vision of his grandfather's cobbling block breaking open conveys with great clarity and effective simplicity the theme of fertile energy (the squirming little nails are like seeds or spermatozoa) being released to undergo further transformation. This is indeed a "luminous" moment of writing in which imagination assimilates the past and sets itself up as the basis of the emergent self:

> Extraordinary . . . The big block—I found it
> years afterwards in a corner of the yard
> in sunlight after rain
> and stood it up, wet and black:
> it turned under my hands, an axis
> of light flashing down its length,
> and the wood's soft flesh broke open,
> countless little nails
> squirming and dropping out of it. (*One,* 27)

The epilogue to *One,* italicized like the prologue to indicate its framing nature, recapitulates the various steps of the voyage and some of the distinctive moments of the individual poems. The zero phase connected to the Terrible Mother is evoked by "the great cell of nightmare" rising in pallor—the malignant zero of the moon we find, for instance, in "Nightwalker," or "Endymion." The woman whose "lank hair . . . stiffened and moved by itself" like the snakes on Medusa's head, impersonates all the "ancient women" whose threats must be faced and assimilated in order to reach stage one of the process of growth. The heart breaking open and sending a fierce beam is like the sacred heart of "38 Phoenix Street" and the cobbling block of "His Father's Hands," both of which are symbols of assimilation and acceptance of the process. The speakers of the poem, squirming, hissing, wriggling, and writhing, remind us of the speaker of the prologue, the snake.

The second part of the epilogue reassesses the process of the descent into the land of the dead, "the fall . . . cradled . . . in a motherly warmth" followed by the assimilation and transformation: "it coils on itself, changing / to obscure substance." Finally there is a recognition of one's identity as "nightmare-bearing tissue," and a recognition that this is the common reptilian and human lot. Stage two of Kinsella's numerological system, the sharing and communicating with others, is still far to come and the poem underlines the estrangement of the travel companions: "their ghost-companionship dissolves back / into private shadow, not often called upon" (*One,* 28). With this epilogue, Kinsella confirms the nature of *One* as a sequence about the speaker's first inheritance.

A Selected Life (1972) and *Vertical Man* (1973)

The death of Sean O Riada, "Ireland's foremost composer and musician" (*FD,* 59), and a great friend of Kinsella's, inspired him with two very personal elegies, "A Selected Life" (1972) and "Vertical Man" (1973), in which the new voice of his poetic writing made itself heard for the first time. Realizing that the two poems contained no public celebration of his friend's personality and achievement except for a few solipsistic images of the legendary musician, Kinsella appended a fifteen-page memoir to the republication of the two chapbooks in *Fifteen Dead.* The group of poems and notes form a coherent whole which sketches out Kinsella's concept of death and creativity. As in the many other elegies he wrote, the sense of waste and the stark horror that death entails are paramount.

"A Selected Life," set after the funeral, has the immediacy of fresh grief. It mixes rebellion at the brutality of death and a few memories of his friend's personality. Kinsella's first reaction to the death of O Riada is bitter and grating, as we can see in this striking passage in which he projects his sense of the indignity of death through the image of a rat killed during the excavation of his friend's grave:

> A rat lay on its side in the wet,
> the grey skin washed clean and fleshy,
> the little face wrinkled back in hatred,
> the back torn open. A pale string
> stretched on the gravel. Devil-martyr;
> your sad, mad meat . . .
> I have interrupted
> some thing . . . You! Croaking
> on your wet stone. Flesh picker. (*FD*, 24)

The "shocking mess" is enhanced by the contrast with the opening of the poem, in which the musician was remembered alive and full of animal energy, "thin as a beast of prey," "cruelly" striking the skin of the *bodhran* (the Irish drum) with his nails.

Details of the funeral day—the drizzle, the croaking crow, the funeral bell—may be conventional literary elements, as Kinsella himself points out in the postscript; yet together with the cruder details, such as "that hole waiting in the next valley" or the description of the body "packed and ready," they enhance the sense of the irrevocable deadness of a dead body.

Some relief is offered, however, by memory. The poem evokes movingly O Riada's instruments and the evenings in the workroom listening to Mahler's "Das Lied von der Erde" ("A contralto fills the room / with Earth's autumnal angst") or Strauss's *Der Rosenkavalier*. The few recollections of their bohemian circle of friends "fumbling at the table, / tittering, pools of ideas forming," of the drunken nights, of his friend's idiosyncratic personality ("Pierrot limping . . . in black overcoat and beret") are short-lived; darkness and decay swallow them as they swallow the body: "swallowed back: animus / brewed in clay, uttered / in brief meat and brains, flattened / back under our flowers" (*FD*, 26).

The poem ends poignantly with the thought of "His first buried night . . . Unshuddering" and a multilingual toast: "*Salut* / Slán. / *Yob tvoyu mat'*. / Master, your health" (*FD*, 27).

The other poems dedicated to O Riada—"Vertical Man" (1973), "Out of Ireland" (1987)—contain Kinsella's characteristic countermovement toward a position of acceptance; but in "A Selected Life" the pain is raw and unrelieved.

"Vertical Man," written on the first anniversary of O Riada's death, is a more complex poem. The arcane numerological system of unity, the quincunx, appears in it for the first time, and intertextuality provides an intricate game of reverberations with quotations from Plato, Wordsworth, and earlier Kinsella, and a loose translation of the poem used in Mahler's "Das Lied von der Erde."

In the elegy, set in Philadelphia one year after O Riada's death, the narrator, wrought up by the sirens in the street and the bourbon, senses his friend's presence in the room:

> I thought we had laid you to rest
> —that you had been directed toward
> crumbling silence, and the like
> It seems it is hard to keep
> a vertical man down. (*FD*, 28)

A lifelike conversation starts between the two friends over a drink, bringing back to life "the sour ancient phrases" about their art, the pain and the search, and the endless series of new beginnings, each "as lonely, as random, as gauche and unready, / as presumptuous, as the first" (*FD*, 29). But this time Kinsella offers his friend a new "plot" which has brought him clarity and understanding in a sudden, blazing vision. After one of his usual order-inducing routines, a look at "the charts pinned on the wall," and a self-devouring prayer, suddenly the charts "come crawling to life again" (*FD*, 30) and reveal, as Kinsella explained in his commentary on the poems in *Fifteen Dead*, the "plot" to "the long sequence [he] had been working on during the day" (*FD*, 72):

> At a dark zenith a pulse beat,
> a sperm of light separated wriggling
> and snaked in a slow beam down
> the curve of the sky, through faint
> structures and hierarchies
> of elements and things and beasts. It fell,
> a packed star, dividing
> and redividing until it was
> a multiple gold tear. It dropped
> toward the horizon, entered

> bright Quincunx, newly risen,
> beat with a blinding flame and dis
> appeared . . . I stared, duly blinded
> An image burned on the brain
> —a woman-animal: scaled,
> pierced in paws and heart,
> ecstatically calm. (*FD*, 30)

Although this vision is couched in the same language and images that accompanied Kinsella's earlier moments of clarity, the approach is new because the image of light does not spring directly out of the images that precede it, but is superimposed as a mystical, visionary element, quite separate from the context. Indeed the speaker realizes that the hazy mysticism and esoteric nature of his project seem rather to pertain to his friend's domain, not only because he is a ghost but because of his spiritual propensities in life: "If the eye could follow that, accustomed to / that dark . . . / But that is your domain" (*FD*, 31).

The poem ends in music, with the triumphant notes and words of "Das Lied von der Erde," and the ghosts of O Riada and Gerry Flaherty playing and singing:

> He stepped forward through the cigarette-smoke
> to his place at the piano
> —all irritation—and tore
> off his long fingernails to play.
>
> From palatal darkness a voice
> rose flickering, and checked
> in glottal silence. The song
> articulated and pierced. (*FD*, 33)

A Technical Supplement

Published first as a Peppercanister in 1976, and then as part of *One and Other Poems,* "A Technical Supplement" represents yet another turning point in Kinsella's career. It is halfway between a poem in twenty-four parts and a sequence of twenty-four poems compactly organized. Everyday objects and places (a slaughterhouse, a factory) replace symbols and symbolic landscapes; metaphors of descent into the abyss of exploration and conquest give way to those of anatomical dissection and probing. The poet abandons the dense trance-like language and imagery for a precise, almost scientific tone, and the speaker of the poems may optimistically affirm "we are out of that soup / into a little brightness" (*One*, 43). In spite of the dark tone of the first poems, there is a certain optimism in the sequence, a belief that the cold-blooded inflicting of pain and death may offer a glimpse of understanding.

The sequence is intended to be a "technical supplement" to Diderot's *Encyclopédie*, much like the volume of plates that accompanied the original edition. (Six anatomical plates from Diderot's work accompanied the Peppercanister edition of the poems). The poems, like Diderot's encyclopedia, have the ambition of contributing to the progress of human knowledge ("au progrès des connaissances humaines") and they are inspired by Diderot's passion for precision, which is the hallmark of enlightenment. The sequence is encyclopedic in its content, ranging from anatomical studies and descriptions of operations and dissections, to literary criticism and do-it-yourself projects, with a few self-reflexive poems thrown in to emphasize the fact that all the different forms of technical investigation are metaphors for the artistic act. The purpose of plates and poems is made clear by the opening invocation to the blessed William Skullbullet: "let our gaze blaze, we pray, / let us see how the whole thing / works" (*One*, 32). The whole sequence, *A Technical Supplement*, consists of a game of mirroring and seeing the multiple facets of the things observed (dying, writing, the self), conveyed by the tropes of mirrors and knives.

The opening group of poems concentrates on the physical body, listing encyclopedically various attempts to undo its integrity and various forms of dying. The speaker of II, the second poem, delights and shudders in imagining a flayed body submitted to his dissecting attention, and to the dialectical process of "containment and separation" to which he subjects the muscular system:

> It would seem possible to peel the body asunder,
> pick off the muscles and let them
> drop away one by one writhing
> . . . .
> Except that at the first violation
> the body would rip into pieces and fly apart
> with terrible spasms. (*One*, 33)

Poem III examines the progressive decomposition of a dead body to reveal the skeleton ("a light architecture. / No stress against no stress") and the skull. It is a process of interiorization, "the pent energy released inward," and of emptying out: "[t]he whole interior of the body / became an empty dry space," "the brow went blank," he departed "leaving a mere shell." In the end, the skeleton becomes a "serene effigy," but also an emblem of passivity and blankness, which, however, rules over fertility and activity. Three stanzas enumerate paratactically the many places of bustling energy where the emblem of death may be seen; it may be at "the sources of streams," "on car bonnets, on the prows of ships and trains," or "attached to our women . . . down their dark bosoms" (*One,* 35). As the phoenix demonstrates, emblems of life and death are indissolubly linked.

Poems IV and V examine the processes of cutting a body with a blade (V) and piercing it with a knife (IV). The act of pushing the sharp point ever deeper is examined in chilling slow-motion:

> Persist.
>
> > Beyond a certain depth
> it stands upright by itself
> and quivers with borrowed life.

> Persist.
>
> > And you may find
> the buried well. And take on
> the stillness of a root.

> Quietus. (*One,* 36)

The short poem is full of intertextual references which expand its meaning. Hamlet's bodkin is evoked by the word "Quietus." The association of death with roots links this poem with the preceding one, underlining the biological nature of the process. The poem also looks forward to the long knives "inserted, tapping cascades of black blood" (*One,* 37) out of the slaughtered animals that appear in VI. But there is one more, very important reference.

Genette in *Palimpsestes* wonders whether it is legitimate to continue to refer to features of the text which have been suppressed by the author—such as the Homeric titles of the episodes of *Ulysses,* which disappeared after the first edition.[18] In this case too, two of the eight plates chosen for the Peppercanister edition (but eliminated from successive editions) could function as chambers of resonance. One is the table depicting the trephination of a skull, and the other, the one on the frontispiece of the pamphlet, is of a quill in the hand of a writer. The two probing instruments have the same effects: they penetrate, separate, and inflict pain ("nerve-strings fraying / and snapping and writhing back," One, 36); they may find "the buried well" of ink or blood, or bring death. Or both. The poem repeatedly asserts the analogy between writing, searching the mind, and inserting a knife to kill, heal, or discover.

Kinsella's urge, which sent him peering at the skies for a pattern of light in his first phase, and into the depths in search of integrity in his Jungian phase, takes on a new form in this group of poems: that of a scientific and precise investigation of all the data.

There is a certain complacency in the unemotional choice of repulsive details in the description of slaughtering in VI. Kinsella's disinterested examination of the various ways in which the animals are hung, slaughtered, gutted, and cut-up in "Swift's slaughterhouse," gains meaningfulness by the homonymy of the meatpacker with Jonathan Swift. The Dean, too, had wielded the pen like a knife, in a pitiless way, to expose and heal, as, for instance, in "A Modest Proposal." The conclusion of the poem—"At a certain point it is all merely meat, / sections hung or stacked in a certain order" (One, 38)—also applies to the other poems exploring the unsentimental probing and dissecting of the anatomist to whom physicality is all.

In VII, the writer wonders whether the cruel probing and exposing implicit in his, or Swift's, kind of writing is legitimate, even if it is all fiction:

> Vital spatterings. Excess.
> Make the mind creep. Play-blood
> bursting everywhere out of
> big chopped dolls. (One, 39)

After the tour de force of poem VI, with its "excess" and exhibitionism, Kinsella might rightly wonder about its legitimacy, since sensitive souls could be upset, as a little girl would stumble away and sob in seeing her doll gutted and spilling sawdust.

The theater of cruelty shifts to the natural world in the next two poems. VIII describes the slow process of a lizard, "a living thing swallowing another"; and IX pictures an aquarium populated with threatening creatures such as the "leopard shark," "two morays," "gross anemones," a crayfish, and a crab, each depicted in vivid and horrid detail. Again the poet feels that describing such shocking sights may not be appropriate, and wonders how to do it:

> How to put it . . . without offence
> —even though it is an offence
> monstrous, in itself. (*One,* 39)

With poem X, the mood changes and the meticulous probing and destruction have, at least apparently, a purely healing, reconstructive aim. The poem opens with the same words as "Good Night"—"It is so peaceful at last" (*One,* 41; *NLD,* 48)—and describes in precise detail some do-it-yourself projects in the speaker's house: building a landing on the stairs "flooded with sun and blowing gauze," scraping and treating the wood, cleaning out the garden, and fixing a banging door. The reconstructive peace of building and cultivating is enhanced by the memory of the child's accepting "the psyche in its sweet wet" in the earlier poem, and of those other "landings" through which Ireland's First People brought the country into existence. Like the earlier poems, this is a founding poem, a poem of origins. The mood of achievement, though troubled by a few intimations of disturbance ("little scratching sounds," "scurrying of wireworms and ribbed woodlice"), is enhanced by the poem having a definite closure, an unusual feature in Kinsella's poetry of the 1970s:

> We have to dig down;
> sieve, scour and roughen;
> make it all fertile and vigorous
> —get the fresh rain down! (*One,* 42)

The action, which refers as much to gardening and house-repair as to the act of writing, is reinforced by poem XI, which acts as a sort of closure for the section preceding it, as well as for the whole phase of searching and discovery in Kinsella's career:

> We have shaped and polished.
> We have put a little darkness behind us,
> we are out of that soup.
> Into a little brightness.
> That soup.
>
> The mind flexes.
> The heart encloses. (*One,* 43)

The sequence then continues in this affirmative mood, celebrating how the heart and the creative mind can absorb and transform darkness, cruelty, even nightmare. The central poems each contain an aphoristic closure; XII ties in with the invocation to "see how the whole thing works." Now that the investigation has been completed, "[t]here at the unrewarding outer reaches, the integrity of the whole thing is tested" (*One,* 44). The lyrical XIII, appealing to all the senses, concludes with the double cry, "I see. / I see" (*One,* 44). XIV resumes the cruel images of the first poems in the sequence: the tired, aching eyes are dreamt of sur-realistically as "a dish of ripe eyes" ready to be squeezed by a "groaning iron press." But out of the nightmare and the menace of blindness come again the affirmation of vision: "I pulled a sheet of brilliant colour / free from the dark" (*One,* 44). XV confronts the speaker's creativity, the muse, seen as "a sad prowler on our landing." Creativity is also "a soft fruit, a soft big seed" (*One,* 45), which the poet can squeeze or pierce (like the eyes/grapes of the previous poem) to draw the wine of seeing. The metaphor of piercing links this poem on the power of the pen to the ear-lier poems on sharp dissecting or piercing instruments.

The changes in life, love, and career are celebrated with open delight in XVI:

> A few times in a lifetime, with luck,
> the actual *substance* alters: fills with
> expectation, beats with a molten glow
> as change occurs; grows cool; resumes. (*One,* 45)

Liquid images of molten ore and the tide contrast with the solid images holding one back: the "thousand mirrors" in the shorescape, the "elements of memory . . . stalking one another" in a nearby pool, and more concretely, "the touch under the shirt" (*One,* 45). The substance alters because of the separations taking place (the ripping apart of the body in II; the loosened fibers in III; the rupture in the skin, the separation of the cells, and the fraying of the nerves in IV; the gutting in VI; and so on).

The next poem, XVII, contrasts in a balanced way images of life and nourishment ("the smell of hot home-made loaves"), with images of death suggested by pictures of Viking spearheads lying near the corpses of invaders and victims at Islandbridge. To the imagination, they emanate a "shiny-stale smell . . . like dried meat. / Man-meat, spitted" (*One,* 46). The sharp, piercing weapons, and the masses of meat to which death reduces man and animal alike, connect this poem to the opening section of the sequence.

XVIII also contains a contrast, this time between the "passive watch-fulness" of Asia, with its deserts and the poppies from which opium is made, and the bustling activity of a factory. The poet in XVIII explores various levels of language, from the lyrical, ample rhythms of the description of the Asian cities—"Trembling / in the golden wind"—to the brisk series of verbs describing the stoking-up of the factory furnace, a human body in disguise: "Grind it up, wash it down, / stoke the blind muscular furnace." Technological nouns oddly match lyrical (and typically Kinsellan) adjectives in the description of the workers' dealings with "hissing navels," "flickering dials," and "shimmering flywheels." The jolly factory worker enjoying his lunch ("fresh bread, / ham, a piece of cheese, / an apple, a flask of coffee") and "giving "a skip up the shop-floor" (*One,* 47) elicits the most colloquial language. Deliberate plainness of language is also found in XIX, a poem which starts by listing the simple pleasures of life, and continues with an analysis of the real pleasure of "sitting down to a serious read." The act of reading is seen as "a mingling of lives," a bringing to bear of "all that you are / and have come to be," establishing "a nexus / wriggling with life not of our kind." The other's act of writing, as one's own, means "to stop in flux, living" and hold "that encounter out from / the streaming away of lifeblood, time-blood" (*One,* 48).

Poems X–XIX constitute a happy interlude from the obsession with death, which returns modified in the final poems of the sequence. XX resumes the subject and some of the old psychic vocabulary in a vision of life as tending inexorably towards death: "And so the years propel themselves onward / toward that tunnel, and the stink of fear." The speaker, however, immediately amends his wording to "the years propel themselves / onward on thickening scars, / toward new efforts of propulsion"

(*One,* 49). By focusing on new beginnings, painful though they may be, Kinsella concentrates on the living process (seeing, writing, reading, changing, working), and on seeing "how it all works." Wanting to find out "how the whole things work," leads to a constant reflection on the act of writing. Not by chance is the plate chosen for the frontispiece of the Peppercanister edition that of a writing hand. XXI is specifically about the art of a colleague, possibly Kavanagh. The pose of the outcast, the "energy wasted / grimacing facetiously inward," the use of "ineffective" big words such as "'Love' 'Truth,'" etc., offered with force / but self-serving," are all condemned. But there is also great admiration for the poet's true achievement: the ability to "grant everlasting life" to the memory of "one crust of bread," or the capacity, "Emotion expelled, to free the structure of a thing, / or indulged, to free the structure of an idea" (*One,* 49–50). Once again, Kinsella is using a persona—the other poet—to express truths applying to himself. Kinsella, too, in his poetry, and especially in this sequence, grants "everlasting life" to simple objects and simple moments, and attempts to strip away emotion to achieve the enlightened and detached glance of the encyclopedist, offering, as was Diderot's intention in *l'Encyclopèdie,* a general picture of all the endeavors of the human mind.

The final three poems deal with division and remind us of Kinsella's concern for the split identity of Irishmen and Irish poets, which is the inspiring force of his seminal essay "The Divided Mind" and the rest of his prose work. XXII, the most impressive illustration of division, involves a surrealistic mirror reflection of the head "opening / like a rubbery fan," until, after a series of splittings, "two faces now returned my stare" (*One,* 50–51). The whole process is observed with equanimity and precision; mirroring is one of the central metaphors of the sequence and of Kinsella's poetry.

XXIII, another poem on self-division, is linked to IV, V, and VI by the images of knives and slaughtered animals. The experience of division in oneself ("a great private blade / was planted in me from bowel to brain"), however, permits the knowledge of both aspects of reality, of all those contradictions which can only be resolved in death—evoked by the "tiny delicate dawn-antelope" being swallowed by the "night-staring jerboa." The central stanza, in perfect symmetry and simplicity, lays down the two faces which coexist once the blade has been accepted:

> From that day forth I knew what it was to taste reality
> and not to; to suffer tedium or pain

> and not to; to eat, swallowing with pleasure,
> and not to; to yield and fail,
> to note this or that withering in me,
> and not to; to anticipate
> the Breath, the Bite, with cowering arms,
> and not to. . . . (*One,* 52)

The final short poem, XXIV, resumes the image of the fall: "It is time I continued my fall. / The divider waits, shaped / razor sharp." Unlike in the poems of *Notes,* the fall is now cradled "in a warmth of flesh / twinned, glaring and growing." (*One,* 52). After the pause of contemplation represented by *A Technical Supplement,* the cellular process of twinning, transformation, and growth continues. The final image, an image of the embryo in the womb, is totally positive.

Song of the Night and Other Poems

Song of the Night and Other Poems (Peppercanister #7, 1978) is comprised of a prologue and five long poems each divided into sections. The prologue is unusual in that it deals with a specific childhood memory framing more abstract poems, instead of the contrary, which is the case in *Notes.* The narrator remembers being carried home half-asleep by his father one night, hugging his father's "night-smelling overcoat," and, as he passes black hedges and twinkling lampposts, letting himself "loosen with his steps" and be carried "homeward, abandoned, onward to the next shadow" (*One,* 54). The intermittence of darkness and light, suggesting prison bars or the grill of *Notes,* appears repeatedly in various forms throughout the poem, as images of a cage or the shadow of stems; it is also transposed in the alternance of high and low tide, dream and wakefulness. In each of the poems, there is something corresponding to the hugging of the overcoat, an act of reliance on someone or something which helps the narrator overcome his fear of the alternating patterns.

The traveler resurfaces from his immersion into darkness carried by a male protective figure, and lets light and shadows flicker by him, abandoning himself to love and creativity. A sensation of peace and trust pervades the whole sequence. As in the case of Jung's early childhood memories, recounted in *Dreams, Memories, Recollections,* the episode is an "initiation into the realm of darkness" and has the purpose "to bring the greatest amount of light into the darkness" (*Dreams,* 30).

"C. G. Jung's 'First Years,'" based on Jung's account of early childhood memories and dreams, which initiated him into "the secrets of the
earth" (*Dreams,* 30), functions as another framing poem. Sections I and
II paraphrase Jung's memories of the Rhine's "dark waters" whitening
at the Falls (another alternance of light and dark), and of his nurse's
song and her sallow skin. This woman, wrote Jung, "became a component of my anima," and "came to symbolize for me the whole essence of
womanhood" (*Dreams,* 23). The child's hazy speculations about Jesus
and burial are translated by Kinsella as the image of Jesus "eating the
dead." Jung's first trauma, the vision of a Jesuit, a man wearing
women's clothes, is represented as a figure toiling down a hillside like a
"witchbat" with arms outspread. Both of Kinsella's reinterpretations
hold the archetypal terrors connected with religion and the fear of darkness and burial. The culminating scene in the poem is a recounting of
the dream which, in Jung's words, "was to preoccupy me all my life"
(*Dreams,* 26): the vision of a gigantic phallus, which, in Kinsella's
words, becomes "a pillar of skin . . . enthroned / in an underground
room," evoking the standing stones of his own racial-archetypal world
(but see "The Oldest Place"). Jung's initiation, as related here, corresponds to the speaker's own walk through the night in his father's
arms. As that walk leads to the comfort of the homecoming, so, after
the asterisk, the poem reflects an acceptance of the implications of the
dreams and the dispelling of their terrors. The "sleeve-winged terror /
shrank like a shadow and flapped away" (*One,* 55), and the speaker of
those dreams, having followed "staring crumbs" through "the tree-
darkness," assumes the throne which had been that of the "pillar of
skin." Jung's dream itinerary in Kinsella's account is similar to the personal and ancestral progress through underground tunnels into the
light, narrated in so many poems.

"Anniversaries" celebrates three different moments of the poet's life
and of his relationship to Wordsworth's "shades of the prison-house."
"1955," in two parts, is about the year of the poet's wedding. The event
is seen first by an observer, noticing the happy couple giving up all resistance and getting "into a cage / of flowering arches full of light." Then,
as the point of view changes to the first person plural, the narrators see
this early stage of their union as indeed a primordial stage in the evolution of the human species and of their love, "on whom Nature had as yet
/ worked so little" (*One,* 57–58): The apelike lovers "preened and shiv-
ered / among pale stems / under nodding grain," and climbed trustingly
up "the tissuey stems" of trees (*One,* 57–58).

"1956" is the year of the publication of Kinsella's first book, and in this section of the poem he returns to the theme of the creative impulse, after "Baggot Street Deserta," "Worker in Mirror at His Bench," and the many other self-reflexive poems. In "1956," the self abandons itself to impulse, as the persona of the poet crooks his "foot around the chair leg / and his fingers around the pen" (*One*, 58), much as the child hangs onto his father, or the lovers to the tree they climb. As the writer lets himself be immersed in light and music ("the star-dome / creaking with music / at absolute zero / across the bankrupt night"), letting go of stress and pre-occupations, the book he is working on materializes as a blackbird or bat:

> A book came
> > fluttering out of the dark
> > and flapped
> > at the window. (*One*, 59)

Kinsella, who has often insisted on the painfulness of the creative process, shows here that creativity can come as easily as love, when resistance is put down.

"1975" comes in two versions, both representing the harmony of the loving couple through the trope of the flight of two birds of prey. In the first version, the birds come to perch, their claws "curled as one, / around the same outer branch / steadily, as it shook" (*One*, 59). The same safety of the child clinging to his father (or, in the preceding poem, of the fingers crooked around the pen) is implicit in this image of oneness. Stems and branches, which in some poems cast threatening shadows, breathe here "dust-gold" and are symbols of fertility: "loaded / stems dipped everywhere / under mouse-fruit . . ." (*One*, 60). In the alternative version, the sense of harmony is mitigated by menace: the lovers in flight are "supported on each other's presence" but the claws are "murderous," as the lovers, threatened by the bars of light and shadow in the stubble, feel "the urge to strangle at them with our feet!" (*One*, 60). The whole poem, with the reminder that the birds have the capacity of "living on their own waste," reads as a corrective to the optimistic series.

"Artists' Letters," one of Kinsella's own favorites, is another love poem exalting the "desperate full-hearted abandon / to all the chances of one choice" (*One*, 61). The poem apparently does not make high claims for love as do "Nightwalker" or "Phoenix Park"; love here is termed "foolishness," "young idiocy," and rashness in "braving" the risks

of throwing oneself into the adventure. Yet, in the end, the poem is one
more celebration of the oneness which emerges out of the ordeals and
the terrors symbolized here, in the final stanza, by an open toothless
mouth, threatening and attracting; a repeat appearance of the ancient
women and the grandmother of "Tear":

> A toothless mouth opens
> and we throw ourselves, enthralled, against our bonds
> and thrash toward her. And when we have
> been nicely eaten and our parts
> spat out whole and have become
> 'one', *then* we can settle our cuffs
> and our Germanic collar
> and turn back calmly toward distinguished things. (*One,* 62)

The textual strategy adopted for introducing this paean on love is the
accidental finding of a "fat packet of love letters, / old immediacies in
elastic bands." Avoiding emotion and keeping the language deliberately
flat and conversational (echoes of Auden are still to be detected at this
late stage), the narrator evokes the foolishness, and yet the courage, of
the enterprise of putting everything into "one throw," "one offering."
The poem evokes different stages of the love affair, even recreating in
embarrassment the old emotions and physical sensations:

> I shook a letter open from
> its creases, carefully, and read
> —and shrugged, embarrassed.
>
>   Then stirred.
> My hand grew thin and agitated
> as the words crawled again
> quickly over the dried paper. (*One,* 61).

But the love relationship is also an emblem for the act of writing. The
letters appear indeed as "artists' letters"; they are, as writing is, an
accompaniment to life, and reflect the different stages of evolution of the
poet's writing. The poet mimes and mocks the artificiality but also the
passionate confessional uses of his youthful writing:

> Character stripped off
> our pens plunge repeatedly
> at the unique cliché, cover
> ache after ache of radiant paper
> with analytical ecstasies,
> wrestle in repetitious fury. (*One,* 62)

The letters are also seen as having a pragmatic effect: they bodily project the writer toward the object of his desire, to "storm," "badger,"
"cajole," and "force her," "to accept our suspect cries / with shocked and
shining eyes." A third stage, of achieved maturity, is hinted at when "the
young career . . . moves toward authority," and "the spirit [is] shaken
into strength / by shock after shock of understanding." Then the letters
"suddenly shudder and *display*! Animal. / Violent vital organs of desire"
(*One,* 62). The stages of literary creation remind one of the various masks
of the creator in "Worker in Mirror, at His Bench."

"Tao and Unfitness at Inistiogue on the River Barrow" also concentrates on a moment of peace, of the "heart, ecstatically calm." Kinsella
returns to the old textual strategy of describing an excursion on foot and
by boat; echoes of "A Country Walk," "Downstream," and "Tara" can be
detected. The day's outing (divided into "Noon," "Afternoon," and
"Nightfall") takes the family through the usual images of confusion of
Kinsella's universe: "nagging" black flies snarling "off pats of dung";
Woodstock "gutted by the townspeople and burned to ruins"; "old angers
and rumours"; ghosts of "Black and Tan" (*One,* 63–64). Yet the description of disturbing sights and events is punctuated by Taoist maxims inviting to peace ("Move, if you move, like water." "Be still, as though pure.").
Moreover, the poem is dominated by images of the tide, suggesting as in
the preceding poems of the sequence, the alternation between states of
being. In the backdrop, "unseen eggs" of mayflies and their nymphs re-
create life. All these positive signals "cancel" the current of destruction
which had been perceived in the visit to the site. Out of the confrontation
with darkness and confusion, and the tension of opposites, the poet and
his family achieve a moment of understanding and harmony:

> We drifted, but stayed almost still.
> The current underneath us
> and the tide coming back to the full
> cancelled in a gleaming calm. (*One,* 66)

The concluding poem of the sequence (and its title poem), "Song of the Night," is the apotheosis of Kinsella's meditations on darkness as leading to light, warmth and love. Two nights and two continents, representing two aspects of the poet's *Weltanschaung,* are compared. Night in Philadelphia is all urban sounds, "a compound bass roar . . . breaking in a hiss of detail . . . interrupted by brief blasts and nasal shouts / guttural diesels"; it is "without wave-rhythm / without breath-rhythm." The result is "terrible pressure" (*One,* 68).

Across the ocean at Carraroe, where the poet and his family once took a camping holiday, night offers an experience of sounds and sights which duplicates the ebb and flow between two contrasting poles of Kinsella's poetic universe. Not by chance is tide so central in this poem: its absence is noted in the sounds of Philadelphia, while "the incoming tide" at Gorumna island is seen as the essence of the night:

> At night-time,

> in the wind, at that place,
> the water-wash lapped at itself under the rocks
> and withdrew rustling down the invisible grains.
> The ocean worked in dark masses in the bay
> and applied long leverage at the shore. (*One,* 69)

In this setting, darkness reveals emblematic visions of light and harmony. As the narrator and his family make their way to the edge of the ocean with an unhooked camping lamp to do the dishes, this simple object of daily use provides what, in previous work, had been numinous revelations of the quincunx or other complex stellar patterns: "A cell of light hollowed around us / out of the night." The wife, with the instinctive feminine awareness of the significance of this moment of harmony, becomes the focus of the epiphany:

> She was standing in a sheltered angle,
> urgent and quiet. 'Look back . . .'

> The great theatre of Connemara,
> dark. A cloud stretched in folds

across the sky, luminous
with inner activity.

Centred on the beached lamp
a single cell of cold light,
part land and part living water,
blazed with child voices. (*One*, 70)

The harmony expresses itself in a "new music . . . . That old / body music. *Schattenhaft.* SONG OF THE NIGHT . . . "; Mahler's music as an expression of Jung's world of shadows. The curlew's song responds to this music, "poignant" and "hauntingly beautiful," but also evoking the curlew's "threadbare cry of common loss" of "Baggot Street Deserta." Out of darkness and common loss, in this poem, the poet wrests an understanding of the tidal nature of things: darkness encloses cells of light, laughter, and music, but also sinister "scalps of heaped weed," grating and cranking noises, and bat-blackness. The poem is closely connected with the movement in and out of light of the prologue, and with the account of Jung's "initiation into the realm of darkness." But, beyond that, it ties in with all Kinsella's early poems in which the conjunction of opposites is the main theme; as epitomized in the "thought of fires in the hearts of darknesses," in "Phoenix Park" (*SP*, 109).

The sequence, *Song of the Night*, represents both Kinsella's emergence out of the darkness of a subterranean and subconscious world, represented by the Jungian phase, and a return to an earlier phase of searching. Enriched by the lessons drawn from reaching down into self and myth, the poet closes the cycle by returning to favorite images of light in a totally positive spirit.

Chapter 6
Peppercanisters, 1988–1994

The remaining Peppercanister chapbooks, published at a rate of one every two years, were gathered in two volumes, *Blood and Family* (1988) and *From Centre City* (1994). Unlike *Notes* or *One,* these volumes have no real unity (except the unity all of Kinsella's poetry shares) but they are a convenient way of making his revised "work-in-progress" more accessible. A few features, however, set them off from the preceding phase of Kinsella's production. While the Jungian aspect recedes, a Joycean naturalism becomes more evident; rather than having mythical or fantastical settings, many of the poems are set in Dublin. *Blood and Family* and *From Centre City* share with the preceding volumes the technique of the sequence, here brought to perfection. But while the overall structure becomes more and more elaborate, the diction is simplified, almost flattened, imagery is sparse, and the versification unobtrusive, with a preference for very short lines. The total effect is of extreme compression and density. In these two volumes, Kinsella proves himself a master of the medium, but remains as elusive as before.

The poems in the two volumes are dominated by the relationship with others, often exemplary figures through whom the poet confronts himself. The elegiac poems, *The Messenger* and "Dura Mater," commemorate Kinsella's own parents, while intellectual fathers and their legacies are summoned up in *Her Vertical Smile* (Gustav Mahler) and *Out of Ireland* (Scott Eriugena); both sequences also feature Sean O Riada. The shorter poems of Part I of *From Centre City* celebrate the memories of Valentin Iremonger, W. H. Auden, Jack B. Yeats, De Valera, Egan O'Rathaille, and others, who in their different ways achieved what Kinsella himself tries to achieve through his art: understanding and a sense of order. The two volumes also feature a number of negative figures who achieve, by contrast, the same result. Thus, after the personal phase, Kinsella returns to the portrait phase of his early poetry. The spirit of place also plays an important role in this phase as the titles of some sections indicate.

Blood and Family

Blood and Family gathers together five Peppercanister pamphlets brooding on personal experience and relationships with other important figures and loci in Kinsella's life.

The Messenger *The Messenger,* written in memory of his father, mixes naturalistic evocation, personal emotion, and psychological analysis, but also continues in the ponderous explorations of the subconscious and its symbolism, making some of its parts akin to *Notes from the Land of the Dead.*

The poem starts at the end, from the anguished awareness of the decay affecting both the father ("your tomb-image / drips and blackens") and the speaker ("A suspicion in the bones / as though they too could melt in filth"). It then backs up to evoke other degraded images of his father: the old man invoking his own mother in his agony, "the Self sagged, unmanned"; or the last days of the invalid, "corded into a thick dressing gown," rambling on about his "last battle" at Guinness, "the impulse at its tottering extreme." Even the funeral seems to diminish the man's stature: a representative from Guinness honors the dead man through the memory of his father and through his continuance in his offspring, but not as himself. To this the son reacts strongly: "In his own half fierce force / he lived!" and he proceeds to find moments in his father's life when he affirmed himself and truly existed. The process is symbolically equated to finding "a pearl in muck" (*B&F,* 3); the pearl of identity, and the slime of disappointment and decay, are the dominant images in the poem.

Stage by stage the poem goes back to the father's childhood, his youth, his union battles, and the son's own conceptions ("I *think* this is where I come in . . . "). There is no chronological order in the succession of such moments when the disappointments of life and the insult of final decay are redeemed by a glimmer of courage or understanding; rather they are arranged in a succession of moments of increasing intensity and brightness.

By so doing, Kinsella effects for his father the process of regression and introspection which characterized a whole phase of his own poetic self-therapy, and which the old man never undertook for himself. In language that mimes a psychologist's, the poet explains his father's self-inflicted repression: "every positive matter that might endanger—but also enrich— / is banished." As a consequence, his "Self is islanded in fog"; he is seen as a Cannibal / Caliban, who "lifts his halved head and bellows / with incompleteness," or as "a dragon [that] slashes its lizard wings uneasily / as it looks out and smells the fog / and itches and hungers in filth and fire" (*B&F*, 7). It is the son-therapist's duty to retrieve the "cysts" absorbed into the psyche, those moments of "goodness" which would have given the father his sense of self.

To the father's playful question to his children in the period of young parenthood, "Who'd like to see what *I* have?" the poet answers ponderously:

> *I* would. And have followed
> the pewtery heave of hindquarters
> into the fog, the wings down at heel,
>
> until back there in the dark
> the whole thing
> fell on its face.
>
> and blackened. . . . And began
> melting its details and dripping them away
> little by little to reveal
>
> him (supine, jutjawed and
> incommunicable, privately
> surrendering his tissues and traps).
>
> And have watched my hand reach in under
> after something, and felt it
> close upon it and ease him of it.
>
> The eggseed Goodness
> that is also called
> Decency. (*B&F*, 8)

Thus the father, who has failed to achieve individuation in his own lifetime, is seen as a winged prehistoric animal moving clumsily towards its extinction. Yet the "wings down at heel" are also the wings on Mercury's heels; the messenger god to whom the father has been com-

pared in some of the glorious moments of his life, and whose effigy dec-
orates the frontispiece of the Peppercanister edition. The pitiless description of the father's decay, linked to the opening verses of the poem,
reflects Kinsella's obsession with waste; while the recognition of the
"eggseed" or "milkblue / blind orb" (the pearl), is of the same nature as
the revelations through egg symbolism in *Notes,* or the finding of organic
tissue at the bottom of the cup of ordeal in "Phoenix Park."

The process of descent and regression itself is described in the diction
of Kinsella's earlier phase, thick in symbolism; but as memory travels
"inside" and "deeper," it returns with vignettes of his father's life in the
naturalistic style of Joyce's epiphanies. Each vignette corresponds to a
pearl shimmering with the light of his father's sense of self. The glory of
having formed Guinness's first union and the disappointments following
are epitomized by a heraldic blazon: "on bright prospects / sable: a
slammed / door" (*B&F,* 6). Other unadulterated moments are the excite-
ment of his father's participation in election campaigns for the Left, and
his walking out of church in the middle of Mass when the priest started
telling his congregation how to vote. In the private area, a culminating
moment in the father's life is the love-making on an August evening in
the grass, when the poet is conceived. The drop of semen entering the
womb (exclaiming "I am all egg") has its analogue in the dragonfly
evolving from "bloodied slime" into a "winged! weightless and won-
drous!" shimmering insect. The evolution from a "place of excrement"[1]
to a thing of beauty, such as the dragonfly, is the mystery which is at the
center of the poem. Similar transformations also give dignity to the
father's drab life.

As the regression continues further back in time, we see John Kinsella
as a young boy helping his father cobble in the dim light of his den on
the Guinness barge, while entertaining glorious political dreams. He
raises his arm to lift the hammer "with Marx, Engels, Larkin / howling
with upstretched arms into the teeth / of Martin Murphy and the
Church" (*B&F,* 13). The final and brightest scene is the evocation of the
young boy's first job delivering telegrams for the post office. The image
of the young messenger pedalling off proudly "with a clean pair of
heels," lends its title to the sequence and justifies the picture of Mercury
on the frontispiece of the Peppercanister chapbook. As Hermes /
Mercury is the messenger of the Gods to the underworld and a mediator
between the world of the living and that of the dead, so the figure of his
father, lovingly brought back to life, has allowed the poet to get in touch
with his own past and the world of the dead.

In the final section of the poem, the poet, reconciled with the apparent sense of failure in his father's life, can contemplate his being taken to his rest with equanimity and a sense of continuity. The final image is that of the grandchildren, "colourful and silent," following the coffin and confirming the cyclical course of birth, life, death, and rebirth suggested by the symbol of the pearl. Moreover, understanding the miracle of how the perfect beauty and purity of the pearl is created from muddy water and a coarse shell, helps the poet overcome the sense of filth and waste of the opening section:

> *A cross grain of impotent anger. About it*
> *the iridescent, untouchable secretions*
> *collect. It is a miracle:*
>
> *membrane and mineral in precious combination.*
> *An eye, pale with strain, forms in the dark.*
> *The oddity nestles in slime*
>
> *functionless, in all its rarity,*
> *purifying nothing. But nothing can befoul it*
> *—which ought probably to console. (B&F, 15)*

Songs of the Psyche   *Songs of the Psyche,* first published in 1985, is the longest and most complexly structured sequence in *Blood and Family*. It starts with a naturalistic prologue (three "preliminary settings" made up of several childhood vignettes), continues with an invocation, followed by thirteen lyrical poems constituting the core of the sequence; a group of eight interrelated poems "on matters of love, friendship and the self,"[2] called "Notes," closes the sequence. Kinsella's design for his oeuvre, expressed in "Invocation" as "the subsequent bustling in the previous" (*B&F*, 23), is illustrated in this poem. More than any other poem, *Songs of the Psyche* is a palimpsest of previous texts "bustling" in the new text: the poet quotes his previous work, alludes to earlier, more fully developed themes, and evokes ancient myths and literary works. All this contributes to the density of a text which, at first sight, appears deceptively thin because of the simplicity of the language and the shortness of the lines.

The three poems in the section "Settings" are about a child's search for knowledge and his budding sense of identity. "Model School, Inchicore" modulates from the child's early certitudes ("I am going to know everything," and "God will judge / our most secret thoughts and actions") to an intimation of the sour taste of writing:

> The taste
> of ink off
> the nib shrank your
> mouth. (*B&F*, 20)

The next two poems, about his grandparents' homes, are centered on the books found there. "Phoenix Street" is about his father's books—"Ruskin and Engels and Carlyle; / Shakespeare in tiny print"—but also about "the insurance collection book": an epiphany of his father's whole career. *The Messenger*, the subjacent poem, had shown the father moving from bookish aspirations ("his dark nest / stirred with promises") to the mediocrities of a workaday life, symbolized in this poem by that other kind of book. "Bow Lane" focuses on disappointments coming to the child from the adult world in matters of faith and knowledge. As his Uncle Tom lay dying of cancer, he whispered, "'Jesus, / Jesus, let me off.' But nothing worked." This to the child was a proof that prayers were to no avail. In other circumstances, Tom Ryan refused to "tell the print" of the fascinating pictures of capuchin monkeys in the grey animal book, once again denying the child the certitudes that should come from the adult world.

The thirteen contemplative lyrics following, develop some of the intuitions achieved in the earlier phase, "the previous," but also revisit and rewrite previous work. The emphasis is laid on how long the process of coming to see has taken:

> Why had I to wait until I am graceless,
> unsightly, and a little nervous of stooping
> until I could see
>
> through these clear eyes I had once?
> It is time. And I am
> shivering as in stupid youth. (I, *B&F*, 24)

The songs chart the various phases that lead to this simple realization. First the traveler, "a character, indistinct," "settled back and / turned inward" (*B&F*, 24), like the magus of *Notes,* or the voice in *A Technical Supplement,* saying: "The beginning must be inward. Turn inward. Divide" (*One,* 45). Kinsella's dealings with experience had for a long time also taken place in the realm of introversion, which he had conveyed by the metaphors of "burrowing" and "eating." The process, leading to "the shallowest peace," is also rehearsed in this poem: "ill-chosen spirits . . . cower close / on innermost knowledge" and "must burrow," "must eat" (IV, *B&F,* 25). The speaker of the poem imitates his descent into the "inner earth" by using his magical arts—divining "at a crack in the dirt" like the Cuman Sibyl, or pronouncing the incantation on the number nine in poem III. Like the narrator of *Notes,* he also traces back the steps of his birth, standing shivering, "where I was born" (I, *B&F,* 24); symbolized in turn by a door or a "grin of stone" (VI, *B&F,* 26), "a crack in the dirt" (II, *B&F,* 24), and a scar in a tree (VIII, *B&F,* 27). The journey backwards, in other words, had taken him to the brink of access into woman and the feminine in himself.

"[I]nnermost knowledge" may be achieved through love and fusion with the other sex: This is another stage of the process. The sequence contains in fact a number of love poems burdened with second meanings. One of them evokes with lightness and delight the meeting of lovers and the cancellation of duality that comes through love. The poem anticipates a more intense experience, which is the subject of a lyric in *Out of Ireland:*

> It was something
> to take a little of the spring
> out of a person's step . . .
> She offered me her hands.
> I took them in mine
> —averse
>   but it was enough:
> we were no longer two
>
> but a third. (VII, *B&F,* 26–27)

Poem VIII, a revisitation in Jungian light of *Wormwood,* returns to the image of the "Two trees grown into one" of the earlier poem, with the heart-carving grown thick. The tree of the poet's early dreams and nightmares is surrounded now by emblematic flowers representing the various phases of his love, which he, like mad Ophelia, assigns appropriately:

> gold for the first blaze
> red for the rough response,
> dark blue for misunderstanding,
> jet black for rue,
>
> pale for the
> unfinished children
> that are
> waiting everywhere. (VIII, *B&F,* 27)

The final flower is for the Caliban-like incomplete beings, caught in a crack of the tree, and represented in this and other poems as searching to complete their identities.

The rest of the central sequence is about the completion of identity through a transformation which also implies the absorption of pain and destruction. Night foxes dream of the cistern hiss of the snake (IX). A silk maggot turned into "a great delicate self," "a great moth of prey" (X, *B&F,* 28–29), makes the poet "writhe in memory" of similar epiphanies: the one in "Chrysalides," also witnessed in a kitchen, and the transformation of the dragonfly as an emblem of conception in *The Messenger.*

Poem XIII compresses into two italicized tercets the whole paradoxical process of immersion into darkness, with its ambivalent connotations:

> *I woke suffocating,*
> *   slipped through a fault*
> *into total dark.*

No.

> *I came to myself*
> *   in the middle of a dark wood,*
> *electric with hope.*

Like Dante's traveler, after getting lost in his *"selva oscura"* ("in the middle of a dark wood"), Kinsella's traveler also returns to light— though not as assertively as in the lines that conclude Dante's *Inferno:* "*e ritornammo a riveder le stelle*" ("and thence came forth to look once more upon the stars").[3] In the psychological and creative processes, darkness is the key element, both positive and negative, for "*in potentia* all things." One must immerse oneself into it in order to be "thrown up . . . into a state of peace." It is "a matter of negative release," and the whole poem, through antinomies and paradoxes, illustrates the poet's capability of subsuming chaos and confusion.

Poem XIII, the central section of the sequence, concludes with various "previous" visions of Self summoned "firstly into being" out of "organic darkness." The vision is a summa of Genesis, *Lebor Gabala Erinn,* and Kinsella's own poetic universe:

> an upright on a flat plain,
>   a bone stirs
> in first clay
>
> and a beam of light struck
>   and snaked glittering across a surface
> in multi-meanings and vanishes.
>
> Then stealers of fire;
>   dragon slayers; helpful animals;
> and ultimately the Cross. (*B&F,* 31–32)

Yet to this evolutionary view of the genesis of the self and creative imagination, the poet opposes the doubt that there may be some other form of access to identity:

> Unless the thing were to be based
>   on sexuality
> or power. (*B&F,* 32)

The final "Notes" are glosses on various points touched upon in the main body of the sequence. In Kinsella's gnostic interpretation, God creates "out of the ache / of *I am*":

thinking

a mouth
to My kiss
in opening

let there be
remote. (*B&F,* 33)

Mouths and openings, grins, smiles, and kisses are omnipresent in the poem (and in the macrotext) as accesses to the underground and to the sexual fusion, from both of which identity emerges. Love, seen as "refreshment / in the recognition of pattern," and as affection for children, brother, and friends, is the subject of the other notes. The final three notes concern the self, which is present even in the titles: "Self Scrutiny," "Self Release," and "Self Renewal." The three poems are closely linked to the "previous," and each of them appears as a gloss on a preceding poem, especially on *A Technical Supplement.*

"Self Scrutiny" expresses identity through consciousness of the body in "its composite parts." The objective attention to individual organs (bones, eyes, ears, tongue, "thumbs and digits") brings us back to the encyclopedic spirit of *A Technical Supplement.* "Self Release" uses sarcasm to affirm the power of the speaker's sexuality, bothersome though it may be to his woman companion. By ironically proposing to deaden his sexual identity, by pulling down "a clean knife-shaft into the brain . . . until there is / glaze and numbness in 'that' area," Kinsella resumes the image of pitilessly plying the knife in self-surgery, which had been exploited in "Clarence Mangan," "Sacrifice," and poems IV and XXIII of *A Technical Supplement.* In spirit rather than in imagery, it also establishes a connection with the poems of tormented love in *Wormwood.* "Self Renewal" resumes the mirror symbolism of *A Technical Supplement* and "Mirror in February." The quester finds his identity in the bitter and solitary watching of himself "in a lonely mirror"; "recovering" himself through confrontation with other lonely watchers and the "icy" contact of brow against mirrored brow. "[T]he memory of a couple / of fading eye diagrams" remains, clouded over, in the mirror.

Reflecting oneself in mirrors—or such forms of mirrors as constituted by other people, one's former self, or one's previous work—allows, in this poem, the recognition of one's self, even if in diagrammatic form. In this umpteenth poem of quest for knowledge of self and creativity, self-reflexivity (in both its acceptations of seeing one's image reflected and of reflecting creatively on one's creative process) seems to have the final word. The sequence opens and closes with a reference to eyes: The secret to seeing is to use one's eyes. Immersion into darkness, or the exploration of the secrets of birth and the subconscious, have only been steps towards this simple realization. "It was time," as the speaker of the poem often repeats.

Her Vertical Smile   Starting with an epigraph drawn from Kinsella's own memories of how O Riada introduced him to Mahler (*One*, 65), *Her Vertical Smile* (1985)[4] gives an account of a performance of *Song of the Earth*, the Austrian composer's masterpiece. The poem, a metapoetic achievement if ever there was one, is itself structured like a piece of music, in five movements, three of which bear musical names— Overture, Intermezzo, and Coda. The performance functions as the allegorical structure of the poem, while a doubt voiced in *Songs of the Psyche* as to the possible relationship of "the thing" with sexuality or power is its philosophical grounding. Point by point the performance is compared with the sexual act, a textual strategy which allows the poet to give vent at times to an unexpected bawdy and comical vein, and at times to introduce a mystical note in his views of creativity.

The great contralto's aria, expressing "that lovely heartbeat of the whole world," (*B&F*, 43) sets the tone for the ensuing speculations on the relationship between creator and creation. God, Mahler, and O Riada are fused into one as they listen "to a last echo fade," an echo "out of nothing." The intense music, "released from all earthbound tonalities" and detached from its creator, appears to the poet as the epitome of artistic achievement. In rather domestic imagery, he wishes: "If only we could wring our talent out, / wring it and wring it dry like that" (*B&F*, 43). What fascinates Kinsella about Mahler (and, probably about O Riada too) is something we find in his own oeuvre:

> the force of will
> we find everywhere
>   in his strange work
> the readiness to embrace risk,
>
> tedium, the ignoble,
> to try anything ten times
> if so the excessive matter can be settled. (*B&F*, 44)

Kinsella's work too, and especially *Her Vertical Smile,* contains a good deal of "tedium" and the "ignoble"—the prosy and the bathetic—coupled to the heightened and the audacious. But, especially, as by now should have become clear, Kinsella dares to repeat himself, to return again and again to the same theme in order to "settle" the "excessive matter." Kinsella's poetry too is based on an unresolved cycle of pattern and formlessness, quest and appeasement. The words applied to Mahler perfectly fit his oeuvre too:

> every rhythm drained
>
> into nothing, the nothingness
> adjusting toward
> a new readiness. (*B&F,* 44–45)

The relationship of the conductor with his music is expressed through sexual tropes, and the extended metaphors describing the performance in the various parts of the poem are at times as subtly bawdy as the title of the sequence itself. The semantic field of man-woman relationships is exploited in full in describing Mahler conducting, and culminates with the double entendre of "his baton explores / her core of peace" (*B&F,* 44). In the "Intermezzo," the analogy between sex and music is resumed and we find such heavy-handed tropes as "the baton withdrawn. / A timed excision," and "'Tuba! Double basses!' / There is a prolonged emptying / of the writhing contents" (*B&F,* 51). After the sexual and musical climax comes the realization that "something magnuscule has been accomplished," something indeed that requires the invention of this neologism: a mystery is consumed in the depths, as "the entities that made it possible / are locked together still" (*B&F,* 51). The mystery of (pro)creation, as elsewhere in Kinsella's oeuvre, is conveyed by the image of spermatozoa "teeming" and "swarming" toward their encounter with an ovocyte, and affirming "*I am ! I am*" (*B&F,* 52).

Besides the relationship of creativity with sexuality, Kinsella also explores its links with power. Mahler's music is the expression of a certain social climate in Vienna at the turn of the century, which contributed to the outbreak of World War I. By the narrative device of turning from the performers to "the excited young," who responded enthusiastically to Mahler's music and were soon to become cannon fodder, Kinsella muses on the paradox of the coexistence of great art and murderous politics.

Semantic choices that apply both to dancing and politics—"Entente. Volte face." (*B&F*, 45)—reproduce the lightheartedness of the age. To these, Kinsella adds the rhetoric of World War I poetry—we hear echoes of Rupert Brooke[5] in "a field that will live for ever in glory" (*B&F*, 46)—and Joycean sarcasm—"the Empire / turns once more toward its farrow" (*B&F*, 46).[6] Thus Kinsella mocks the idealism which preceded the First World War, observing it from the vantage point of our knowledge of its uglier realities. Talk of harmony and the strategies of "white gloved / and glittering bellied elder[s]," is contrasted to "the tangled woebegone / the morning after" (*B&F*, 46), and the "bannerets of our own selves / dangl[ing] on wires along / irregular rivers of our own making" (*B&F*, 49).

In the "Intermezzo," he quotes a patriotic letter by an intellectual declaring, "I have set my mind now / to the service of the German cause." (*B&F*, 50). The shock at the revelations about Heidegger's position vis-a-vis the Nazis was strong among intellectuals of the late-1980s. Kinsella in this poem shares George Steiner's idea that the great humanistic tradition of the West has failed to humanize the world, and indeed has contributed to the horrors which have beset it. He perceives clearly that Mahler's music "had been elicited from precisely this matter"—the emperor's warring plans. Yet the musician was intensely aware of a world dominated by pain, death, doubt, and despair (as Kinsella was to be later), and through his art he was trying to establish some ultimate ground for existence.

What stands out in this painfully ironic, metapoetic meditation is the indifference of art, its inability to solve anything, and its deceptiveness. Music, as all great art indeed, has only the power to induce a sense of order and harmony:

> Was there ever one chasm closed
> but another opened
> on our case

> —however the medium,
> blood-bearing in itself,
> might seem temperate and good?

> Or our Music Master
> fold the terms of the curse
> back upon itself

> in sensible figures in the air
>> so the blood might beat at our temples
> with the pulse of order
>
> (let it be
>> only even as
> the work passed). (*B&F,* 47)

The ultimate goal of art—the glimpse of order to which Kinsella's own poems are committed—is mocked as an illusory "happy ending": It is like "a Man and a Woman" in a final glittering Hollywood embrace (*B&F,* 47). And its happy beginnings—a "Patriarch-Mother" relationship, described ironically through Michelangelo's Adam, on the roof of the Sistine Chapel—are equally illusory.

The useless horror of war, equated with a sense of waste among the life-bearing cells "knocking against one another" like an army of soldiers in "bloody passageways," elicits a sense of perplexity, quite unusual in a poet who made waste the source of his brightest illuminations:

> (waste
>> a part of the process,
> implying life):
> . . . .
>
> and that from even this matter
>> (as of man's head rammed against stone
> and woman a mad animal)
>
> we might yet make a gavotte
>> to feed
> the everlasting Ear. (*B&F,* 53)

In this case, the sad connivance of art with power provokes Kinsella to express indignation at the thought that one might make music out of such suffering.

The structure of the poem is less straightforward than this schematic explication suggests. The poem moves back and forth from one musical phrase to another, jostling among its three thematic cores, each polysemically subsuming the others. Using different media (a letter, the description of a photograph, pastiches of war poetry) and tonalities, as a musician would use different instrumentation, Kinsella conducts the experiment of applying musical form to meditative poetry.

The poem ends with a rhapsodic evocation of the contralto's song—"the open air / a single throat / thrown wide / in a gasp of / alarm and praise" (B&F, 54):

> And central to the song's force is
>   an awareness
> . . . .
> of her two nutrient smiles:
>
> the one with lips pouted soft
>   in half wet love
> in earnest of
>
> that other,
>   dwelling upon itself for ever,
> her vertical smile. (B&F, 55)

While the link between art and power is shown to be powerful and pernicious, the sexual roots of this triumphant song are, on the contrary, worth celebrating.

Yet the poem is not quite complete. In the "Coda," the poet, having become one with the conductor, mocks everything that has been said before in a slapstick gesture that has annoyed more than one critic:

> Nine are the enabling elements
>   in the higher crafts
> and the greatest of these is Luck.
>
> I lift my
>   baton and my
> trousers fall. (B&F, 55)

Her Vertical Smile is an ambitious and uneven achievement, both in conception and in the mixture of tones. McCormack points out that in

Mahler's First Symphony, there is a similar blend of the rhapsodic and the parodic, but that "the various strategies of *Her Vertical Smile* . . . bring together the Sublime and the Crass in a way which jeopardizes any steady perception of such notions."[7] The poem follows the flow of thoughts and emotions of someone listening to a musical performance, and this may explain its oscillations and its apparent uncertainty about the significance of art. The familiar theme of art canceling out contradictions in a momentary unity, is parodied by too much insistence on violent swerves from one mood to another, and by charging each word with too many levels of signification. Rather than "concealing his art" (a recommendation Kinsella follows in *Out of Ireland*), he seems ironically to lay it open by revealing its structure of juxtaposition and intertextual reference. Yet the poem appears remarkably unfocused, especially compared to the one that follows it, *Out of Ireland.*

Out of Ireland   *Out of Ireland* is probably Kinsella's greatest achievement of the last two decades. Its individual poems are closely interlaced in an organic whole which acquires added significance by incorporating former work ("Wormwood," "Phoenix Park," "Nightwalker," "A Selected Life," "Vertical Man") through direct quotations and allusions. By so doing, Kinsella mimics the polyphonic structure of early Irish music. Theories on polyphony, as expounded by Giraldus Cambrensis and Scott Eriugena, constitute a necessary part of the sequence and are worked in, intertextually, in the epigraph and the prose section, "Precedents and Notes." The "metaphysical love sequence," which has a mystical quality reminiscent of T. S. Eliot's *Four Quartets,* reaffirms the centrality of love in the new perspective offered by Jungian analysis. As in the preceding poem, moreover, Kinsella draws a parallel between love and the artistic act.

The poem is structured temporally and spatially around a visit to Sean O Riada's grave in the churchyard of Ballyvourney. In a forward and backward movement, rather than a descent, the artist/lover enters the graveyard and the world of experience, has a brief illumination through love, and emerges with a fresh purpose to resume his pen.

The flight of crows welcoming the visitors as they enter the cemetery, connects this poem with *A Selected Life,* but a more serene tone than in the former elegies reigns here. The naturalistic description of the graveyard, with its "pious litter," a hole gaping in the ground "like a mouth" (*B&F,* 69), and the dead, "Lidless, lipless, opensocketed / and dumb with suspended understanding" (*B&F,* 65), could make this appear as yet another scene of waste. It is, instead, a place of certainties, or rather, to use Kinsella's caveat, "half-certainties." A first certainty, his faith in love, which has been the leading motif of all his poetry, is reiterated by quoting "Phoenix Park":

> *that love is*
> *to clasp simply,*
> *question fiercely;*

Symbolic figures in the graveyard—a crow, a painting of the Black Robber, a stone sculpture of a *sheela-na-gig*,[8] and a gaping hole—proffer other certainties ranging from carnal to spiritual, each oracularly calling "*come and buy.*"[9] But the visitor proceeds towards a different form of knowledge. The "many-sounded / and single voice" of his friend's music reveals a "harmonious certainty: that the world's parts, / ill-fitted in their stresses and their pains, / will combine at last in polyphonic sweet-breathing union," and all Mankind will be "silent in a choir of understanding" (*B&F*, 61). "Seamus of the Smart Suit" joins the ancestral voice of Scotus Eriugena in this belief.

The poet has his own "half-baked" notion, matching Eriugena's, that the experience of love—consigning his will to the woman's flames (as he had already affirmed in "Phoenix Park")—leads to a significant moment of unity and understanding; a Jungian individuation deriving from the fusion of Male and Female:

> and will turn again toward the same furnace
> that melted the union of our will
> to ineffable zero
>
> how many times in its radiant clasp
> (a cancellation
> certainly speechless for a minute or two)
>
> in token of the Union and the Light.
> Until gender returned
> and we were made two again
>
> Male and Female. (*B&F*, 62)

A further certainty lies in the survival of O Riada's spirit in his music. Although this too is temporary—his spirit is "in one piece still / (just for a little while, / and only just)"—for the time being his figure can be seen "cavorting . . . along the scruffy skyline," as his "Grieving solos fade / and twine on echoes of each other" (*B&F,* 63), filling the poem with a Dionysian energy.

But finally, as Eriugena, a misunderstood and unsuccessful prophet, teaches: "Nothing certain of this world / . . . / except for certain impediments." The visitors leave behind their intimations of the harmonious resolution of dissonance:

> and it grows dark and we stumble
> in gathering ignorance
> in a land of loss
> and unfulfillable desire. (*B&F,* 64)

The poem, however, ends on a positive note. As the visitors exit, the dance of the dead is at their feet, but they can turn their backs to it with the confidence of having acquired a new power to write.

Kinsella's poem enacts some of the features Giraldus Cambrensis attributes to Irish musicians: "a concord achieved through elements discordant" and the ability to "glide so subtly from one mode to another," joining "grace notes" around "the steady tone of the heavier sound." Kinsella imitates the polyphonic mode by rewriting the earlier work into the later; by blending prose and verse, naturalistic elements and visionary ones; by integrating quotation and original text; and by achieving a counterpoint of modern versus ancient. But, more especially, the polyphonic effect is in the matter of the sequence itself: the momentary unity coming from writing (as well as from love) promises to heal all divisions and contradictions—death and the survival of the dead, Male and Female, "the two languages interchanged"—as dissonance is harmonized into polyphony. The same approach was used in *Her Vertical Smile,* but here Kinsella does it less ostentatiously, "concealing his art" as his Irish forebears did, and modulating skillfully from one mode to another.

St. Catherine's Clock   *St. Catherine's Clock,* a close-knit sequence first published in 1988, represents a further chapter in Kinsella's search for a sense of identity in significant past experience; but here the search is conducted not through a process of psychic analysis but, rather, spatially and temporally. In the central poem of the sequence, the protagonist asserts: "I always remembered / who and what I am" (*B&F,* 79). This awareness is achieved by revisiting Thomas Street (around which Kinsella spent much of his childhood) through memory and paintings evoking its history.

In the epigraph, the poet is represented as a fisherman choosing and lifting the fish "against the light" for "the bowel-piercing hook" (*B&F,* 68). Similarly, the poet chooses significant moments in history and autobiography—each section bears a date—rambling through time, as the "prowler" of the prologue, to conclude the opening poem with the words "I see" (*B&F,* 69).

St. Catherine's clock, beating the hours, marks the passing of time, points out the simultaneousness of past and present, and helps structure the poem into its three sections. Symmetrical short lyrics—"Thomas Street at the first hour," "Grand Canal Place, at the second hour," and "About the third hour"—mark the contrapuntal alternations from present to past. The different events which happened in the same place have all affected the speaker's identity and contributed to the stratifications of self.

The attempt to pierce through such significant moments is conveyed by images of sharp objects which are metaphoric representations of poetic imagination—the fisherman's hook, the syringe, the pen, the clock hand (dripping blood on the frontispiece of the Peppercanister edition)—and which are another unifying factor in the poem. Things are elusively known and even more elusively represented.

As many of Kinsella's other self-reflexive poems, "St Catherine's Clock" also contemplates the different forms of representation through which the self is known. The poem implicitly compares different linguistic and pictorial approaches, becoming, above all, a study of how the various media of representation all fail to give us real understanding; deceptiveness and subjectivity seem to characterize human attempts to couch understanding into words or paint. The poem, in its own polyphonic structure, also includes a variety of voices; dry irony mingles with the controlled lyrical tone and the flat description.

In the first poem, Kinsella, by applying terminology belonging to the semantic field of writing to his description of a drug addict, comes close to suggesting that poetry, painfully piercing and briefly blissful, is like the escapism of drug addiction:

> In a corner, a half stooped image
> focused on the intimacy
> of the flesh of the left arm.

> The fingers of the right hand are set
> in a scribal act on the skin:
> a gloss, simple and swift as thought,
> is planted there.
>
> The point uplifted, wet with understanding,
> he leans his head a moment
> against the glass.
>
> > I see. (*B&F,* 69)

The "understanding of some kind," which as he often repeated, should be the goal of the poetic act, seems as deceptive as the understanding that comes with a heroin shot.

The next two poems, dealing with two pictorial representations of historical events which took place in Thomas Street during the 1803 insurrection, emphasize the unreliability of all kinds of narrative. An engraving by George Cruikshank, representing the killing of Lord Kilwarden and his nephew by the mob supporting Robert Emmet, is the subject of Kinsella's first description. Cruikshank's is an ironical and partisan form of discourse depicting the killers as "a pack of simians, / their snouted malice gathered into the pike-point entering his front" (*B&F,* 71). On the other hand, the execution of Robert Emmet, which took place close to where Lord Kilwarden had been murdered, inspires "a non-contemporary nationalist artist" to a rhetorical representation of the severed head "brandished aloft." The image matches the patriotic rhetoric of expressions such as "the altar of truth and liberty" and "the lamp of light extinguished," culled from Emmet's "Speech from the Dock"—itself an apocryphal text, the original version of which is not known, and into which tradition has incorporated much nationalist rhetoric. Each fabulation is colored and made unreliable by the special concerns of those who produce it or transmit it, and takes us further away from a true knowledge of reality.

A third engraving, by James Malton, represents the place bustling with street life and dominated by a familiar figure—the old hag or *cailleach:*

> Centre, barefoot,
> bowed in aged rags to the earth,
> a hag

> toils across the street
> on her battered business,
> a drained backside
>
> turned toward St Catherine. (*B&F,* 73)

A sense of uneasiness is created by other grotesque figures: the "children or dwarfs," the "couple of mongrels worrying the genitals out of each other," and, especially the shade waiting for the old woman "against a dark cart humped man-shaped / with whipstaff upright." The menace of "a solitary redcoat . . . handling the entire matter," is played down, as the painter seems to have set him down "with unconcerned fingers." The print represents yet another voice, detached and noncommittal. As the familiar places of Kinsella's universe can be guessed in the background—"a distant dream / of Bow Lane and Basin Lane"—we are made to realize that the present is present in the past, and all the voices, deceptive though they may be, intermingle to create a kaleidoscopic sense of identity.

The poems following, revert to autobiography to complete the puzzle of one's identity. The long section entitled "1938" paints precisely etched domestic scenes from the poet's childhood through which he searches for the elusive truth. We are in the same territory as in *Notes* and *One,* only without the Jungian jargon and with a touch of humor. The search begins by facing once more the prototype of all the old women and *cailleachs* of Kinsella's poetry: the grandmother whose candy shop near St. Catherine's church is the focus of the memories in the earlier volumes. Represented among fascinating objects, the boxes from India, the embossed scales and their weights, the "silver and black eyeballs / and glassy twisted coloured sticks" in the glass jars, the old woman retains the mystery and slight menace of her earlier appearances, as she rules over aunts and uncles with an iron fist. It is in the shades of the back room, or "The empty Back / between the backs of the people's houses," that the young child goes through various formative experiences, apparently unconnected with one another or with the preceding historical scenes. They are moments of desecration and cruelty (swatting a fly against the picture of the Sacred Heart, dropping a stone on striped perch in the river, skipping around burning rubbish), but, especially, moments in which sexual knowledge is approached. As in the historical prints, three different kinds of discourse about sex are explored. There are the erotic fantasies with the rhetoric of pulp literature, as the young boy, "the flesh in nightmare," dreams about "The balm of a clouded breast . . . / The musk of a stocking rolled down / over her pale knee." There is the picture-book metaphoric experience of arousal and transformation:

> A little boy, some kind of an uncertain
> shade, started trying to get up
> with wings dragging.
>
> Then upright in beauty,
> his pinions touched with the red firelight.
> He turned his golden head. (*B&F,* 78)

Finally there is the childish, matter-of-fact recognition of one's sex and identity, of sex discovered with his little brother:

> One night we scrounged up together
> and felt the little eggs in each other.
>
> and I always remembered
> who and what I am. (*B&F,* 79)

The final view of Thomas Street includes past and present, as in a river flowing toward some haven. The water of the fountain by which the poet stands in the present, questioning the night, and Emmet's blood trickling from the scaffold, both flow into it; and from this composite stream emerges the speaker's self, once more represented as a winged creature:

>   a river
> coiling its potent flood
>
> between high salt block walls,
> carrying a brand new soul
> struggling with wet wings
>
> to flourish a while in freedom
> on the surface of our recollection. (*B&F,* 83)

"Inch by inch," time is beaten by the clock in the turret, as "a tooth on the big measuring wheel / reengaged." And as the third hour rings, a mysterious figure "all dressed up / in black, like a madwoman," crosses the marketplace "reading the ground." This is Jonathan Swift himself walking to nearby St. Patrick's and adding the shadow of his literary legacy to the multifaceted picture. This composite personification of his heritage reads the ground as the poet has been reading the ground of his origins, St. Thomas St., sending us further and further back in an attempt to make some sort of representation possible. Each of the pictures and autobiographical vignettes by itself is untrustworthy; together, they offer a multifaceted view, almost a visual polyphony, of reality which might be trusted.

The sequence which had opened with the act of seeing and writing, closes with the act of reading. All the mad and sane figures of this long gallery of portraits are characters of a text through which the author attempts to know himself.

From Centre City

From Centre City (1994) which, as Kinsella revealed, "is probably going to be the last of the Peppercanister books" (appendix, p. 195), collects One Fond Embrace (1988), Personal Places (1990), Poems from Centre City (1990), Madonna and Other Poems (1991), and Open Court (1991). Kinsella has extensively revised the texts of the chapbooks and in the process their titles have disappeared. The volume is organized into five sections, with "One Fond Embrace" acting as a prologue, establishing the tone, and indicating the main concerns of the volume. Thus From Centre City has more unity than Blood and Family, which is composed of discrete units.

All five sequences deal with autobiographical material, taking in events and figures of the poet's adult life rather than the world of his childhood. The literary establishment plays a big role in the collection and several poems are dictated by the memory of the deceased. The whole volume is firmly set in central Dublin, and is a celebration and castigation of the multifarious world Kinsella felt so strongly about after his long residence there, along the canal.

"A Fond Embrace"   In "A Fond Embrace," Kinsella bids a bitter-sweet farewell to the urban world he is about to quit, as he prepares for his move to the country and a new phase of his life. Matching farewells to writing accompany the speaker's frustration with city life. The poem starts with an exhausted rejection of the poetic act: "Enough / is enough: / poring over that organic pot" (*CC,* 1). The refusal is reiterated midway in the poem: "And I want to throw my pen down. / And I want to throw myself down / and hang loose over some vault of peace." (*CC,* 3). In the end, however, when the angry encompassing glance to his fellow Dubliners has turned into an embrace, the poet declares his willingness to turn all he has experienced into poetry.

The poet's encompassing glance takes in the whole microcosm of the city, and focuses with sarcasm and scorn on a gallery of Dublin personalities and institutions. The diatribe is interrupted by a few structural hinges: the repeated declarations about his writing, and the recurrent convivial welcomes to his guests/victims—the embrace of the title. After each interruption, the listing starts again with increased violence and the poem gains power by the sheer accumulation of items and spleen. However, as Kinsella indicates at the beginning of the poem, we are all participants in " a process that requires waste," and in the end, even scorn becomes a necessary ingredient of "the organic pot" (*CC,* 6).

In the first part of the prologue, the embrace takes in the speaker's immediate surroundings:

> this hearth and home
> . . . .
> our grown and scattered loves
> And all this place
> where (it occurs to me)
> I never want to be anywhere else. (*CC,* 1)

There certainly is fondness and tenderness here. But as his glance moves outward, the tone becomes less idyllic as it encounters hypocritical social workers, developers, speculators, and, especially, "urinal architects" and planners turning "a bungled city . . . into a zoo" (*CC,* 1). The anger against brainless city renovation, which had already made itself known in "A Country Walk," peaks in a denunciation of the notorious Dublin scandal of "our city fathers," who, ignoring Viking archeological finds, laid flat "an enduring monument to themselves, / an office car park sunk deep in history."[10] Crude invective ("May their sewers blast under them") and a sense of co-responsibility ("We were the generation / of positive disgrace") ebb in a convivial and eucharistic tone, as fellow citizens of all walks of life are invited to the speaker's poetic table as much to eat as to be eaten:

Fellow citizens! I embrace
your grasping manners, your natural behaviour,
as we thrive together for an instant
. . . .
The moment is at hand.
Take one another
and eat. (*CC,* 4)

It is a banquet, indeed, in which the fare is the whole Irish society. In
a series of eighteen apostrophes, all starting with "You," followed by an
adjective or an adjectival clause, Kinsella builds up a typology of despi-
cable individuals. Like a judge, he is pointing "a stiff midfinger in stern
warning" against contemporaries and figures of the past whose proto-
types could easily be recognized by people close to Dublin society, but
whose identities are kept veiled in the poem by a certain degree of
vagueness. Some of the sketches will be developed into fuller portraits
in the rest of the volume. This is for Kinsella something like Chaucer's
prologue to *The Canterbury Tales,* or a prologue to his own *Inferno,* in
which enemies and a few friends are pinned down through a characteristic sin. The portraits are less detailed and concrete, and of course
much more sketchy (most of the invectives are contained in a tercet),
but they are just as virulent; and the symmetrical structure of each
apostrophe creates an effect of cumulative energy of which a few quotations can give but a pale idea.

You, capering, predatory, inexhaustible
in ideas, the one thing certain
we will never know what was on your mind.

You with your bedtime mug of disappointment
—the loser in every struggle;
always on the right side.
. . . .
You, in morose inadequacy,
settling your contemporaries in order of precedence,
denying what you still might: discern. (*CC,* 5–6)

A new cumulative and symmetrical list is articulated around a slightly different pattern starting with "one" and followed by an adjectival clause (e.g., "One, withered and erect, satisfied / that poetry is anything extruded in pentameter"). Kinsella had used this repetitive and symmetrical device before, in "The Good Fight" and "Butcher's Dozen."

What all the objects of the speaker's sarcasm have in common are hypocrisy and self-importance. There is a Roget's Thesaurus-like display of adjectives and participial verb forms with negative connotations such as "peremptory," "presumptuous," " predatory," "insistent," "commanding," "elbowing your way in," "muscling," "hectoring," and "lecturing."

The sarcastic mood peaks when the speaker turns his attention to the North/South conflict and comes up with a new "modest proposal" of equally hyperbolic violence as the Swiftian one:

> everything West of the Shannon,
>
> women and children included,
> to be declared fair game.
> . . . .
> Unparalleled sport
>
> *and in the tradition.* (CC, 9)

After an ironical evocation of Christ's words at the Eucharistic meal—"Have love for one another / as I have loved the lot of you"—the final arrow is pointed against Ireland herself, "our holy distracted Mother / torn between two stools" (*CC*, 10).

The final "Enough" is an exhortation addressed by the speaker to himself to stop this self-destructive exercise and return, after giving vent to frustration, to his Diderot-like enlightened attitude. Once more a Kinsella poem ends with the comforting truth that even loathing, ugliness and waste are part of the food a writer needs to fuel his creativity (represented here as the writing hand pictured on the frontispiece of *A Technical Supplement*):

> Enough.
> That there is more spleen
> than good sense in all this, I admit

—and back to the Encyclopaedia I go.
Diderot, my hand upon it.
The pen writhed

and moved under my thumb
and dipped again
in its organic pot. (*CC,* 10)

In spite of this final determination, and the preceding eucharistic and accepting words (which are not to be taken in utter sarcasm since the embrace, indeed, is fond), the poem leaves an impression of bilious and unjustified hatred directed indiscriminately against one and all. Some of the sarcasm may be incisive and some of the lines memorable, but the vagueness of the objectives together with the hyperbolic hatred they elicit leaves a sense of unbalance and imprecision.

Section I   Section I of *From Centre City* (formerly *Personal Places*) takes the word "embrace" at face value. The speaker thinks with fondness about what he is about to leave, those people and "personal places / that receive our lives' heat / and adapt in their mass, / like stone." The spirit, however, is quite different. The sarcastic tone of the prologue can only be heard in two poems of section I. In "Night Conference, Wood Quay: 6 June 1979," after a victory following a sit-in against the construction of a parking-lot on the site where Viking remains were found ("the swift crane locked /—and its steel spider brain—by our mental force"), we hear an echo of the bitterness of the opening poems in the description of the adversaries as "White-cuffed marauders" with "Visages of rapine" (*CC,* 25). In "Apostle of Hope," urban discontent surfaces in such descriptive touches as the "lair of a town," "this sick place," and the "Grossness" of an advertising panel with "Man the Measure cruciforked / upon His wheel" (*CC,* 14). Yet, even more than in "One Fond Embrace," the hatred is subsumed, though tentatively, into something positive:

Forgive. Forgive.
The impulse, ineradicable,
labours into life. Scrutiny;
manipulation toward some kind
of understanding; toward the Good.

> The Process as it hath revealed
> its Waste on high.
>
> > Let our hate reach that. (*CC,* 14)

In the rest of the sequence, instead, there is a contained lyrical emotion, as the speaker's familial and literary past is revisited in terms of past words and contexts. Continuity as a source of enlightenment is actually emphasized in the opening poem of the sequence by the affirmation that these remembered places "absorb . . . the radiance of change in us, / and give it back / to the darkness of our understanding" (*CC,* 13). The poems of this phase also "absorb the radiance" of previous work.

"Seven" opens with a short poem on a butterfly, which, while establishing the delicate understated tone of the poem, also creates a sense of continuity with the past through its imitation of ancient Irish devices. The alliterative skipping rhythm of "Will you *d*ance at my *d*oorway, / *perch* at my *porch*?" or the prolonged one of "*F*oxglove and their *f*aded *f*lames nodded," bridges the gap of the broken tradition. The third section of this poem on early morning emotions is enriched by lexical and contextual memories of the dawn in "Another September." There is, however, now a tender realism instead of personifications and abstractions in the description of the lovers waking up in the "fragrance" of dawn:

> Our thoughts touched in waking,
> holding her live underarm,
> honest hand on a tender tit.
>
> A pigeon repeated its elaborate, brainless murmur.
> The bedroom curtain inhaled
> and filled with light. (*CC,* 16)

The final prayer is addressed, "in the name of the Father . . . of the spirit and . . . of the senses," to a woman's sex:

> deign, O crushed lips, pursed
> in the woman dark
> where'er you walk

> to separate
> beneath this kiss. (*CC,* 16)

The unabashed allusion, however, gains significance from the memory of the many celebrations of sexual intercourse, even if the mystical vision of love of, for instance, *Out of Ireland,* is far from the intention of this poem. On the contrary, the final image, "the pair of cars / parked ill-matched in the yard" (*CC,* 17)—a synecdoche of the couple—exemplifies the new, subdued, and unrhetorical ruminations on old themes.

"Rituals of Departure" recalls the earlier poem "Ritual of Departure" even in its title. Melancholy, personified in the more recent poem as "retiring with her finger to our lips," reigns in both. The condition of the exile is communicated through the device of focusing on some pathetic details: the "sticks of furniture" and "a dozen silver spoons" clasped by a string in the earlier poem; the "strapped suitcases" and crying children "strapped" in the car in the later poem. The intertextual reference to preceding poems embedded in the present one dilates its meaning. As the ending of the poem confirms, "other rituals of departure, / their ashes dying along our path," lie behind this one, making life a series of "personal places" left behind.

Figures of the literary world evoked in this sequence also help stress continuity. Indeed "Brothers in the Craft" dwells on the "conspiracy" existing "in the creative generations" between "the mature and the brilliant young." The poet traces his own line of descent from Austin Clarke back to Yeats and Thomas Mann. "In Memory," a poem of great simplicity and moving beauty in its plain, conversational tone, illustrates the solidarity of a literary generation mourned in the person of Valentin Iremonger[11] who is remembered as the one at whose feet they all gathered. The melancholy sense of waste is perceptible in the description of the admired poet-civil servant who once "managed both careers," and later lost some of his poise, becoming "aroused and self-devouring." The mourners, "our people among the others /—everybody everywhere with white hair," share in the sense of waste. There is residual sarcasm in the description of some mourners with their shortcomings, but the tone, matched by the phonic and structural features of the poem (fairly regular unrhymed quatrains of mostly iambic trimeters and tetrameters), is one of equanimity and balance.

"Dura Mater," an elegy for a deceased mother, is complicated by the memories of painful parental relationships and threatening women offered by the psyche. Moreover, the two sections dedicated to the mother are completed by two more poems: one on the father at the funeral, and one on the son in his relationships with others. The emphasis is thus shifted from the elegiac core.

The pronoun "I" is never mentioned in the first three sections of "Dura Mater" (unlike in "The Messenger" or "In Memory"), nor are the mourner's feelings directly stated, but the lexical choices denote a mixture of fear, resentment, and pity in the son. "[H]er long nails / held out," suggest the witch or the bird of prey, and her " fuzz of navy hair" and her "cheek of withered silk" suggest an old doll. Homely details such as the slippers, and the kitchen smelling of potatoes and boiled meat, are not sufficient to dispel the uneasiness due to the hardness of her "pursed mouth" and the "bad temper in her eyes." The title, with its semantic ambiguity (dura mater is the outer membrane enveloping the brain but also the Latin equivalent of hard mother), also confirms this perception of the mother's personality, as does the reading of her hidden thoughts: "Will you look at him. How do you stick him at all."

The climax of the poem (as of several others in this collection) is the kiss, which the old lady offers in an unwilling and unmotherlike manner: "Stiff necked, she put up her pursed mouth / at her grown young . . . / And offered and withdrew, a Cupid's Bow puckered" (*CC*, 23). In spite of the returned kiss on the cold body, a sense of hardness and rejection remains, especially when the mother is addressed with the biological and alienating term "Dura Mater," and "stone" as an epithet is repeated twice:

> The withheld kiss returned
> onto her stone forehead. Dura Mater.
>
> To take it, a seal on her stone will,
> in under the screwed lid. (*CC*, 23)

A portrait of the father at the funeral reverses all the traits of the mother: he stoops forward whereas she stood stiffnecked, his eyes are soft while hers were "bad tempered." Each feature of the description is matched by its corresponding opposite. Finally, poem IV introduces the son and the pronoun "I" stands assertively at the beginning of four of the verses. This part of the poem represents the young man establishing new parental relationships with a mysterious figure, full of power and authority, whom Brian John identifies with Yeats.[12] Thus the whole familial trinity has been called into question.

The final poem of the sequence, "At the Western Ocean's Edge," represents an "embrace" of the poet's own tradition and stresses continuity with the past in various ways. A previous poem by Kinsella on this same subject ("The Poet Egan O'Rahilly, Homesick in Old Age") also depicted the eighteenth century poet in his own "personal place"—the ocean's edge. Both poems make large use of O Rathaille's own words (especially, from "The drenching night drags on"), incorporated into the poem through Kinsella's own translation. Kinsella also resumes mannerisms of his early style, like the use of personifications ("Dame Kindness, her bowels torn") and abstractions, such as we find in "Death of a Queen" (1956). As in the 1956 poem, successive waves of disintegration confront the central character, whose face is set "beyond the ninth shadow." Thus there is continuity with himself as well as with the earlier poet, who has become one of Kinsella's most effective personae. In describing O Rathaille's work, Kinsella remarks on distinctive features which are close to his heart: "—the energy of chaos and a shaping / counter-energy in throes of balance" (*CC*, 26).[13] Finally, the poem also stresses continuity with Yeats and Lady Gregory, who, like Kinsella, were attracted by "mental strife, renewal in reverse, / emotional response, the revelation"—all qualities they discovered in Cuchulain, a figure who, like O Rathaille, fought against the sea. This is indeed a poem about "predecessors in the craft."

The former contexts of many of the poems in this sequence cannot be entirely banished; they come to enrich the poem, pointing out that Kinsella, faithful to himself, continues to develop in a cumulative process the chief themes of decay and mortality, the stance of acceptance, and the vision of final unity in death.

Section II   Section II, formerly *Poems from Centre City,* evokes individuals and incidents connected with the poet's residence near the canal and amplifies the brief sketches of *One Fond Embrace.* "Administrator" and "Social Work" are two instances of the process of amplification, but the milder satirical vein takes away much of the bite without adding efficacy. The mockery is as much about the speaker as about his antagonist in "A Portrait of the Artist." As the two argue heatedly about art and beauty (much as their Joycean antecedents did), on the other side of the canal, two prostitutes suggest a different concept of the uses of beauty. The technique of a collage of two contrasting scenes which dovetail into each other, is one readers of Kinsella are familiar with; here it enhances the contrast between an ideal seen in an ironical light and the squalor of reality.

"The Back Lane" illustrates Kinsella's ability to objectify such squalor through a painstakingly precise description of detail:

> I stirred a half brain of cauliflower
> > with my foot, on wet paper
> against the corrugated tin and the neglect next door. (*CC,* 36)

Next to such passages, we find the most ponderous abstractions ("prejudice veiled as justice"), but also the emotion of a brief moment of visionary clarity:

> I stopped at the junction
> > in a first smell of water off the Canal,
> and allowed myself a prayer with open arms.

Kinsella's love for the features of his city inspires him with a prayer whose spirit of "local watchfulness" and "totality of response" can be recognized as the inspiring force of the whole volume *From Centre City:*

> Lord, grant us a local watchfulness.
> > accept us into that minority
> driven toward a totality of response,
>
> and I will lower these arms and embrace what I find.
> (*CC,* 38)

The emotion about "hearth and home . . . and all this place," which had made a timid appearance at the opening of "One Fond Embrace" before becoming submerged by sarcasm, finds vent in poems about particular places close to the poet's heart. The descriptions are as detailed as those denouncing "the slovenliness of the City." "The Stable" presents an image of the neighborhood as it used to be before "the local roughs" came in. It is through the carefully described activities of one of its inhabitants—old O'Keeffe taking care of his horse in the stable of the back lane—that we get the measure of a decent, self-sufficient, ungreedy Dublin. When O'Keeffe got sick and had to give up the stable, "handing over with the key" a special kind of hold, Kinsella transformed the place into his working room. This is the kind of radiance mentioned in the introduction to the preceding sequence, a radiance absorbed by personal places and given back. Kinsella's poetry in this volume often consists of capturing this radiance which can throw light "to the darkness of our understanding."

The reader, however, risks remaining in the dark if he is not given some vital facts about the biographical background (as, in this case, about the transformation of the stable, inhabited by the memory of O'Keeffe, into the artist's workroom). The problem becomes even more evident in "Household Spirits," another positive poem, on which a thrush, its beak reddened by the juice of berries, is consulting "the cannibal committee downstairs." There is evident amusement in the poet keeping his readers guessing at the significance of these comical and grotesque household spirits:

> grinning nude with ibis,
> a squat goose extruding a skull,
> a scaled midget glaring. (*CC*, 34)

The knowledge that Kinsella possesses a collection of aboriginal art from Australia may dispel all curiosity but removes the mysterious, threatening atmosphere of the poem. Many poems in these collections suffer from this dilemma: If information is given, the poem may turn banal; if withheld, it may be incomprehensible. Yet several of the poems gain in their power over the reader by their open-endedness. Kinsella himself often has upheld the indeterminacy of his poems. Discussing a reviewer who complained, "The last what?" about his little poem, "The Last," Kinsella commented: "It seems to me that you must use your wits or the poem loses some of its voltage. Jack Yeats is the last survivor of the artistic renaissance and De Valera is the last of the political giants of the time."[14]

Certainly the reader must use his wits to penetrate the density of several of the poems in the sequence in which people and places are weighted with symbolism; and the technique of superposition or association of two different scenes or images does not easily yield its *raison d'être*, which may only exist in the poet's dreams or memories. "The Stranger" is such a poem; the link between the description of the speaker's antipathy for the stranger and the self-reflexive sections of the poem is tenuous. Only by reading this poem as an ironical meditation on the process of scrutiny and understanding which the poet has undertaken, does the poem signify. The stranger's "face / Arab close up," is seen as a symbol of otherness which disturbs the dream (present in this and the preceding sequences) that all waste and anger provoked by people and institutions may be subsumed in an embrace. Kinsella offers almost a parody of his art, with its obsession for pattern and order, and its devices drawn out of "the school dark":

> Once, at an upper window, at my desk,
> with the photographs and cuttings pinned in fury
> around the wall, and tacked across the blind,
>
> I found a structure for my mess of angers,
> lifted out of the school dark:

Next to this approach is another: dreaming up a Beatrice or Muse-like "kindly beauty" at the side of the poet sleeping by a stream, which might enable the production of order and interpretation:

> A simple form,
>
> adjusted simply with the situation;
> open to local application; weakened
> by repetition; ridiculed and renewed
>
> at last in parody. My pen quickened
> in a pulse of doggerel ease. (*CC,* 40)

But these approaches appear vain. The confrontation with the stranger, a figure of Otherness, with its archetypal and stereotypical suggestions of threat—the stranger "close upon our heels," a harbinger of "evil luck or early death" (*CC,* 39)—shakes the persona of the poet from his idyllic dream of order and interrupts his easeful writing, "Leaving my fingers stopped above the paper."

Section II closes with "In Memory of W. H. Auden," a commemoration of the impression the poet of the 1930s made on his younger colleague. The frame of reference is "Baggot Street Deserta." In the earlier poem, the speaker had laid aside the will to work after "the spent attack" (*SP,* 26) and gazed at the sky; similarly, the speaker of this poem is at his window sill "above the dark channel of Baggot Street" turning away from "a tangle of concerns." The new poem is more specific and attributes the ability to combine the real and the imaginary to the influence of Auden, discovered as "a stone-bright dead light" in the sky, "a ghost of brilliance / staring down out of the Thirties /—rapt, radiant with vision and opinion, / flawed with the final furrows" (*CC*, 43).

Matching the words, "Lost—turning away," of the initial move to the window with "Found—turning back into my den," by which the speaker signals his vision, the poem ends with perfect closure: the resumption of creative work, "my fingers finding their way / back about their business, with the taint upon them" (*CC*, 43). The poem is an apt closure for these three sequences, in which Auden's lesson of applying imagination to reality and blending "vision with opinion" has been faithfully followed.

Section III   Section III, formerly *Madonna and Other Poems,* opens with the assertion that it is "better to leave now," far away from the "travail and vexation of spirit." The speaker bids farewell to city life, termed as "this loving upset," but also likened to a doorjamb stained with hate and leading to "my blind fingers forsaking your face" (*CC*, 47).

Choosing the title "Madonna" for a poem on his female companion, expresses reverence even if she is evoked in a sensuous rather than mystical tone. Assonance and consonance underline the sensuousness of her high heels, her "meat sweet," and the long "brushful" of hair held out in the light. Their moments of sexual intimacy breathe "concern and familiarity," "pleasantry and fright;" yet passion is present in the "piercing presences exchanged" in intercourse and in the "stubborn memory" of "her tender, deliberate incursions."

"Morning Coffee" assesses the Self in two ways: through the various myths that make it up and through physical awareness of the speaker's own body. Starting with the stories of the First People and their "smell of blood and milk," and the figure of Cupid, his darts "returning furious to my heart," the narrator uses the Narcissus myth to assert the self-reflexive nature of literature. The reflection in the water of the well, in fact, is quite familiar to the speaker:

> You, lifting your face
> like a thirsty thing to mine,
> I think I know you well:

    of character retiring,
      settled in your habits,
      careful of your appearance;

      with eyes open inward;
      restless in disposition;
      best left alone. (*CC*, 51)

In the second part of the poem, the narrator, sitting in a coffee-shop described in minute detail, takes stock of himself by feeling at his throat "with thumb and finger. The shaved leather"; or by remembering "holding the affected wrist / too long under the scalding tap, / sharp with pain and pleasure" (*CC*, 52).

One of the finest poems in the volume is "Visiting Hour, in which the speaker lies in a hospital bed while bodily sensations mix with hallucinations. The lace curtains of the "high Victorian window" become the drapings around the sensuous body of a female figure, both lover and mother:

And she was there, at the crimson drape,

one thin hand out, denying. The other
pulled the lace away from her pale thigh
and the dark stocking with the darker border,

in the pale motherly places
—the sac of flesh and fervour where we met
and nourished each other for a while. (*CC*, 53)

Praying for the woman to "accept me in your medicine dark," the man shows that he has completed the process of individuation and can be made whole by fusion with the woman. But the process is also self-reflexive: phrases such as "awareness turned inward" and fingering his "mental parts," suggest the act of writing; while yielding to his healing fantasies is an act of reading which can make and unmake reality. The patient is well aware that when he wakes again he will be "rereading the lace curtain, / and turn back to the nothing in the doorway" (*CC*, 53).

"At the Head Table" is another portrait of the mature craftsman, assessing his personal and artistic achievement:

> I have devoted
> my life, my entire career,
> to the avoidance of affectation,
> the way of entertainment
>
> or the specialist response.
> With always the same outcome.
> Dislike. Misunderstanding. (*CC,* 54)

We can recognize here some traits of Kinsella's own personality, as there were some in Narcissus' reflection. As in "Worker in Mirror, at His Bench," the handicraft becomes the symbol of Kinsella's own conception of art: it is a "lovely beaker / with the slim amphibian handles"—a synthesis of the cup and snake symbolism that has dominated his poetry. Oppositions of concave and erect, female and male, zero and one, converge in the object, which also bears the imprint of the tradition which brought it about: the "marks of waves and footsteps / somewhere by the sea," are the imprints of the First People. The cup's decoration, with its insistence on the "web of order" and the "system of living images," is a compendium of his *ars poetica:*

> —in fact a web of order,
> each mark accommodating
> the shapes of all the others
> with none at fault, or false;
>
> a system of living images
> making increased response
> to each increased demand
> in the eye of the beholder,
>
> with a final full response
> across the entire surface
> —a total theme—presented
> to a full intense regard. (*CC,* 55)

At a literary banquet, the craftsman lifts the cup in a toast to an angry mother-Muse, wishing that the same harmony that reigns in his art may also rule in their relationship. As in the case of "Worker in Mirror, at His Bench," the public occasion, and the figure of the artist limping from one guest to the other, takes away some credibility from his glib artistic creed.

Open Court, the concluding section of the sequence, returns to the bitter invective of the opening *One Fond Embrace.* The rhymed couplets of Pope's satire give a classical edge to Kinsella's sarcasm about the literary establishment. Using the same technique as in *Butcher's Dozen* and *One Fond Embrace,* Kinsella presents a series of cruelly etched portraits of literary personalities and their followers (students, journalists, lecturers) interacting and getting drunk in a Dublin pub. A "ruined Arnold," "a ruined Auden," and "a ruined, speechless Oscar Wilde" are slumped in the bar next to a character parodying Kavanagh, who declares to his admirers:

> When I was a growing boy
> and bent my back in ditch and dung
> it wasn't mockery that flung
> my holy body down one day
> in ecstasy upon the clay.

> Accursed pity
> I ever came to Dublin city,
> packed my bag and left behind
> the very source I came to find. (*CC,* 62–63)

The final scene of the merry crowd ejected from the pub into the lane—as "a man, with brush, behind our backs / sweeps our waste across our tracks, / wipes his feet and bolts the door / against us" (*CC,* 64)—concentrates the poet's disgust for the vainness and hypocrisy of his colleagues in craft.

An equal disgust transpires from the surrealistic desert scene, "Dream," in which deformed and slightly obscene monstrous creatures devour each other. The final three short poems are set in the countryside, and each depicts a turning away "in refusal" (*CC,* 69), and breathes calm and contentment. In "I left the road where a stile entered the wood," the walker faces a bat, a "little leather angel / falling everywhere" (*CC,* 67). The second poem pictures a human couple at peace, "silent in the morning cold, / our bodies and body hair clean," and at one with "Our raven couple" which flies together away, "on the high rock shoulder" (*CC*, 68). The third short poem is more specific about what is left behind: it is not only the bustle and ugliness of "our foul ascending city," but also the spirit of its people and literati that have been lambasted in some of the preceding poems. Just a few words are sufficient to stigmatize the sort of attitudes the speaker has resented most: "the hissing assemblies. / The preference for the ease and the spurious /—the measured poses and stupidities" (*CC*, 69). The final pastoral image closing the volume is of the speaker "on a fragrant slope," holding "a handful of grass / sweet and grey to my face" (*CC*, 69). The closing lines promise a turning away from the bitter spirit which animated *From Centre City* and the introspective mood of what preceded it, and a move toward a more bucolic and peaceful world.

Chapter Seven
Political Kinsella

Ever since Yeats transformed the violent political reality of his days into myth, there had been an enforced intimacy between literature and politics, reflected in a political stance in the production of Irish poets. Yet by the time T. K. Whitaker's economic program of the 1950s had resolutely turned Ireland toward the world and made economic growth the dominant concern, heroic stances and nationalism had become obsolete. Kinsella, together with many of his contemporaries, turned his back on outright political poetry. Even the tensions created by the situation in Northern Ireland left him apparently detached—with one major exception. On the occasion of the death of thirteen civil-rights protesters in Derry, in what came to be called Black Sunday, Kinsella gave vent to his political feelings in *Butcher's Dozen;* his active political engagement stopped at that. In his poetry, we only occasionally find the fusion of private feelings and political fervor that characterized the poetic flowering in the North. And yet, Kinsella's poetry is grafted on a profoundly political awareness of his country's predicament.

One important aspect of Kinsella's lifelong *sui generis* political engagement has been to point out the rift in his own culture due to the British colonization, which succeeded in wiping out the Irish language and making a whole body of literature inaccessible to most. This, in Kinsella's eyes, is the cause of the "divided mind" an Irish poet is heir to—and which obliquely inspires his poetry, but quite explicitly inspires the rest of his work. His essays, anthologies, and translations attempt in various ways to bridge the gap between English and Gaelic culture even while revealing at every stage the vainness of the effort.

As an interpreter of a lost heritage, Kinsella knows all too well his country's cultural losses, its mummified romantic past, and the ruins and shabbiness that reflect them. As a former civil servant and a civic-minded person, he is fully familiar with Ireland's "unfinished business" and the indignities of an economic policy opening the country to new forms of imperialism. In the face of "history as an expression of disorder," poetry as a system of order, however, appears inadequate.

Political Poetry

Kinsella's response to Ireland's divisions and tragic history appears in the general sense of waste, violence, and loss pervading his poetry. The tropes and imagery of his poetry, the landscapes and cityscapes of ruin and decay, and the personal stories of division, deprivation, and death are some of the oblique ways in which an awareness of "dislocation and loss," both in the personal and historical domains,[1] manifests itself. Kinsella came gradually to realize that it was not enough to reveal, as he had always done, the mutilations of the present through subject matter and imagery, while at the same time trying to impose patterns of order or seeking epiphanies of unity. By mid-career he realized he had to get rid of the more external manifestations of order which tend to aestheticize and simplify the lacerated reality, and to search for new strategies of expression. Disorder and formlessness used as expressive strategies are a way of refusing totalizing visions. Kinsella, like many post-colonial writers, had to recognize that the resolution of contradictions, points, as Eagleton has argued in his Field Day pamphlet, "to the effective impossibility of the whole project."[2] The ironic tone of much of Kinsella's public poetry reflects his awareness that his belief in poetry as "a tool for eliciting order," or at least for "tidying substance," is fundamentally in contrast with his political stance. Another aspect of Kinsella's commitment is the political satire transpiring from many of his poems about Ireland. Finally there are his two overt political poems, *Butcher's Dozen,* on an episode of the strife in Northern Ireland, and *The Good Fight,* on John F. Kennedy's assassination.

The two poems are very different from each other. *Butcher's Dozen* is topical and violent; *The Good Fight,* philosophical, and inspired by a general sense of social justice. The latter took ten years to write and is one of the more experimental poems in Kinsella's canon; the former, quite traditional and accessible, was written and published in just a few weeks.

Butcher's Dozen   On 30 January 1972, thirteen peaceful Irish civil-rights demonstrators were killed in Derry by the British army. An official British report (the Widgery Report) on the massacre followed, trying to whitewash the army's role and throw the blame on the demonstrators. Kinsella's *Butcher's Dozen,* written and circulated in 1972 as a response to the report, came as a surprise. It was disconcertingly different in content and tone from the sophisticated, experimental poems the poet was composing at that time, and different in general from the guarded and indirect political comment offered at all times by his poetry.

Starting with its title, which plays on the saying "baker's dozen," the poem is crudely sarcastic, embarrassing, even, in its invective. Its clumsy resumption of an old device, the use of personifications (capitalized), also comes as a shock. Its rough doggerel and strained rhymes contrast with the search for natural rhythms apparent in the blank verse of *Nightwalker and Other Poems* and the free verse of *Notes*. But as Kinsella writes in the postscript to *Fifteen Dead,* where the poem was republished: "The pressures were special, the insult strongly felt, and the timing vital if the response was to matter, in all its kinetic impurity" (*FD,* 57).

Kinsella never regretted writing the poem, considering "it was exactly what was needed."[3] The poem also represents "a living use of the dual Irish tradition," to which he turned at a time he felt it was necessary to repudiate the British; by refusing their established literary forms he was also implicitly repudiating their hypocrisy. The models he chose were the *aisling*—the political visionary poems never quite extinct in Ireland— and Merriman's parody of the form in *Midnight Court.*

The plotline of the poem is simple and follows the traditional line of development of the *aisling.* As the narrator walks through Bogside in the rain, one month after the massacre, the ghosts of the dead protesters rise, one by one, and start speaking, with scathing irony: they underline their innocence and the British soldiers' bad faith and denounce the lies of the Widgery Report. All thirteen protesters speak, some alone, others in groups, and each speaker has a different personality and a different tone of voice. The narrator adds details of the grim setting and offers brief, gruesome descriptions of the appearances of the individual ghosts, giving an emotive and visual touch to a poem which is, on the whole, rather discursive. By not tempering the one-sided and at times hysterical invectives of some of the ghostly speakers with more balanced comment, the narrator implicitly makes them his own.

The first ghostly speakers start mildly: one points out the fact that they were not armed—he "lost his life for throwing stones" (*FD,* 13); another, that their attack was so nonaggressive that they were shot in the back as they were fleeing—"Careful bullets in the back / Stopped our terrorist attack" (*FD,* 14). A third victim reports that he was accused of carrying explosives and weapons which, however, had not been detected by the doctor who examined him. Biting irony and simple rhymes bring out the contrast between the bad faith of the report and reality: "Yes, they must be strict with us / Even in death so treacherous" (*FD*, 14), concludes one of the ghosts ironically.

In a crescendo, the next speakers launch into harsher attacks and their voices range from invective to angry political analysis. One specter comes to the heart of the matter and accuses the judges—"Who prate of Justice, practise greed / and act in ignorant fury" (*FD*, 14)—of contradicting the facts and whitewashing the army by throwing the responsibility on the innocent protesters. "Where's the law that can't be changed?" the ghost comments cynically. His diatribe ends with a challenge to England to "Spread the lie with all your power," and the prophetic warning that since the world is not "blinded by your smoke . . . . The truth will out, to your disgrace" (*FD*, 15).

In a rising tone of anger a "joking specter" analyzes the causes of the strife in a series of pastiches. He echoes the song of *Macbeth*'s witches, stirring their brew, to point out how the "Irish stew" contains the even deadlier ingredient of colonial rule:

> Ropes and rifles, feathered nests,
> Some dried colonial interests . . .
> . . . .
> Tongue of serpent, gut of hog
> Spiced with spleen of underdog.
> . . . .
> Boil it over, make a mess.
> A most imperial success! (*FD*, 16)

The Roman imperial policy of "divide and rule" is punningly echoed by the British Empire's "divide and ruin," and the much greedier new Caesars are accused: "You came, you saw, you conquered. . . . So. / You gorged" (*FD*, 18).

Kinsella, then, turns to outright political analysis through the words of this same ghost. England's policy of ignoring the protests of the oppressed unless they are made violently, is tantamount to inciting violence:

> England, the way to your respect
> Is via murderous force it seems;
> You push us to your own extremes.

You condescend to hear us speak
Only when we slap your cheek. (*FD*, 17)

Another ghost, as violently articulate, lashes out against colonial rule:

My curse . . .
On gentlemen who loot a land
They do not care to understand;
Who keep the natives on their paws
With ready lash and rotten laws. (*FD*, 17)

Yet even more indignation is evinced by how the rulers turn the colonized "against their own kind," and by how, when they have had enough, they leave all their mess behind; including political mistakes, unkept promises, and, especially, the hated loyalists, described in violently offensive terms:

An Empire-builder handing on.
We reap the ruin when you've gone,
All your errors heaped behind you:
Promises that do not bind you

. . . .

Good riddance. We'd forget—released—
But for the rubbish of your feast,
The slops and scraps that fell to earth
And sprang to arms in dragon birth.
Sashed and bowler-hatted, glum
Apprentices of fife and drum. (*FD*, 18)[4]

Finally, the thirteenth ghost offers words of pacification and common sense, including the loyalists in his understanding: "Love our changeling! Guard and mind it. / Doomed from birth, a cursed heir, / Theirs is the hardest lot to bear." Once the English will have left, he believes, they too "may settle down for good / And mix themselves in the common blood," since "We all are what we are, and that / Is mongrel pure" (*FD*, 19). Although the narrator of the vision does not take sides, giving the last word to a more balanced victim shows that some of the anger in which the poem was composed has subsided.

Butcher's Dozen is an odd poem, powerful at times in its striking visions of the rising bloody ghosts and the raw impact of their invectives, but also singularly lacking in emotion and sounding too much like a political treatise in iambic tetrameters.

The Good Fight   *The Good Fight,* a poem for the tenth anniversary of the assassination of John F. Kennedy, was published as a Peppercanister chapbook in 1973 and reissued as part of *Fifteen Dead* (1979).[5]

In the poem, which is neither eulogistic nor commemorative, Kinsella sets side by side a view of Kennedy's personality to one of his presumed killer, Lee Harvey Oswald. The poem rather simplistically contrasts the privileged leader and the underprivileged killer, deliberately ignoring the findings of the Warren Report and the hypothesis about a conspiracy. Kinsella himself in his commentary accepts the assumption of Oswald's guilt "for the purpose in hand" (*FD,* 75). Truth to the spirit of history, thus, appears less important to Kinsella here than the theme of social justice, and *The Good Fight* differentiates itself widely from the many other poems about the assassination.

In *The Good Fight,* which is a patchwork of quotations from different sources (clearly identified by Kinsella in his commentary), Kinsella's taste for intertextuality reaches a climax. Made up in large part of excerpts from Kennedy's speeches and interviews, Oswald's diaries, and books and articles on both personalities, it constitutes an interesting experiment in poetic collage. Individual passages may suffer too much in rhythm and diction from their prose origins, but the poem works as such for its ampler musical structure (as many Kinsella sequences do). It is a sort of grandiose oratorio in many voices and styles. Paratextual elements highlight the complex structure, and the use of different fonts for different speakers makes this the closest thing to concrete poetry.

Part I, which starts like a fairy tale with "Once upon a time," presents Kennedy at the height of his power. Like Prince Charming or Superman, "Shock-headed, light footed, he swung / an invisible cloak about him" (*FD,* 38). His charisma comes through as he is shown in action among the reporters and his advisers, or talking to the crowds during the election campaign. In Kinsella's deliberate attempt to scale him down, nothing is said about his presidency. Thus it is the rhetoric of oratory, much of it Kennedy's own, which sets the tone of the poem. Excerpts from the president's speeches and from Plato's political considerations in *The Republic* and *The Laws,* enhance the figure of the successful leader and heir of a privileged position; what he actually achieved is not mentioned in the poem. Thus, the power of language plays a dominant role,[6] and the "Appropriate Performance . . . [the] almost perfect / working model" (*FD*, 39) of Kennedy's speeches is contrasted to the basic syntax of Oswald and the inarticulateness of those who comment on the assassination.

The use of the first person plural, especially in the speeches, underlines the sense of community surrounding Kennedy, and his awareness of his public function and personal power. In contrast to this, Oswald's loneliness is signaled by his obsessive use of the pronoun "I," which is often in a dominant position at the beginning of a verse. While the section on Oswald will dwell on his loneliness, Kennedy's speech on the New Frontier exalts togetherness:

> 'Ever free and strong
> we will march along, going to meet
> the harsh demands of the West, building
> a new City on a New Frontier.
> Where led and leader bend their wills together
> in necessary rule. . . .
> The eyes of the world upon us!' (*FD*, 38)

The whole section has a journalistic rhythm which tries to reproduce the breathlessness of the climate of the campaign and the rhetoric of its speeches. Excerpts from popular songs of the time, as the one just quoted, add to the lively campaign atmosphere reproduced in the poem. The only time when allusion is made to Kennedy's political role is when he is said to be "Not commanding. Steering."

Part II draws a sympathetic portrait of Oswald, based, as Kinsella acknowledges in his note, on an article by John Clellon Holmes, "The Silence of Oswald," published in *Playboy* in November 1965. Oswald is presented as the opposite of Kennedy—a member of the underprivileged classes leading a life of routine and alienation. Although this portrait too depends on intertextual references, it presents more authorial intervention. A device revealing the author's intentions is the repetition of some specific grammatical patterns. The passage beginning with "And though the night passes" (*FD*, 42–43), is a thirty-line compound sentence containing twenty-four clauses each introduced by the coordinating conjunction "and." Parataxis here highlights the simple-minded repetitiveness of Oswald's miserable and lonely life in Dallas. The routine of buying "bread and tomatoes / milk and meat," climbing "the dirty stairs," lighting the gas, and taking "possession of his neighborhood" is enhanced by the flat everyday language and the simple repetitive syntactic structure. The description of Oswald's life gains momentum and poetic power by this enumeration of senseless and glamourless acts. The second passage—purportedly Oswald's diary and containing actual excerpts from it—is also structured around the repetition of a simple declarative verbal pattern. Each stanza starts with a present-perfect verb in the first person suggesting an attempt at action ("I have stood out," "I have glided," "I have watched," "I have seen," "I have forgotten") and ends with an expression of failure or doubt: [I have] "not known what city," "I will drown," "knowing content nowhere," "I have forgotten . . . what city . . . what father . . . But not what hunger" (*FD*, 43–44).

The series ends with a statement validating the negativity of all these actions:

> I have seen myself, a 'thing'
> in my own eyes, lifting
> my hand empty and opening
> and closing my mouth
> in senseless mimicry
> and wondered why I am alive
> or why a man can live in this way. (*FD*, 44)

The political impact of the poem lies in the justification Oswald's apparently senseless act receives because of his lack of privilege and his awareness of being an alienated and reified being. Kinsella's imaginative rendering of the diary emphasizes Oswald's hopeless life, his exclusion, and difference:

> I believed once that silence
> encloses each of us.
> Now, if that silence does not
> enclose *each,* as I am led
> more and more to understand
> —so that I truly am cut off,
> a 'thing' in their eyes also—

> I can, if my daydreams are right,
> decide to end it. (*FD*, 44)

As an alternative to suicide—"'A sweet Death,' (to violins)"—Oswald imagines "reach[ing] out and touch[ing]" (*FD*, 44–45) Kennedy or some such figure of power. The section ends with a telling comment drawn from Plato: "Democracy cries out for / Tyranny; and the Tyrant becomes a wolf instead of a man" (*FD*, 46). On these two concept words, man and wolf/beast, Kinsella elaborates an e. e. cummings-like game of permutations: he typographically sets out two columns of contrasting words derived from the two original ones by anagrams or substitutions. Hidden meanings, which are central to the themes of the poem, thus emerge. From *man* we get *team*, but also *mean* and *meat; beast* gives *best* and *brains.*

Part III describes with some irony the public shock and the show of spectacular grief at the news of the assassination. Then "matters settle down," emotion subsides "with surprising swiftness," like "a fish, flung back, that lay stunned, shuddered into consciousness, and dived back into the depths" (*FD*, 48). The superficiality of the people is epitomized by the "chic . . . Aphrodite in Washington" for whom this crime "spoiled everything" (*FD*, 47). The last section, Part IV, reflects linguistically the disarray of whoever, poet or reporter (the TV talk-show announcer David Frost is the supposed speaker of these words), tries to assess the events and establish comparisons between the two actors, "the one so 'heroic', / the other so . . . " (*FD*, 49). This section is also a collage of clichés, platitudes, and unfinished sentences miming the inability of words either to assess or react properly to the events.

The whole concluding section asserts a most Kinsellan truth: the valuableness of waste, uncertainty and division. The final attitude is in clear contrast with Kennedy's animating belief that "All reasonable things are possible." The speaker of this section pragmatically knows instead something that might "disappoint Plato," and which stems parodistically from Hegel: "all *un*reasonable things / are possible. *Everything* / that can happen will happen . . . " (*FD*, 49). Instead of finding "balance" and "harmony," the poet suggests, "it is we, letting things *be*, / who might come at understanding. / That is the source of our patience." "Fumbling from doubt to doubt . . . our papers" may mirror "a primary world / where power also is a source of patience" (*FD*, 50).

Butcher's Dozen celebrates the power of language to dissemble; *The Good Fight,* to oppress and alienate. In both, language is a political instrument. But Kinsella also affirms once more the power of language to allow, "fumblingly," some sort of understanding.

Evaluation of Kinsella's Cultural Role

Cultural critique   A more effective aspect of Kinsella's political commitment can be seen in his acts of repossession of the Irish-language tradition; the dispossessed being both the natives who have lost their voice and the Anglo-Irish culture deprived of its cultural specificity by assimilation into the British canon. Kinsella's anthologies and translations are his active contribution to a cause which might be termed anti-revisionist.[7] His merit does not only consist in having selected, translated, and saved from oblivion a number of texts from the storehouse of the Irish past, but also in having protected them from being, as David Lloyd puts it, "mediated, interpreted and dominated" by the Other, the English in this case.

Kinsella's two seminal polemical papers from the 1970s, "The Irish Writer" and "The Divided Mind," became, as Luke Gibbons points out in *The Field Day Anthology of Irish Writing III,* "something of a manifesto for a new generation of writers wishing to free themselves from the shackles of faith and fatherland."[8] A book called *The Dual Tradition* (1995), and a number of shorter statements in the form of articles and interviews, indicate a consistent but evolving attitude on the subject.

Kinsella's two essays, both covering more or less the same ground, emphasize the pernicious consequence of the long colonization. In the first place, Kinsella objects to a view of Anglo-Irish poetry as "an adjunct to English poetry" (*DM,* 208), and makes a plea for what he calls his "broken tradition" (*IW,* 66). While not offering him the "air of continuity and shared history" (*IW,* 59; *DM,* 209) that the monolingual Irish literature had and English still has, this broken tradition has the advantage of effectively linking him with what is most significant in the past of his nation—the fact that "that past is mutilated" (*IW,* 66). The Irish writer's "divided mind" is, indeed, a "vital reality"; the division is "a considerable part of his imaginative substance" (*DM,* 211).

By claiming this bilingual and mutilated tradition as his birthright, he affirms the "otherness" of the Irish tradition and its canon, and effectively dissociates them from the dominant British culture and that Anglo-Irish line of descent traced by Yeats, which was, as Kinsella wryly comments, separate from "the main unwashed body" (*IW,* 64).

While recognizing that Irish poetry in English "has never been isolated from English poetry, much to the benefit of poetry in general," Kinsella also points out that "the separation between the two languages was never complete, and neither was the connection between the two literatures" (*DM,* 208). The plight of the modern Irish poet, thus, is that as he looks back he may either find the mainstream of English tradition—in which, in spite of the language, he is "unlikely to feel at home" (*DM,* 209)—or "a thousand years full of riches and variety"; a tradition, also, in which he would not feel at home, because he could only accede to it by "an exchange of language and an exchange of worlds." The Irish poet is confronted "with a great inheritance and simultaneously a great loss" (*IW,* 59; *DM,* 209), and Kinsella can appropriately declare, "I stand on one side of a great rift, and can feel the discontinuity in myself" (*IW,* 59).

Gradually, Kinsella has abandoned the rhetoric of deprivation and the allusions to fracture, rift, and division to talk about duality and enrichment; and has thus become the advocate, in theory as well as in practice, of what he came to call the "dual tradition" of Irish literature. The elaboration of the concept of a dual tradition is one of the most important events in his life, argues the poet: "we have to look back and make sense of that body of interlocking accident, back as far as possible into the detectable past."[9] The "attempt to present the totality of a poetic tradition, taking into account the literatures in both languages" (Fried, 10), has led to his new book, *The Dual Tradition,* and his editorship of *The New Oxford Book of Irish Verse,* which gave large space to the Gaelic tradition in translation. The emphasis in both works is on the simultaneous presence of the two trends: "Ireland's history discounts continuity of any kind. But there is a poetic response to the complex experience and it exists in two languages. The two bodies of response interact among themselves in some extraordinary ways" (O'Driscoll, 1989).

Kinsella certainly does not suggest "a return to the past for its own sake," but there is "that part of the imaginative activity of our fathers, and their fathers, which refuses to go away. It enriches and stays active in the present, and it will give a character to what we do to the present as we turn it into future. It is . . . a dynamic phenomenon."[10] This, to him, is the tradition that needs preserving and he has effected it in various ways, but especially through his anthologies and his translations.

The anthologies   In order to appreciate Kinsella's originality and the impact of his work, his anthologies and his translations have to be gauged in comparison with similar works and in the light of the larger debate about the making of the Irish literary canon.

Thomas Mac Donagh, the poet and critic who lost his life in the Easter Rising, had probably been the first to propose equal rights for literatures in both languages. But the trend to separate the two literatures perdured. Thus there were anthologies or histories of Irish literature in English, and anthologies and histories of Irish literature in Irish. Yeats' own *Oxford Book of Irish Verse* (the first of the three Oxford Books on the subject) only contained works originally written in English, while Donagh McDonagh's second *Oxford Book of Irish Verse* included only a handful of translations from the Irish (published under the name of the translators, as if what counted were the resulting English poems). Kinsella's *New Oxford Book of Irish Verse* (1985) gives equal space to both traditions under the same cover, and represents, even graphically, the coexistence of the two traditions in the alternation of English and Irish poems in the middle section of the anthology. This goes against the impression left by many earlier collections that the Irish tradition had been silenced and supplanted by an English one. In focusing in *An Duanaire* on a neglected age (1600–1900), when poetry was in decline, Kinsella wants to reclaim a body of literary production not as accomplished and valued as the earlier bardic poetry, but just as Irish and important.

Kinsella's anthologies go well beyond the task of proving the existence of a tradition. By their choices of material and their translation style, they also attempt to isolate some identifying patterns; paradigms that might explain the past and predict the future. The content of *An Duanaire*, thus, is as polemical as the choice of the period examined. The number of lyrics of personal and cultural loss, for instance, emphasizes, as Kinsella notes, that loss "is not a question of mere individual complaint but of the dispossession of an entire caste"[11] The racy, unsentimental tone and the unexpected wording and imagery, which Kinsella strives to preserve, add a sense of a different tradition. Kinsella avoids creating English analogues—poems that will stand by themselves; he wants to create poems that will stand simultaneously with the original.

This purpose (although not substantiated by the physical presence of the facing version) made his *New Oxford Book of Irish Verse* very controversial because Kinsella almost exclusively used his own translations for the rather substantive Irish section of the anthology (much more substantive than other similar collections). Kinsella defends himself against the criticism of having ignored other valuable translators, and thus suppressed the entire history of the reception of these poems, by saying: "the translations did not exist," there were only "loose versions" or "complete falsifications of atmosphere and tone" (O'Driscoll, 64).

In both anthologies, the kind of literature selected illustrates Kinsella's desire to recover the "unwashed body" of a popular Irish literature and transform it into "a usable past." The mocking, the Rabelaisian, the democratic aspects which had been largely excluded by preceding editors, give access to a larger world "full of oxygen" (*NE,* 30–35).

The translations   Kinsella's translations are his major contribution to the preservation and diffusion of an Irish canon. Although not a native speaker, Kinsella has translated extensively from the Irish. He started his career with *Faeth Fiadha: The Breastplate of St. Patrick* (1954), *The Sons of Usnech* (1954), and *Thirty-three Triads* (1955), to which he added his greatest title of glory, the translation of the national epic tale *Táin Bó Cuailnge.* He also provided most of the translations for his two anthologies.

Kinsella defined his translation of the great Irish saga as "an offering to the past" (*IW,* 60) and "an act of responsibility" (Haffenden, 112). The translation, over ten years in the making, tries to provide accurate readings of the original text while preserving its spirit. This important epic relates the tribal warfare started by a raid to steal a herd of cows (the full title *Táin Bó Cuailnge* means "The cattle raid of Cuailnge"), and features the legendary Cuchulain, who by the end of the nineteenth century had become a symbol of heroic Ireland. The saga had not been translated in the nineteenth century, in spite of Cuchulain's popularity as a heroic figure, because it was considered embarrassing and politically incorrect. The several versions it went through in the early 1900s were unsatisfactory and incomplete. In his introduction to *The Táin,* Kinsella explains that he had to undertake the translation to counterbalance "the romanticized, fairy tale, versified, dramatized and bowdlerized versions of the Ulster cycle."[12]

Previous translators hoping to graft romantic material onto the repertory of British literature had translated for an English audience and tried to make their texts as English-sounding as possible. Nationalist translations had been equally unfaithful to the original, focusing on romantic or heroic themes only and "beautifying" the original according to the canons of the day, which believed in the sublimity of Ireland's heroic age and attempted to present Irish culture as dignified.

The reasons for the neglect and mishandlings of the translations are evident on a first reading of Kinsella's version: this saga was most unconventional by the canonic standards of the epoch. Not only was it often incoherent, uneven, and redundant (having been transmitted in three different recensions), it was also unliterary in its mixture of five different varieties of prose and verse. Its oral-tale rhythms and blatantly sexual, scatological, and grotesquely humorous content made it quite unsuitable to the purposes of earlier translators.

The different spirit animating Kinsella's translation is well apparent in a comparison of his version with other versions of this major Irish saga. His version tries to shun the patterns imposed by the colonizers and the Nationalists, and has the courage to reflect the alien tone and the primitive, native incoherence of the original without bending it to the aesthetic standards current in the Western world. Encouraged by the precedents of Joyce and Flann O'Brien, Kinsella accepts as part of the tradition the inglorious and outrageous behavior of his characters, and the sexual and scatological details. Thus Kinsella conveys the "otherness" of Gaelic culture and the sense of a lost world, while at the same time establishing an ancestry for a racier modern Irish literature.

In a time of historical revisionism, Kinsella's cultural critique has had enormous influence and political reverberations. Kinsella's advocacy, in theory as well as practice, of what he came to call the "dual tradition" of Irish literature, counteracted the action of revisionists by demonstrating how much had been lost and how serious the loss had been.

Kinsella is well aware that Douglas Hyde's advice to de-anglicize Irish culture is not tenable, but neither should the country ignore its Gaelic past or deny its fragmented and divided reality.[13] As a consequence, Kinsella has put forward the vision of a tradition which sees the two linguistic trends as equally important, running parallel, at times ignoring each other, but also, on occasion, fertilizing each other, and both part of the heritage of an Irish poet.

His activity as a translator and an anthologizer, which runs parallel to his efforts to channel Irish culture toward a modern and cosmopolitan vision, is the best proof of Kinsella's involvement in a sort of political action which is not the less radical for its being unobtrusive. Kinsella works under no illusion: the past is not retrievable nor can the tradition be healed. He only seeks to establish links with "the significant past" and to reclaim the tradition in forms closer to the spirit in which it was composed. Since revisionism would either refuse the past or diminish its importance by making it a mere decoration, Kinsella's honest and respectful attitude toward the original texts he has translated has the value of an anti-revisionist, political move. Though not showy, all this corresponds to a definite political stance, or rather as Kinsella specified, to a "just response."

Chapter 8
Kinsella's Place within the Tradition

Kinsella has always appeared as an isolated figure, a poet with a restricted audience, who does not acknowledge any kinship with the poets of his generation and despises most of them. With a certain pride, Kinsella deems that he does not belong to the literary scene: "I do not think I am outside but that the others have lost the way."[1] At the time he wrote "the Irish Writer," he believed his fellow writers could "show me nothing about myself except that I am isolated" (*IW,* 59). In recent work, such as *One Fond Embrace* and *Open Court,* he has mordantly satirized the literary establishment.

But for all this, Kinsella is neither isolated from his "mutilated past" nor from the present. Moreover, in "Brothers in the Craft" (*From Centre City*), he includes himself in a "conspiracy" in "the creative generations" between the "mature and the brilliant young," which has Irish and cosmopolitan connotations:

> Again and again, in the Fifties, 'we' attended
> Austin Clarke. He murmured in mild malice
> and directed his knife-glance curiously amongst us.
>
> Out in the dark, on a tree branch near the Bridge,
> the animus of Yeats perched.
> Another part of the City,
> Tonio Kroeger, malodorous, prowled Inchicore. (*CC,* 19)

His whole career, in fact, proves that he is well-rooted and able to assimilate and transcend different models in totally original creations. At the start of his career, Kinsella had avoided the obvious Irish models, Yeats especially, and turned to English and indeed international models. He was not too dissimilar then from the British poets of the 1960s, granted the differences of individual talent and the isolation in which he worked. His poetry, like theirs, was traditional, alien on one side to the modernist experiment, but also to the ample vision of Yeats; on the other side, he eschewed the explicit factualism and documentation of American confessionalism, the sense of poetry in process of the New York school, and the intense, visionary mode of the oracular poets. His themes were modest and narrow; the tone, introspective, diffident, and sometimes elegiac in a minor key. He carefully avoided metaphysics as well as visionary modes and larger political or religious concerns, even while demonstrating awareness of the social and historical context in which he was writing. Like Larkin and Davie, he was urbane, but less philosophical than Hughes, and more spontaneous and apt to unload his feelings in a poem.

The Parnassian quality of many poems of his early phase reflects Kinsella's declared admiration for Auden's "grace under pressure" and his ability "to emerge . . . whatever the pressure, with a poem of grace, beauty, charm, seductive rhythm—all those superficial things" (Haffenden, 102). But to Auden he also owes the many ironic devices he uses, especially in his early poetry, his self-mockery, even the jocose use of different verse forms such as the doggerel.

During his stay in the United States, the influence of American poets helped him loosen up the forms of his poetry. The single most important influence, to his saying, was that of William Carlos Williams. Under the influence of confessionalism and Lowell, whom he greatly admired, he wavered between projections of the romantic lyrical "I" and a more realistic "I,"[2] favoring in the end Roethke's non-confessional approach to the autobiographical subject. Kinsella's insistence on precision of detail in his autobiographical flashes, coupled with his reticence about central facts and causes, are both functions of his crypto-confessionalism.

By affirming in "The Divided Mind" that "every writer in the modern world . . . is the inheritor of a gapped, discontinuous, polyglot tradition" (*DM,* 216–17), Kinsella claims a place among the high modernists. Modernist poetic strategies such as allusions, lack of exposition, and switching rapidly from one subject or image to another characterize *Nightwalker and Other Poems,* and, even more so, *Notes from the Land of the Dead* and the successive collections. "The land of loss" is not only the title of a section of *Out of Ireland*; it also describes the landscape—lacking in coherence and cultural values, corroded by decay and fragmentation—which Kinsella has depicted throughout his career and which finds its counterpart in Eliot's *Waste Land.* Yet Kinsella's poetry is too personal and thus in contrast with the impersonality of high modernism.

The Irish modernist Joyce was "definitely his early hero," as Kinsella declared to a class of American students (Johnston, 33), and he invoked his assistance in "Nightwalker," calling him "Watcher in the tower." Kinsella's urban poetry and his grappling with the actual details of personal and public life owe much to Joyce: "His relationship with the modern world is direct and intimate. He knows the filthy modern tide, and immerses himself in it" (*IW*, 64). This seems to have been Kinsella's aspiration too. Joyce encouraged Kinsella by his example to create from the materials he had at hand, and to transcend them by making them part of a system of order which went far beyond their provincial manifestations.

Pound, with whom, among the modernists, Kinsella claims the greatest affinity, has had an active influence on his poetry. He admires "the way Pound could handle so satisfactorily what happened to him," turning poetry into "the accompaniment to a life lived"; but although Kinsella's poetry is doing something similar, "it doesn't pretend at that kind of completeness" (Fried, 6).

Irish critics have warmly debated whether Kinsella belonged to a local tradition. In *Celtic Revivals,* Seamus Deane sees his poetry as "a testimony to the enabling strength of a tradition, a sense of continuity which is greater than the sense of fragmentation" (Deane, 145). Gerald Dawe sees him instead as finding few consolations in that same tradition and trying to "literally make himself."[3] But Kinsella, while being his own man, has fully assimilated the tradition within his poetic imagination and integrated the public and the private—so much so, that he could subscribe to Heaney's words: "on the one hand poetry is secret and natural, on the other hand it must make its way into a world that is public and brutal."[4] The mixture of public and private, indeed, is a characteristic trait of modern Irish poetry and Kinsella is no exception in his emphasis on it. Although Kinsella did not make Ireland his myth and theme, as Kavanagh says Yeats did, he wrote after Austin Clarke and Kavanagh had dispelled the mists of rhetoric about Ireland, and thus he could "cast his mind" on the present and the past of his country without having to worry about "the indomitable Irishry."

In discussing the effect of teaching a course in Irish studies for his American students, Kinsella pointed out the creative relationship with the tradition:

> When reading historical and geographical studies of the Irish tradition for
> the programme we run here in conjunction with the Pennsylvanian uni-

versity where I teach in the autumn, I find great tendrils reaching out and connecting. There are times when it's almost impossible not to write a poem.[5]

The whole tradition, past and present, myths and realities, is part of Kinsella's subject matter. His poetry interacts with a petty Ireland as well as with a nation which has not realized that violence is not redemptive. He does this in the voice of the tradition, the bitterly satirical tone of the bilingual eighteenth-century tradition of Swift, O Bruadaire, O Rathaille, and Merryman.

Because of the way his poetry has reflected and interacted with the present, and has assimilated the past in a totally original construct, Kinsella has produced a most remarkable body of poetry. The various traditions he has used have helped him shape a very distinctive kind of poetry which keeps developing in a unitarian and organic way, absorbing new developments and old themes but remaining true to itself in spite of experimentation and changes.

Although Kinsella recognizes that "there is no great popular response" to his poetry, he continues on his proud, solitary way; a poets' poet, yet rooted in tradition.

Appendix

Excerpts from 14–15 August 1993 Interview

The following interview between Thomas Kinsella (TK) and Donatella Abbate Badin (DAB) took place in Kinsella's study on 14–15 August 1993, shortly before the publication of *The Dual Tradition* and *Collected Poems*.

DAB: In your earlier essays on the broken tradition, you put the accent on the "divided mind," on loss, on the rift. Now, instead, you put the accent on the enrichment deriving from a "dual tradition." Can you briefly trace the process that took you from a sense of division to a sense of enrichment?

TK: It was a process of relaxation. Recognizing that it is not necessary to abandon one aspect of Ireland's literature in order to deal with the other. Accepting ourselves as we are. We have a dead language with a powerful literature and a colonial language with a powerful literature. The combination is an extremely rich one. I don't see why it's necessary to separate the elements.

DAB: So you moved from pessimism to optimism.

TK: Yes, and to accepting all the parts as they are, and all benefitting by whatever is there. I lift my hat to the Christian Brothers. I hated their work at the time but it gave me access to Irish literature in the Irish language. There is another subdivision. Old Irish, the language of *The Táin*, is virtually a different language from modern Irish. I found myself in practice managing two separate Irish languages. Why not do it again with the modern literature, in English? It is not necessary to give up anything.

DAB: You have frequently mentioned your almost completed book on the dual tradition. Could you talk a little bit more about this project?

TK: It is a presentation of the idea of an entire tradition and of the entire literature of the country.

DAB: Is it a history of Irish literature?

TK: No. It is an essay on an idea. Seamus Deane has produced a very useful short history of Irish literature. There is no need for another one. And there are specialized books on the literature in Irish. Mine is neither of these; it deals with an idea of the dual tradition from its origins, finding whatever unity survives into the present. It has to do with colonialism, politics, prejudice, and the possible absorption of these things enriching our view of the literatures in both languages. It's a short essay, about a hundred pages, reduced to its proper form. But it begins at the earliest beginnings and includes the development of the colonial relationship between Ireland and Britain.

DAB: How would this compare with your early statements on the subject, the essays "The Divided Mind" and "The Irish Poet" of the 1970s?

TK: It will have them as component chapters. They are partly where the idea worked itself out.

DAB: Have you written anything on the subject in between?

TK: No. I did not want to write anything until I had a view of the entire situation. I have managed this. I think it is ready for publication.

DAB: Throughout your life you have been engaged in redeeming a lost tradition by translation, wide diffusion through anthologies, books such as the one you are writing, public talks, or programs on TV. This commitment is eminently of a public nature. On the other hand, your poetry is of an extremely private nature. Your public commitment is to make accessible what was inaccessible, while the hermeticism of your poetry makes inaccessible what might have been accessible. Do you see a contradiction between these two commitments? A sort of dual tradition in your soul?

TK: The poetry, as far as it's driving anywhere, is driving inward. That is where it wants to go. The other has to do with the relationship between writer and reader; it is not connected. It is more an intense hobby.

DAB: They are not, then, of equal importance.

TK: They are of equal importance. Like the dual tradition itself, they may wind up expressing a larger whole.

DAB: I would like to come back to what I called the dual tradition in yourself. The public and the private. It's like the yin and yang, and I don't know where the fusion point is.

TK: They are not separated. They are a joint response to everything. If it is significant, I want to handle it. If it is internal, so be it; if it is external, likewise. I want to deal with them on their own terms.

DAB: And there are fusion points, I imagine, between the public commitment to the tradition and the private reinterpretation, such as, for instance, in "Finistere."

TK: Yes, and there is a recent poem, "In Memory," for Valentin Iremonger. This is the kind of poetry I want to write. And in what is probably going to be the last of the Peppercanister books, I think I have found a form where the external "plot" continues, while giving an opportunity for the exploration of many matters, including the internal.

DAB: Preparing the volume of *Collected Poems* must be an important moment. You are in a position to survey your entire production and see lines of development.

TK: It certainly has its peculiarities. I thought the *Collected Poems* was going to be a simple matter, assembling the work and sending it off. But it's not like that. I can't let some of the things go the way they are. Looking at what I have permitted myself in the past is extraordinary.

DAB: But you must allow yourself to have been young.

TK: I suppose so.

DAB: What is it you resent most about your early production?

TK: Pointless elegance. Let it earn its place as elegance, or beauty, or whatever, but let the thing talk straight. The poems of my own that I am most embarrassed by are the ones that have been most enjoyed for their rhyme and rhythm and beauty. But in the opportunity for a *Selected Poems* they all disappear. They are not necessary.

DAB: So it means rewriting everything.

TK: Not everything. I am startled, in the other direction, by some of the things I managed to write many years ago.

DAB: It must be difficult to revise once the impulse is gone.

TK: It is possible to relive the moment and see it straight. It is a long process.

DAB: But how about the technicalities of revising? How do you keep yourself from actually rewriting a poem completely, instead of trying to do it from the point of view of your former self? Do you rewrite? Do you discard?

TK: It is a matter of accurate reading, and judging the poem on its own terms.

DAB: Do you try to rearrange the order in which the poems will appear or do you respect the order in which they were first published? Do you try to group your early poems in sequences? Do you try to bring out the ruling preoccupations of the different stages of your career?

TK: I don't worry about this too much. When it comes to categorizing or grouping, the chances of error and confusion are high.

DAB: Do you have a sense of continuity as you look at your early poems and the later stages? Do you see a line of development?

TK: As with your life. You know, you live through a thing and it is finished, and you can scarcely remember. Some parts are clear, some parts disappear.

DAB: Do you remember why you wrote some of these poems?

TK: I have a feeling that I wrote some of them because I wanted to write.

DAB: For some time now you have been composing in sequences. You have been very careful to point out that you are not writing poems in isolation. Now sequences are held together by some central preoccupation or mood.

TK: Yes, but there are also individual cases, like the poem "In Memory." But I did try one extraordinary exercise in which I attempted to plan all the future work in immense detail.

DAB: You mean your numerological plot?

TK: It was numerological, emblematical, historical; it was philosophical, extremely complicated, and very satisfactory. At one time the charts covered the whole wall.

DAB: Was it planned for a long poem, like Pound's *Cantos*?

TK: It was a plan for a career.

DAB: And did it work?

TK: It was totally useless. I think not a single detail was ever used in a subsequent poem.

DAB: Why do you think it hasn't worked, was it too closely planned?

TK: The insistence made it not work. The poetic response went somewhere else.

DAB: Have you then abandoned the numerological pattern?

TK: It seemed, finally, that I was imposing a pattern. . . . I never reached three. . . . Four would be a totality, an achieved stability, a total career, the understanding of the outside world. The quincunx would be the penetration of that, into the center, to find the utter basis. It is the circle and the zero, and everything else. It was a very useful device for enlarging the state of mind, but it had no use for individual pieces of work.

DAB: Yes, and you could not start writing about three if you are not ready for that and you were still exploring.

TK: And the particularities you mentioned earlier, they keep getting in the way. They are the important thing, otherwise I can't see the subject as important.

DAB: Do you feel it is important for a reader to know the circumstances in which a poem was written? Your poems are rooted in particularities, in the raw material of your life, but you keep your tracks well hidden. Do you think it is important to know those circumstances for a correct understanding? Or do you feel that the thing should remain veiled, that the raw material should not come to the surface?

TK: No, that would simply not occur to me. What I aimed at were those particularities, and I think that the thing communicates on the basis of particulars. If you do not earn your generalities, they do not count, or it becomes rhetoric. I think I got some of these ideas from reading Joyce. I would find some of Yeats's particularities unacceptable, like "I pace upon the battlement and stare . . . ." I don't believe it. He shuffled along the battlements—he was not a god or a god-like figure, and that bothers me.

DAB: But you keep it really to a bare minimum. The poems seem to have one topical meaning for you and Eleanor, or whoever was involved in them, and they have another for the reader.

TK: But I feel that the poems relate and accumulate among themselves. The particulars accumulate and in the development of the sequence, or of a whole career, the thing will assemble. T. S. Eliot operates in this way, it seems to me. But you get unprocessed particulars even in "Prufrock."

DAB: I was rather thinking of the poems in the confessional vein. Lowell, for instance, gives you all the data you need. You understand what he's talking about.

TK: I am probably uniquely unqualified to talk about this because I am locked inside.

DAB: You mean *you* know what you are talking about.

TK: *I* know what I am talking about.

DAB: But it is difficult for the outside reader.

TK: I have no plans to conceal anything, to confuse the issue, or to send anyone looking somewhere else. But everything needs to earn its place; each essential particular allows something else.

DAB: You must be aware that you are considered a very difficult poet. I have an example. In one version of *Notes from the Land of the Dead*, you had some subheadings—"an egg of being," "a single drop," etc.

Then, in the next edition you withdrew them. I found the headings useful and was bothered by their disappearance.

TK: I think what I withdrew was a sort of facetious journalism. A display of smartness. The headlines are wordplay of a shallow kind, focusing attention only on the journalist. "An egg of being" . . . I don't see that this added anything.

DAB: It gave a clue to what the section of the sequence was about.

TK: But the egg itself was obviously there. It seems to me it is this false journalism which adds nothing.

DAB: What is your relationship to the reader? I feel that you abandon him to himself, that you are not giving him any clues to help him in understanding your poetry.

TK: I require a reader to complete the act of communication. I don't want to entertain. If a person is looking for entertainment or information, or is merely curious, I am not interested.

DAB: Would you agree with those critical positions which sustain that the text, once it is in circulation, as an independent existence, does not belong to the author but to the reader?

TK: I agree completely. From the point of publication the writer is passive.

DAB: So it should not be a transparent window onto the author?

TK: It can be.

DAB: Should I then be asking all these questions: "Why was this written?" "Who is so and so?" Is it useful or should we forget about it?

TK: It can be interesting. But it has nothing to do with the appreciation of the work. The work exists in its own context and that is all. It succeeds or not. The reader responds adequately or not. There is no further control.

DAB: So what is your reaction to the critics' maybe extravagant interpretations of your poems?

TK: It's a free country. I am startled sometimes at the missing of the point. But I am relieved sometimes at seeing them absorbed or responded properly. Once I see this, I realize that I am not talking to myself.

DAB: So you expect some understanding that corresponds to your own understanding.

TK: I expect it to be more or less the same. But then I am usually surprised because the reader is bringing another body of data to bear.

DAB: It is also difficult to get a clear view of your production because it has gone into so many editorial channels, with the Peppercanisters, and so I think the *Collected Poems* will bring in a sort of "collective" reaction, a global look at your poetry.

TK: In which case, I wonder, is it fair to make changes? It has given me a chance to make some changes and improvements.

DAB: Of course, this whole thing is a process and you keep processing it. Are you publishing the Peppercanister sequences as sequences?

TK: They come out in their different forms. Some are sequences. The one I am writing is going to be a long poem. But I think I have come to the end of that way of doing it. The change will be part of the plot.

DAB: I would like to talk a little about the love poetry. Much about it is about love, but very often it is not so much about the beloved as about the sense and significance of love. Is it so?

TK: Can you name a love poem that isn't?

DAB: There are poems which are projected on the person rather than on the response to the person or on the significance of the relationship.

TK: I think a love poem roots the particular in the general. I believe that is what is meaningful. Not to say simply, "How gorgeous you are, how I need you." That is Bing Crosby. There is also the negative case, when things are not going so well. These are love poems too.

DAB: You said the other night that religion is an issue that has been disappearing. Has something else taken the place of religion? Maybe some alternative religion, such as Taoism or some philosophical stance?

TK: Nothing.

DAB: Has the poetry become a substitute for religion? You say it has given a pattern to your life.

TK: No, religion, as normally understood has disappeared totally. I don't see any room for it. Poetry has no connection with the religious impulse. I see poetry as a form of responsible reaction to the predicament one finds oneself in. If a person has an impulse to record the situation, I believe that is necessary, but I have no idea what use it is. It has something to do with continuity, with trying to compensate for the limited life span of the individual. But it's essential to get the matter recorded before one disappears.

DAB: It answers the same impulses which make people turn to religion. One impulse is that of finding a pattern in life, a meaning to life, and the other one to have a continuity after death.

TK: Except there is no impulse toward meaning, or form, or understanding. For instance, I would regard the human being as a worthless and objectionable form of life. I don't see that it is possible, or even desirable, to redeem such a thing. But the experience of an individual *can* be significant and, if the impulse is there, it is a responsible thing to record the particularities of that experience. I don't mean like keeping a diary, but accompanying the record of the experience with a record of the response. It can be fictional, it can be artificial, it can be musical, rhythmic, anything. What need this is answering I am not quite sure, although I am getting clearer.

DAB: You have often mentioned the ordering impulse; the recording is an ordering of experience.

TK: Order does matter and order can be elicited from significant experience, but the temptation to impose order should be resisted. It comes from somewhere else. It can be meaningless and it can be dangerous.

DAB: But at the beginning of your career you tried to impose order.

TK: It was a vague impulse, at the beginning. Religion supplies a ready-made order and when that disappears, it leaves a need for something. But I think it is essential, and a part of the maturing process, to give up any imposed or inherited order.

DAB: When you started writing poetry had religion already lost its importance for you?

TK: It was certainly disappearing. It never formed part of the poetry.

DAB: Yet there is, for instance, a "Christmas Carol." . . .

TK: It is something observed. In "The Bell," in a recent book, the gear inside the church—the darkness, the candles, the bells—are interesting and important. This is not religious.

DAB: It is an aesthetic experience.

TK: It is an expression of need, pathetic in some ways. People in a given place and time need something; they go about finding it and fail. And you get something like the pyramids, cathedrals. There is a big cathedral in North Philadelphia where you see the whole process, the wealth invested in its construction. Now it is a wreck, with one or two people using it.

DAB: Has Taoism ever been important for you? There is, for instance, this poem: "Tao and the Unfitness of Being."

TK: That is just a footnote. I am trying to understand the process.

DAB: Another question one must ask of an Irish poet, or maybe of any Irish person, is about politics. How would you describe your political engagement, if any? Has politics played a role in your poetry?

TK: No. What is involved is more important than a political stance or a religious belief. It is a matter of finding the just response. This is essential. Committed standpoints have nothing to do with justice. From a humane standpoint they are objectionable.

DAB: So you feel you are above parts in looking for justice.

TK: More outside. Or rather, I don't think I am outside, but that the others have lost the way. It is necessary to be as just as one can, to follow the just impulse, and not allow prejudice to interfere.

DAB: A third inevitable question is about the present-day Irish literary scene. I think you are an isolated figure within that tradition, especially compared to other poets who are very much on the scene. Do you see yourself as a poets' poet? A poet with a restricted, very refined audience, a minority?

TK: Again, I think I am unfit to judge. But obviously there is no great popular response.

DAB: You are not popular because you are too difficult.

TK: Most poets are difficult.

Notes and References

Preface

    1.   In August 1993, Thomas Kinsella granted me an interview in his house in County Wicklow. Excerpts from the long conversation, which was taped and checked by the poet, appear in the appendix and are hereafter cited in text. Excerpts from other unpublished conversations will be accounted for in the notes.

Chapter One

    1.   *Contemporary Authors: A Bio-Bibliographical Guide to Current Authors and Their Works,* vols. 17–18 (Detroit: Gale Research Co., 1976), 263. Similarly worded statements about his poetry are to be found in many of Kinsella's interviews and notes. Hereafter cited in text.

    2.   Thomas Kinsella, *One and Other Poems* (Dublin: Dolmen Press, 1979; London: Oxford University Press, 1979), 25; hereafter cited in text as *One.*

    3.   John Haffenden, *Viewpoints: Poets in Conversation with John Haffenden* (London: Faber and Faber, 1981), 111; hereafter cited in text. Information about Kinsella's life is drawn from this and other interviews including the two granted by Kinsella to the author of the present book.

    4.   Thomas Kinsella, *Blood and Family* (London: Oxford University Press, 1988), 13; hereafter cited in text as *B&F.*

    5.   Thomas Kinsella, *Fifteen Dead* (London: Oxford University Press, 1979), 59; hereafter cited in text as *FD.*

    6.   Le Brocquy illustrated, among other works, Kinsella's edition of *The Táin;* while Anne Yeats illustrated the chapbook of *One.* For more information on the history and role of Dolmen Press see Robin Skelton, "Twentieth-century Irish Literature and the Private Press Tradition: Dun Emer, Cuala and Dolmen Press 1902–1963," *Massachusetts Review* 5 (1964), 368.

    7.   Thomas Kinsella, interview by Dennis O'Driscoll, *Poetry Ireland Review* 25 (Spring 1989), 58; hereafter cited in text.

    8.   Quoted in Maurice Harmon, *The Poetry of Thomas Kinsella* (Atlantic Highlands, N.J.: Humanities Press, 1975), 120; hereafter cited in text.

    9.   T. Kenneth Whitaker, a distinguished Irish civil servant, was secretary to the Department of Finance (1956) and author of an influential economic development report (1958) that was the basis for a revolutionary economic program which brought planning and foreign investment to the country. He later became governor of the Central Bank of Ireland (1969), chancellor of the National University of Ireland (1976), and a member of the Irish Senate.

10.   John Deane, "A Conversation," *Tracks* 7 (Thomas Kinsella Issue, 1987), 86; hereafter cited in text.

11.   The previous Oxford anthologies had only included poetry original-ly written in English. Cf., *The Oxford Book of Irish Verse: XVIIth Century—XXth Century,* chosen by Donagh MacDonagh and Lennox Robinson (London, Oxford University Press, 1958).

12.   Eileen Battersby, "Thomas Kinsella: a Poet Between Two Traditions," *The Irish Times,* 3 December 1990.

Chapter Two

1.   Question: "What is it you resent most about your early production?"
Answer: "Pointless elegance. Let it earn its place as elegance, or beauty or whatever, but let the thing talk straight The poems that I'm most embarrassed by are the ones that have been most enjoyed, with rhyme and rhythm and beau-ty. . . . They are not necessary." Conversation with the author, 14–15 August 1993 (Appendix, p. 195).

2.   The 1972 sequence was republished, with the addition of a few poems, as *New Poems 1973* (Dublin: Dolmen, 1973) in Ireland, and as *Notes from the Land of the Dead and Other Poems* (New York: Knopf, 1973) in the United States. The Peppercanister chapbooks are collected in *Fifteen Dead* and *One and Other Poems,* covering between them Peppercanister pamphlets #1–8. *Peppercanister Poems, 1972–1978* (Winston-Salem, North Carolina: Wake Forest University Press, 1979) contains a similar selection.

3.   Thomas Kinsella, "Omphalos of Scraps," interview by Philip Fried, *Manhattan Review* 4 (Spring 1988), 15; hereafter cited in text.

4.   Thomas Kinsella, "The Irish Writer," in W. B. Yeats and T. Kinsella, *Davis Mangan Ferguson?: Tradition and the Irish Writer* (Dublin: Dolmen, 1970), 215; hereafter cited in text as *IW.*

5.   Statement. *Poetry Book Society Bulletin,* no. 55 (December 1967).

6.   Thomas Kinsella, *Selected Poems 1956–1968* (Dublin: Dolmen Press, 1973; London: Oxford University Press, 1973), 65. References to Kinsella's early and mid-career poetry will be from this volume, when possible; hereafter cited in text as *SP.* References to poems not quoted in *SP* will be from the cumulative volume *Poems and Translations* (New York: Atheneum, 1961); here-after cited in text as *PT.*

7.   Donatella Abbate Badin, "'Tissues of Order': Image Patterns in the Poetry of Thomas Kinsella," *Annali di Ca' Foscari* 29 (1990), 5–26.

8.   Floyd Skloot, "The Song of Thomas Kinsella," *The New Criterion* 8 (March 1990):7.

9.   Tom Halpin, "Foundations for a Tower?" *Poetry Ireland Review* 35 (Summer 1992), 27–28.

10.   In James Vinson, ed., *Contemporary Poets, 1975* (London: St. James; New York: St. Martin's, 1975), 834. Kinsella declared: "It is my aim to elicit

order from significant experience, with a view to acceptance on the basis of some kind of understanding. Major themes are love, death and the artistic act."

11. "Soft to Your Places," *SP,* 14.

12. Peter Orr, *The Poet Speaks: Interviews with Contemporary Poets* (London: Routledge and Kegan, 1966), 106; hereafter cited in text.

13. Thomas Kinsella, *Notes from the Land of the Dead and Other Poems* (New York: Knopf, 1973), 44; hereafter cited in text as *NLD.*

14. EPI *(phaino):* show, manifest (V. Oxford English Dictionary).

15. John Whitman, *Allegory* (Oxford: Clarendon Press, 1987).

16. Thomas Kinsella, "Poetry since Yeats: An Exchange of Views" (Transcript of a Panel), *Tri-quarterly* 4 (Fall 1965).

17. Dennis O'Driscoll, "Interview with Thomas Kinsella," *Poetry Ireland Review* 25 (Spring 1988), 63.

18. From unpublished conversation with the author.

19. Gerard Manley Hopkins, "Author's Preface," *The Poems of Gerard Manley Hopkins,* 4th edition, W. H. Gardner and N. H. MacKenzie, eds. (Oxford University Press, 1967), 49.

20. Hugh Kenner, "Thomas Kinsella: An Anecdote and Some Reflections," in *The Genres of Irish Revival,* Ronald Schleifer, ed. (Dublin: Wolfhound, 1980), 181.

21. J. Hillis Miller notices this strategy in the poetry of Thomas Hardy, but certainly Kinsella has taken it to its extreme form. Cf., William Kerrigan and Joseph Smith, eds., *Taking Chances: Derrida, Psychoanalysis, and Literature* (Baltimore: Johns Hopkins University Press, 1984), 144–45.

22. George Steiner, "Roncevaux," in *The Return of Thematic Criticism,* Werner Sollors, ed. (Cambridge: Harvard University Press, 1993), 299–300.

23. Kinsella himself pointed out the link between *Out of Ireland* (1988) and *Wormwood* (1966). But the lifeline can be traced further back to "A Lady of Quality" (1956). Other strands of motifs can similarly be traced throughout his career, as the motif of the persona of the poem looking at himself in the mirror in several self-reflexive poems.

24. Thomas Kinsella, *From Centre City* (Oxford: Oxford University Press, 1994), 55; hereafter cited in text as *CC.*

Chapter Three

1. The Dolmen edition (1988) was followed by an Oxford University Press edition and an American edition (Philadelphia: Dufour, 1962).

2. Calvin Bedient, *Eight Contemporary Poets* (London: Oxford University Press, 1974), 120.

3. Thomas Kinsella, *Poems* (Dublin: Dolmen Press, 1956), 23.

4. Paul Engle and Joseph Langland, eds., *Poet's Choice* (New York: The Dial Press, 1962), 270.

5. Vinegar Hill was the site of the bloody repression of the 1798 revolt against England.

6. Another, completely different poem called "First Light" was published in *Wormwood* (1966), and then, in a revised form, in *Nightwalker and Other Poems* (1968) and *Selected Poems* (1973).

7. Engle and Langland, 270.

8. Statement. *Poetry Book Society Bulletin,* no. 7 (March 1958).

9. The male and female theme has been the object of several critics' analysis. Cf. Arthur McGuinness,"'Bright Quincunx Newly Risen': Thomas Kinsella's Inward I," *Eire-Ireland* 15 (1980); Peggy Broder, "Images of the Feminine in the Poetry of Thomas Kinsella," *Canadian Journal of Irish Studies,* 5(1974):87–94; Carol Tattersall, "Thomas Kinsella's Exploration in *Notes from the Land of the Dead* and his sense of Alienation from Women," *Canadian Journal of Irish Studies,* 16 (1990):79–91.

10. Originally, in *Another September,* the line read "That plants its grammar in her yielding weather." The allusion to writing, much like "communicate again / Recovered order to my pen," of "A Lady of Quality," enhances the contrast between intuitive, "unspeaking" woman and the speaker who adds to his masculine rationality the cold analytical bent of the writer.

Chapter Four

1. Statement. *Poetry Book Society Bulletin,* no. 55 (December 1967).

2. Dillon Johnston, *Irish Poetry after Joyce* (Notre Dame: University of Notre Dame Press, 1985), 108; hereafter cited in text.

3. Gerry Flaherty was one of the great singers of Irish music in the old style (*sean nós*). O Riada and Kinsella had discovered him in Kruger Kavanagh's pub in Dunquin, on the Dingle peninsula, where they were spending a holiday with their families in 1959. After this trip, O Riada started recording Ireland's traditional songs and dance tunes, and founded a group of traditional musicians, the Ceoltóiri Chualann, which was to evolve into the internationally renowned Chieftains. The groups gave wide diffusion to the country's disappearing musical patrimony. Two songs of Flaherty's were recorded just before he drowned.

4. *Nightwalker and Other Poems* (New York: Knopf, 1968), 38; hereafter cited in text as *NOP.*

5. Quoted from Austin Clarke's own "The Abbey Theatre Fire." In *Selected Poems* (Dublin: Dolmen Press, 1976), 45.

6. *Contemporary Authors,* 264.

7. Thomas Kinsella, Preface to "Ballydavid Pier," in *Choice,* Desmond Egan and Michael Hartnett, eds. (The Curragh: Goldsmith Press, 1973), 62.

8. "The Divided Mind." In *Irish Poets in English, The Thomas Davis Lectures on Anglo-Irish Poetry,* Sean Lucy, ed. (Dublin and Cork: Mercier, 1972), 215.

9.   Thomas Dillon Redshaw, "The Wormwood Revisions," *Eire-Ireland* 6 (1972):111–55.

10.   *The Collected Poems of W. B. Yeats* (New York: Macmillan, 1956), 177–80; hereafter cited in text.

11.   The original poem was published in *Downstream* (Dublin: Dolmen Press, 1962; London: Oxford University Press, 1962). The revised version appeared first in *The Massachusetts Review* (Winter 1964) as "Downstream II," and then in *Nightwalker and Other Poems* and *Selected Poems*. In his forthcoming *Collected Poems,* Kinsella will revert to the original longer version.

12.   Kinsella translated Amergin's song for *The New Oxford Book of Irish Verse* and used it extensively in *One.*

13.   James Joyce, *A Portrait of the Artist as a Young Man* (Harmondsworth: Penguin, 1992), 275.

14.   Again, it is M. Harmon who points out that the words "it was a terrible time" were pronounced by Queen Victoria about Ireland at the time of the famine (*op. cit.,* 68).

15.   Richard Crashaw, "In the Holy Nativity of Our Lord God: A Hymn sung as by Shepheards," in *Poetical Works,* L. C. Martin, ed. (Oxford: Clarendon Press 1957), 248–51.

16.   Both George Steiner (*op. cit.*) and Roland Barthes (*Roland Barthes par Roland Barthes,* Paris, Seuil, 1975:78) consider intertextuality an echo chamber.

17.   The apostrophe was taken from "The Ballad of Lord Thomas and Fair Ellinor" in Percy's *Reliques,* III, 1.

18.   Cf., George W. Williams, *Image and Symbol in the Sacred Poetry of Richard Crashaw* (Columbia, SC: University of South Carolina Press, 1963), 54.

Chapter Five

1.   The sequence was reprinted in two commercial and more extensive editions, the Irish *New Poems 1973* (Dolmen: Dublin, 1973), and the American *Notes from the Land of the Dead and Other Poems* (New York: Knopf, 1973).

2.   *One and Other Poems* is comprised of *One, A Technical Supplement,* and *Song of the Night and Other Poems. Fifteen Dead* contained *Butcher's Dozen* and the two elegies for Sean O Riada.

3.   From unpublished conversation with the author.

4.   C. G. Jung affirms that "The unconscious corresponds to the mythic land of the dead, the land of the ancestors." *Memories, Dreams, Reflections,* Aniela Jaffé, ed., Richard and Clara Winston, transl. (London: Collins, 1963), 216; hereafter cited in text as *Dreams.* However, as Dillon Johnston points out, the invaders' landing site in Munster is also known in Irish legend as "the land of the dead" (*op. cit.,* 99).

5.   Arthur McGuinness, "Fragments of Identity: Thomas Kinsella's Modernist Imperative," *Colby Library Quarterly* 4 (1987),187–89. Other excel-

lent analyses of the Jungian influence are the same author's "Bright Quincunx Newly Risen: Thomas Kinsella's Inward I," *Eire-Ireland* 15 (1980), 106–25; and Brian John, "Imaginative Bedrock: Kinsella's *One* and the *Lebor Gabala Erenn*," *Eire-Ireland* 20 (1985), 109–32.

      6. Seamus Deane, *A Short History of Irish Literature* (London: Hutchinson, 1986), 236.

      7. Irish mythology, with its pantheon of five gods—Lug transcending the other four—confirmed the pattern, as did the four rivers of Eden (in "Nuchal (*a fragment*)" 1973) flowing from of the fingers of a reclining woman, a Great Mother archetype. Even the historical Irish administrative divisions reflected this sense of totality in fragmentation: the five provinces, of which Meath was the central one, formed by taking land from each of the other provinces, suggested the pattern of a Quincunx—*Dictionnaire des symboles* (Paris: Laffont, 1982), 200.

      8. C. G. Jung, *The Development of Personality,* vol. 17 of *Collected Works,* R. F. C. Hull, transl. (Princeton: Princeton University Press, 1977), 198.

      9. Brian John, "Thomas Kinsella and the Yeats Inheritance," *Irish University Review* 24 (1994), 255.

      10. *Lebor Gabala Erenn: The Book of the Taking of Ireland,* R. A. Macalister, ed. and transl. (Dublin: Irish Texts Society, 1938–1956). The edition Kinsella draws on for his poems was put together from eleven separate sources by its editor. It gives an account of the history of Ireland and the Gaels through the six successive invasions of Ireland.

      11. Kinsella turned frequently to *The Book of Invasions* as a source for his own poetry. The saga—which represents the Irish nation's collective memory of how different people came from across the sea in successive waves of invasion, assimilation, and annihilation—lends itself to Kinsella's Jungian uses better than the stories of cattle raids and battles of the Ulster cycle, which Kinsella translated in *The Táin.* The repossession of the old tradition became for Kinsella a device to explore self and world. *The Book of Invasions* as hypotext is operative both at the level of stylistic microstructure—verse form, specific semantic choices, incorporation of fragments—and meta-textuality.

      12. Cessair and her people were excluded from Noah's ark because they were thieves. To avoid the Flood, Cessair sailed to a place where no sin had ever been committed—Ireland—hoping thus to be spared. But two of her three ships were wrecked and the contingent landing in Ireland was of fifty women and three men. As the pilot and Cessair's own father, Bith, died of sexual overwork, Fintan alone remained alive to satisfy the sexual demands of his wife and fifty other women. Exhausted, Fintan fled from the women into a cave, where he weathered the Flood and survived throughout the successive invasions in various shapes to retell his story.

13. Italics my own. Cf., "Phoenix Park": *"Deeper* still, *Delicate distinct* tissue begins to form" (*SP,* 110).

14. Thomas Kinsella, interview by Daniel O'Hara, *Contemporary Poetry: A Journal of Criticism* 4 (1981), 14; hereafter cited in text.

15. In a traditional storyteller's repertoire, stories were not grouped according to cycles but according to the subjects with which they were concerned (i.e., births, voyages, invasions, etc.)

16. Alwyn Rees and Brinley Rees, *Celtic Heritage* (London: Thames and Hudson, 1961), 107; hereafter cited in text.

17. Seamus Deane, "Thomas Kinsella: Nursed out of Wreckage," in *Celtic Revivals* (London: Faber and Faber, 1985), 142; hereafter cited in text.

18. Gérard Genette, *Palimpsestes* (Paris: Editions du Seuil, 1982), 10–11.

Chapter Six

1. The same concept is present in W. B. Yeats's "Crazy Jane Talks with the Bishop": "Fair and foul are near of kin, / And fair needs foul. . . . But Love has pitched his mansion in / The place of excrement." *Collected Poems,* 254.

2. Kinsella's description of *Songs of the Psyche* to Floyd Skloot; quoted in Skloot's review of *Blood and Family, Northwest Review* XXXVIII, 1 (1990), 154.

3. *The Divine Comedy,* tr. Dorothy L. Sayers (Harmondsworth: Penguin Classics), 1966.

4. The title is a further indication that the poem is linked to Sean O Riada, whom Kinsella had honored in *Vertical Man.* But there is also a sexual double entendre, as is evident in the final verses of the second movement. Moreover, Hugh Maxton (alias W. J. McCormack) in a review of the poem suggests that it "takes its title from a fifteenth-century Irish language diagram of an eclipse—the diagram is on the title page [of the Peppercanister edition] the sun throwing the shadow (smile) of the earth up the page among the stars." "The Elusiveness of Thomas Kinsella," *Books Ireland* 97 (Oct. 1985), 153.

5. Cf. Rupert Brooke, "The Soldier": "there's some corner of a foreign field / That is for ever England." *Poetical Works* (London: Faber and Faber, 1946), 23.

6. Cf. James Joyce, "The old sow that eats her farrow!"*Ulysses* (New York: Garland, 1986), 1303.

7. W. J. McCormack, "Politics or Community: Crux of Thomas Kinsella's Aesthetic Development," *Tracks* 7 (1987), 73.

8. An Irish fertility cult figure obscenely exposing her sex.

9. In "Precedents and Notes," Kinsella gives us a clue as to the significance of this obsessive call by quoting from *Daily Life in the World of Charlemagne:* "[the Irish] were incomparable learned men. They cried out to a

210 NOTES AND REFERENCES

crowd of customers, 'If anyone desires wisdom, let him come to us and receive it, for we are here to sell it'" (*B&F,* 86).

10. The reference is to a dispute over the Viking remains at Wood Quay, the place where the actual city originated. The administration pretended to ignore what had been found there, played down its significance, and went on with their building plans for a parking lot. Thomas and Eleanor Kinsella were actively involved with the campaign and the demonstrations against the plans.

11. Valentin Iremonger (1918–1988). Poet and diplomat, ambassador to Sweden and India, and editor of the magazine *Envoy.*

12. Cf. Brian John, "Thomas Kinsella and the Yeats Inheritance." *Irish University Review* 24 (1994), 262. John bases his assumption on a description of the character in a former and more extended version of the poem in *Personal Places.*

13. In *An Duanaire,* too, Kinsella talks about O Rathaille using words which could apply to himself: "His poetry. . . is in many ways a result of his efforts to come to terms with the chaos in which he and his people found themselves" (139).

14. From unpublished conversation with the author.

Chapter Seven

1. The words "dislocation and loss" were repeatedly used in "The Irish Writer."

2. Terry Eagleton, "Nationalism: Irony and Commitment," in *Nationalism, Colonialism and Literature,* T. Eagleton, F. Jameson, and E. W. Said, eds. (Minneapolis: University of Minnesota Press, 1990), 35.

3. From unpublished conversation with the author.

4. This particular passage was violently resented by the Unionists who accused Kinsella of being "fascist," "bourgeois," and one-sided. Not only did he insult them heavily, but he also pretended to ignore the innocent Protestants who were also losing their lives in the conflict. A pamphlet called *Kinsella's Oversight* turns the poem inside out, staging the Protestant dead voicing their anger and scorn.

5. *Fifteen Dead* collects poems commemorating Sean O Riada, the thirteen dead of Derry, and John F. Kennedy, the fifteenth death in the series.

6. It is not surprising that Kinsella's most self-reflexive poem, "Worker in Mirror at His Bench," was extrapolated as "foreign matter" from this poem (cf. "Commentary," *FD,* 74).

7. The revisionist trend, which started gaining ground in Irish cultural and historical discourse in the 1960s, has been characterized by a rejection of nationalist historiography and a general whitewashing of colonial responsibilities. The 1966 celebrations of the Easter Rising constituted a sort of watershed, after which, for instance, presentation of de-dramatized versions of the 1916

Revolution or the Famine gained more and more ground. An older form of revisionism has also been at work in the cultural field and has intensified recently. It regards the difficult relationship between modern Anglo-Irish literature and its Gaelic forebears.

After the intoxication with the Irish past displayed by Yeats and the Irish Revival, proto-revisionists started as early as the 1930s and 1940s to undermine the Gaelic cult, denying the continuity of an Irish cultural heritage and denouncing it as yet another Nationalist construction. Their invitation to stop lamenting the loss of language and literary tradition and to channel Irish culture towards a more European and modern vision within a liberal-humanist perspective, was heeded by many with beneficial effect on literature; but also with a loss of cultural specificity and the side effect of a further obliteration of Gaelic language and culture. More recent cultural revisionists, such as Edna Longley, have been pointing out that there has been such an obsession with "decolonizing" literature that aesthetic values have been forgotten; it is time, she argues, to pay less attention to loss and deprivation, and more to creative links with English culture.

      8.   Luke Gibbons, "Challenging the Canon: Revisionism and Cultural Criticism," in *The Field Day Anthology of Irish Writing III*, Seamus Deane, ed. (Derry: Field Day Publications; London: Faber & Faber, 1991), 566.

      9.   From unpublished conversation with the author.

      10.   Thomas Kinsella, "A View of Irish Literature," *A Needle's Eye* (1979), 30; hereafter cited in the text as *NE*.

      11.   *An Duanaire: Poetry of the Dispossessed 1600–1900*, selected by Seán O Tuama (Dublin: Dolmen Press,1981), xxvii.

      12.   *The Táin* (*Táin Bó Cuailnge*) (Dublin: Dolmen Press,1969, 1985; London and New York: Oxford University Press, 1970), vii.

      13.   Douglas Hyde (1860–1945). President of National Literary Society, the Gaelic League, and, in 1938, elected the first president of Ireland. He collected and translated Gaelic folktales and songs. In 1892 he delivered an address on "The Necessity for De-Anglicizing Ireland," in which he advocated playing down English and reviving Irish by creating a modern literature in the language.

Chapter Eight

      1.   From unpublished conversation with the author.

      2.   It is Lowell's distinguishing feature, as Marjorie Perloff points out, to have substituted the realistic convention of Tolstoy and Chekhov with the web of symbolic implications of the Romantic lyric, and to have relied on factual documentation as a metonymy of the larger realities. Marjorie Perloff, *The Poetic Art of Robert Lowell* (Ithaca: Cornell University Press, 1973), 83–88.

3. Gerald Dawe, "An Absence of Influence: Three Modernist Poets," in *Tradition and Influence in Anglo-Irish Poetry,* Terence Brown and Nicholas Grene, eds. (London: Macmillan, 1989), 139.

4. Seamus Heaney, *Preoccupations: Selected Prose* (New York: Farrar, Straus and Giroux, 1980), 34.

5. Thomas Kinsella, interview by Elgy Gillespie, *Irish Times,* 20 June 1981, 14.

Selected Bibliography

PRIMARY SOURCES

Poetry (chronological listing)

Poems. Dublin: Dolmen Press, 1956.

Another September. Dublin: Dolmen Press, 1958.

Moralities. Dublin: Dolmen Press, 1960.

Poems and Translations. New York: Atheneum, 1961.

Downstream. Dublin: Dolmen Press, 1962; London: Oxford University Press, 1962.

Wormwood. Dublin: Dolmen Press, 1966.

Nightwalker. Dublin: Dolmen Press, 1967.

Nightwalker and Other Poems. Dublin: Dolmen Press, 1968; London: Oxford University Press, 1968; New York: Knopf, 1968.

Tear. Cambridge, Massachusetts: Pym Randall Press, 1969.

Butcher's Dozen. Dublin: Peppercanister, 1972 (#1).

A Selected Life. Dublin: Peppercanister, 1972 (#2).

Finistere. Dublin: Dolmen Press, 1972.

Notes from the Land of the Dead. Dublin: Cuala Press, 1972.

Notes from the Land of the Dead and Other Poems. New York: Knopf, 1973.

New Poems 1973. Dublin: Dolmen Press, 1973 (same as the Knopf edition, but does not include "Butcher's Dozen").

Selected Poems 1956–1968. Dublin: Dolmen Press, 1973; London: Oxford University Press, 1973.

Vertical Man. Dublin: Peppercanister, 1973 (#3).

The Good Fight. Dublin: Peppercanister, 1973 (#4).

One. Dublin: Peppercanister, 1974 (#5).

A Technical Supplement. Dublin: Peppercanister, 1976 (#6).

Song of the Night and Other Poems. Dublin: Peppercanister, 1978 (#7).

The Messenger. Dublin: Peppercanister, 1978 (#8).

Fifteen Dead. Dublin: Dolmen Press, 1978; London: Oxford University Press, 1979 (Peppercanister pamphlets #1–4).

One and Other Poems. Dublin: Dolmen Press, 1979; London: Oxford University Press, 1979 (Peppercanister pamphlets #5–7).

Peppercanister Poems, 1972–1978. Winston-Salem, North Carolina: Wake Forest University Press, 1979 (Peppercanister pamphlets #1–8).

Poems 1956–1973. Winston-Salem, North Carolina: Wake Forest University Press, 1979; Dublin: Dolmen Press, 1980 (replaces and expands *Selected Poems 1956–1968,* and includes most of *New Poems 1973*).

213

Songs of the Psyche. Dublin: Peppercanister, 1985 (#9).

Her Vertical Smile. Dublin: Peppercanister, 1985 (#10).

Out of Ireland: A Metaphysical Love Sequence. Dublin: Peppercanister, 1987 (#11).

St. Catherine's Clock. Dublin: Peppercanister, 1987 (#12).

One Fond Embrace. Dublin: Dedalus Press, 1988 (#13).

Blood and Family. London: Oxford University Press, 1988 (Peppercanister pamphlets #8–12).

Selected Poems 1962–1989. Helsinki: Eurographica, 1989 (limited edition).

Personal Places. Dublin: Dedalus Press, 1990 (#14).

Poems from Centre City. Dublin: Dedalus Press, 1990 (#15).

Madonna and Other Poems. Dublin: Dedalus Press, 1991 (#16).

Open Court. Dublin: Dedalus Press, 1991 (#17).

From Centre City. Oxford: Oxford University Press, 1994 (Peppercanister pamphlets 13–17).

Essays and Critical Works (chronological listing)

"Poetry Since Yeats: An Exchange of Views" (Transcript of a Panel). *Tri-quarterly* 4 (Fall 1965):100–113.

"The Irish Writer." In W. B. Yeats and T. Kinsella, *Davis Mangan Ferguson?: Tradition and the Irish Writer.* Dublin: Dolmen Press, 1970.

"The Divided Mind." In *Irish Poets in English, The Thomas Davis Lectures on Anglo-Irish Poetry,* edited by Sean Lucy. Dublin and Cork: Mercier, 1972.

"A View of Irish Literature." *A Needle's Eye* (1979):30–35.

"W.B. Yeats, the British Empire, James Joyce and Mother Grogan." *Irish University Review* 22 (1992):69–79.

The Dual Tradition. Manchester: Carcanet Press, 1995.

Translations (chronological listing)

Longes Mac Unsnig: Being the Exile and Death of the Sons of Usnech. Dublin: Dolmen Press, 1954.

Thirty-three Triads, Translated from the XII Century Irish. Dublin: Dolmen Press, 1955.

The Breastplate of St.Patrick. Dublin: Dolmen Press, 1954; revised as *Faeth Fiadha: The Breastplate of St.Patrick,* 1957.

The Táin. (Táin Bó Cuailnge) Dublin: Dolmen Press, 1969, 1985; London and New York: Oxford University Press, 1970.

An Duanaire: Poetry of the Dispossessed 1600–1900, selected by Seán O Tuama. Dublin: Dolmen Press,1981.

Anthologies

The Dolmen Miscellany of Irish Writing. Edited with John Montague. Dublin: Dolmen Press, 1962.

The New Oxford Book of Irish Verse. London: Oxford University Press, 1986.

Interviews with Kinsella (chronological listing)

Orr, Peter. "Thomas Kinsella." In *The Poet Speaks: Interviews with Contemporary Poets.* London: Routledge and Kegan Paul, 1966.

Haffenden, John. "Thomas Kinsella." In *Viewpoints: Poets in Conversation with John Haffenden.* (London: Faber and Faber, 1981):100–113.

O'Hara, Daniel. "An Interview with Thomas Kinsella." *Contemporary Poetry: A Journal of Criticism* 4 (1981):1–18.

Gillespie, Elgy. "An Interview with Thomas Kinsella." *Irish Times* (20 June 1981): 14.

Deane, John. "A Conversation." *Tracks* 7 (Thomas Kinsella Issue, 1987):86–91.

Fried, Philip. "Omphalos of Scraps." *Manhattan Review* 4 (Spring 1988):3–25.

O'Driscoll, Dennis. "Interview with Thomas Kinsella." *Poetry Ireland Review* 25 (Spring 1989):57–65.

Personal Notices (chronological listing)

Statement, *Poetry Society Bulletin* 7 (March, 1958).

Statement, *Poetry Society Bulletin* 55 (December, 1967).

Statement, In *Contemporary Poets,* James Vinson, ed. London: St. James; New York: St. Martin's, 1975.

Statement, In *Contemporary Authors: A Bio-Bibliographical Guide to Current Authors and Their Works,* vols. 17–18. Detroit: Gale Research Co., 1976:263–264.

SECONDARY SOURCES

Books and Parts of Books

Badin, Donatella Abbate. "Language and Passion in the Poetry of Thomas Kinsella: 'The passion is in the putting together.'" In *I linguaggi della passione,* edited by Romana Rutelli and Anthony Johnson, 199–208. Udine: Campanotto, 1992. Seeking passion and order at the same time is one of the fruitful paradoxes of Kinsella's poetry.

———. "Thomas Kinsella and the Fractured Tradition of Irish Culture." In *Intrecci e contaminazioni,* edited by De Scarpis, Innocenti, Marucci, and Pajalich, 261–72. Venice: Supernova, 1993. Analyzes Kinsella's translations and anthologies as examples of his attempt to heal the rift caused by the loss of a language and a tradition.

Bedient, Calvin. *Eight Contemporary Poets.* London: Oxford University Press, 1974. Examines Kinsella in the context of his British contemporaries, admiring his early poetry and seeing the danger of disintegration in his production of the 1970s.

Dawe, Gerald. "An Absence of Influence: Three Modernist Poets." In *Tradition and Influence in Anglo-Irish Poetry,* edited by Terence Brown and Nicholas

Grene, 119–42. London: Macmillan, 1989. Studies Kinsella, Coffey, and Devlin within the context of Irish tradition.

Deane, Seamus. "The Literary Myths of the Revival: A Case for their Abandonment." In *Myth and Reality in Irish Literature,* edited by Joseph Ronsley, 317–29. Waterloo, Ontario: Wilfrid Laurier University Press, 1977.

———. "Thomas Kinsella: Nursed out of Wreckage." In *Celtic Revivals,* 135–45. London: Faber and Faber, 1985. A comprehensive survey of the various phases of Kinsella's career, putting the accent on the way violence and disorder in his poetry are subsumed into order, and how the sense of continuity is greater than the sense of fragmentation.

Garratt, Robert F. "Poetry at Mid-century I: Thomas Kinsella." In *Modern Irish Poetry,* 167–97. Berkeley: University of California Press, 1986. A thorough review of Kinsella's early and mid-career paying particular attention to "Nightwalker."

Harmon, Maurice. *The Poetry of Thomas Kinsella.* Dublin: Wolfhound Press, 1974; Atlantic Highlands, N.J.: Humanities Press, 1975. The only book-length study of Kinsella's poetry offers a thorough critical introduction to his poetry until 1973.

John, Brian. "Contemporary Irish Poetry and the Matter of Ireland—Thomas Kinsella, John Montague and Seamus Heaney." In *Medieval and Modern Ireland,* edited by Richard Wall, 34–59. Gerrards Cross: Colin Smythe, 1988. On the importance of the Irish tradition, fractured as it may be, for Kinsella and the other two poets.

Johnston, Dillon. "Clarke and Kinsella." In *Irish Poetry after Joyce,* 74–120. Notre Dame: University of Notre Dame Press, 1985. One of the most helpful essays on Kinsella's middle period (up to *The Messenger),* and on how his poetry draws on both incidents of his own life and mythical material.

Kenner, Hugh. "Thomas Kinsella: An Anecdote and Some Reflections." In *The Genres of Irish Revival,* edited by Ronald Schleifer, 179–87. Dublin: Wolfhound Press, 1980. A brief and unsympathetic introduction focusing on the Kinsella effect, "an irruption of violent enigmatic language."

Leersen, Joep. "Tain after Tain: The Mythical Past and the Anglo-Irish." In *History and Violence in Anglo-Irish Literature,* edited by Joris Duytschaever and Geert Lernout, 29–46. Amsterdam: Rodopi, 1988. A comparison of Kinsella's translation of *The Táin* with Lady Gregory's and others, in the context of the image the nation has of itself.

Longley, Edna. "Searching the Darkness: Richard Murphy, Thomas Kinsella, John Montague, and James Simmons." In *Two Decades of Irish Writing,* edited by Douglas Dunn, 118–53. Cheshire: Carcanet Press, 1975. Examines the four poets' self-consciousness about being Irish and their links with British and cosmopolitan culture.

O'Hara, Daniel. "Appropriate Performance: Thomas Kinsella and the Ordeal of Understanding." In *Contemporary Irish Writing,* edited by James D. Brophy and Raymond J. Porter, 65–81. Boston: Twayne, 1983. A study of a few poems as examples of Kinsella's "psychic geography"—the landscape through which Kinsella takes his journeys of experience and understanding.

Rosenthal, M. L. *The New Poets: American and British Poetry since World War II.* London and New York: Oxford University Press, 1967. A thorough introductory study of Kinsella's early poetry.

Articles

Anderson, Mary. "Kinsella and Eriugena: 'Out of Ireland.'" *The Canadian Journal of Irish Studies* 17(1991):39–53. Eriugena's influence goes beyond *Out of Ireland:* his pantheistic philosophy inspires Kinsella's views in "Phoenix Park" and several other poems.

Badin, Donatella Abbate. "'Tissues of Order': Image Patterns in the Poetry of Thomas Kinsella." *Annali di Ca' Foscari* 29 (1990):5–26. Kinsella's repetitive imagery grouped around the two poles of light and decay, gives unity to his apparently disparate production.

Broder, Peggy. "Breaking the Shell of Solitude: Some Poems of Thomas Kinsella." *Eire-Ireland* 14 (1979):80–92. Examines sympathetically the theme and techniques of fragmentation in *Notes.*

———. "Images of the Feminine in the Poetry of Thomas Kinsella." *The Canadian Journal of Irish Studies* 5 (1974):87–94. Kinsella's attitudes regarding women evolve toward considering them as a means to achieve the reconciliation of opposites.

Dawe, Gerald. "In the Violent Zone: Thomas Kinsella's *Nightwalker and Other Poems*." *Tracks* 7 (1987):27–31.

Dunn, Jim. "An Duanaire: A Bridge for the Divided Mind." *Eire-Ireland* 17 (1982):116–26. Assesses the importance of Kinsella's anthology for Irish culture.

Garratt, Robert F. "Fragilities and Structures: Poetic Strategy in Thomas Kinsella's 'Nightwalker' and 'Phoenix Park.'" *Irish University Review* 13 (1983):88–102. Examines the deeper patterns acting as ordering principles of the two poems.

Harmon, Maurice. "By Memory Inspired: Themes and Forces in Recent Irish Writing." *Eire-Ireland* 8 (1973):3–19. Kinsella's and other writers' responses to the new, more liberal and international Ireland.

John, Brian. "Imaginative Bedrock: Thomas Kinsella's *One* and the *Lebor Gabála Erenn*." *Eire-Ireland* 20 (1985):109–32. The groundbreaking essay on Kinsella's use of *The Book of Invasions* to draw a parallel between the early Irish travels and Kinsella's own exploration of the psyche.

218   SELECTED BIBLIOGRAPHY

—. "Irelands of the Mind: The Poetry of Thomas Kinsella and Seamus Heaney." *The Canadian Journal of Irish Studies* 15 (1989):68–92. Examines the process of assimilation of Irish and non-Irish literature, art, and sculpture apparent in the recurrent images used by the two poets.

—. "Thomas Kinsella and the Yeats Inheritance." *Irish University Review* 24 (1994):247–63. For all his early dismissals, Kinsella has come to recognize the pertinence to his own work of Yeats's late poetry, and John emphasizes the many points of contact between the two poets.

Longley, Edna. "The Heroic Agenda: The Poetry of Thomas Kinsella." *The Dublin Magazine* 2 (1966):61–78. A formal and unsympathetic analysis of Kinsella's early poetry underlining its abstract nature and mannerisms.

McCormack, William J. "Politics or Community?" *Tracks* 7 (Thomas Kinsella Issue, 1987):61–77. Kinsella's apparent turning away from contemporary politics is his most consummately political act.

McGuinness, Arthur E. "'Bright Quincunx Newly Risen': Thomas Kinsella's Inward 'I.'" *Eire-Ireland* 15 (1980):106–25. A fundamental study of Kinsella's Jungian background.

—. "Fragments of Identity: Thomas Kinsella's Modernist Imperative." *Colby Library Quarterly* 4 (1987):186–205. A thorough study of Kinsella's psychological and cultural themes in a modernist perspective.

Meir, Colin. "Narrative Techniques in Austin Clarke's 'Mnemosyne Lay in Dust' and Thomas Kinsella's 'Nightwalker.'" *Etudes irlandaises* 8 (1983):57–78. Careful analysis of the narrative principles ruling over the organization of "Nightwalker."

O'Hara, Daniel. "Love's Architecture: The Poetic Irony of Thomas Kinsella." *Boundary* 2 (1981):123–35. Studies some of Kinsella's poems as examples of his ironic response to the "anxiety of influence."

Redshaw, Thomas Dillon. "The Wormwood Revisions." *Eire-Ireland* 6 (1972):111–55. A very thorough study of the *Wormwood* revisions, demonstrating how Kinsella moved from confessionalism to a more impersonal and abstract attitude.

Skelton, Robin. "The Poetry of Thomas Kinsella." *Eire-Ireland* 4 (1969):87–108. An early assessment of Kinsella's achievement and originality.

Skloot, Floyd. "The Song of Thomas Kinsella." *The New Criterion* 8 (1990):41–47. Kinsella's later poetry is part of an ongoing project, the quest for the significance of poetry.

Tattersall, Carol. "Thomas Kinsella's Exploration in *Notes from the Land of the Dead* and his Sense of Alienation from Women." *The Canadian Journal of Irish Studies* 16 (1990):79–91. Kinsella exorcises his alienation from the female, present in his poetry, through his immersion in Irish myth and Jungian psychology.

Tymoczko, Maria. "Strategies for Integrating Irish Epics into European Literature." *Dispositio* VII, 19–20 (1982):123–40. Kinsella's translation of

The Táin is a watershed in the history of translating the text because it makes no compromises with the audience.

————. "Translating the Old Irish Epic *Táin Bó Cúailnge:* Political Aspects." *Pacific Quarterly Moana* 8 (1983):6–21. Studies the political motivations and impact of the different translations of *The Táin,* including Kinsella's.

Index

The Author

Donatella Abbate Badin received her first degree in English Literature from Bocconi University, Milan (Italy) and her Ph.D. from the University of Maryland. She has taught English and comparative literature at Bocconi University; the University of Maryland; Webster University, Geneva (Switzerland); and the University of Sassari (Italy), and is now an associate professor of English at the University of Turin (Italy).

Professor Badin's earlier work primarily concerned Gerard Manley Hopkins, on whom she has published a book and several articles. Her teaching and research interests are principally in the areas of modern and contemporary poetry. She has written on Roethke and Rimbaud, T. S. Eliot and Theophile Gauthier, and other English, American, and Irish poets.

Her interest in the poetry of Thomas Kinsella dates back to the 1970s, when she translated the poet's work into Italian. She has since published several articles on his poetry and his activities in favor of the Gaelic tradition.

Professor Badin is a member of the International Association for the Study of Anglo-Irish Literature (IASAIL) and has contributed to the diffusion of Irish culture in Italy.